GW00762695

The Order of the Ages

World History
in the Light
of a Universal
Cosmogony

ROBERT BOLTON

THE ORDER
OF THE AGES

*WORLD HISTORY
IN THE LIGHT
OF A UNIVERSAL
COSMOGONY*

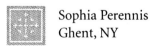

Sophia Perennis
Ghent, NY

First published in the USA
by Sophia Perennis, Ghent, NY 2001
Series editor: James R. Wetmore
© Robert Bolton 2001

For information, address:
Sophia Perennis, 343 Rte 21C
Ghent NY 12075

Library of Congress Cataloging-in-Publication Data

Bolton, Robert (Robert A. N.), 1941–
The order of the ages : world history in the light of
a universal cosmogony / Robert Bolton

p. cm.
Includes index
ISBN 0 900588 31 4 (pbk: alk. paper)
ISBN 0 900588 37 3 (cloth: alk. paper)
1. Time—Religious aspects I. Title
BL65.T5 B65 2001
291.2'4—dc21   2001000430

✠

With special acknowledgement to Ruth Yendell
for her work in correcting and amending the text,
and to Stratford Caldecott, without whom
the idea would never have gone so far.

✠

By the same author:

Person, Soul and Identity
The Logic of Spiritual Values

Contents

FOREWORD

This book is very unusual, so unusual that some people—
many people I should think—will be frightened by it. It is a revolutionary book. It challenges every single orthodoxy of our times right
down to the very basis of modern orthodoxy. And yet it is not 'original' in the sense of introducing some new theory or personal
insight. The author is not just displaying his own mind but recon-
structing and setting out that code of knowledge and way of thinking that is called traditional or Platonic and is acclaimed by some as
perennial, rooted in mathematical truth, expressive of nature and
the human mentality and deriving ultimately from revelation. These
are large claims and this is not the place to argue them. The traditional world-view has the undisputed quality of being constant, the
same in every generation and period of history, unaffected by fash-
ions or other schools of thought. It therefore provides a uniquely
objective standpoint from which to view and analyze the phenomena of these present times.

We think today about progress, and about how much society has
advanced in the last few decades, but the evidence for this could
equally well be used to argue that these are times of extreme deca-
dence, when all natural and human standards have been overturned
and we await the inevitable dissolution of all that the modern mind
has created. Either we are moving toward new, higher standards of
science and civilization or we stand at the very end of an era, on the
verge of Apocalypse. The traditional, premodern view of time is that
it proceeds in a series of greater and lesser cycles and constitutes, in
Plato's words, a 'moving image of eternity'. Obviously linked to these
cycles are the seasons of nature, and they have also been studied in
connection with changes in the human psyche, reflected in changes
of customs and the history of civilizations. One of these is the
period of 25,920 years in which, by ancient reckoning, the sun com-
pletes its course through the twelve houses of the Zodiac (2,160 years

for each house). At which point on this cycle, and indeed on the greater cycles recognized in antiquity, are we positioned today? To this question and many others of immediate and essential interest Dr Bolton brings rare knowledge and understanding. He is no mere prophet of doom, neither does he offer false comfort. Here we are led by the light of reason to approach as nearly as possible the actual truth of things. You cannot expect this to be an easy passage. I certainly did not find it so, but having embarked on the manuscript I soon realized I was in the hands of a trustworthy guide to those questions which haunt everyone's mind about the nature of existence. How, when, and why did the world begin? And how will it end? Or is there no ending or beginning? What is infinity, and are such questions merely about illusions? What part does the mind play in creation? Are we and the universe programed toward a certain end? Are we going in the right direction? How should we think, believe, and conduct ourselves? Where is firm ground? Or should we rather ask, like Socrates, what are the best possible myths to live by?

All that can honestly be given in response to such questions is an introduction to that constant and recurrent world-view which this book uniquely provides. It signals a revolution of the most effective kind possible, a revolution in cosmology, a turning-over of the world which alters our entire view and experience of it. There are many signs that this change is due and already in process, and one of them is this admirable, remarkable book.

In case anyone thinks that this enthusiastic, inadequate appraisal is written just to oblige a friend, I should say that I have never met Robert Bolton and know almost nothing about him, but was enlightened and edified by this high-quality work and wish the same benefits on others.

JOHN MICHELL

1

CONFLICTING
IDEAS OF TIME

CYCLIC TIME AND PROGRESS

The esoteric aspect of time, and the law of metaphysical entropy contained in it, is the subject of this study which has the aim of exploring a radical alternative to what is popularly believed about the meaning of history. The psychological conditions for such an alternative have been provided by the steady decline of a once-universal belief that almost everything was subject to a law of inevitable progress, in the moral realm as much as in the material. This idea tends increasingly to be the doctrine of minority groups with an interest in forcing changes on the public which are mainly for the benefit of their instigators, along with many forms of standardization and encroachment against nature. Belief in progress involves a special evaluation of historical time which has come to seem ever less assured in the wake of a series of geopolitical catastrophes, including the two world wars, the advent of nuclear war, and the overcrowding of the earth. The very technical advances which once supported a belief in progress now show tendencies which can do the opposite.

But no matter how doubtful the progressive view of history may have become, it still seems to many to be the only theory of history which is workable at all, and to be without credible alternatives. Even a bad theory is better than none. Since time is the most fundamental and universal condition of life, one which affects it more intimately than any other, there must be an overall conception of the nature of historical time if the meaning of life is to be understood. Without it, there would be no way of evaluating the results of historical trends, so that good and bad, great and trivial, would be brought down to the same level. Such is the state of confusion toward which present-day opinion is in fact tending, and the waning of the idea of progress has left an ideological vacuum which no rival theory has yet begun to fill. As the once-credible theory becomes beset by its own contradictions, some react by simply making it a political dogma which can be relied on to have popular appeal, but this is to ignore the fundamental problem. If we can assume that world conditions will remain opposed to a revival of this theory, it will be worthwhile to rediscover the conception of time out of which the modern one grew, the one which was typical of times when mankind saw itself as largely unable to control its own fate by material means.

Was there in fact only one premodern conception of time? And if in Europe it was a part of religious orthodoxy, was it something peculiar to Christianity, or was it really something older still, which was adapted to the doctrines of later times? To answer these questions, a significant point of departure is the fact that the Bible is arranged in the form of a world history. This sacred history embodies something essential to the premodern ideas of time, and it is one which was abandoned in the face of what was felt to be overwhelming evidence against it in the form of scientific advances. Not only is the traditional time-scale limited to a few thousand years, but it offers no scope for the idea of material progress, firstly because it is tied to the idea that the beginning and the end of the world are both supernatural events, between which the consequences of the Fall continue alongside salvation history, as if in another dimension. The biblical message is firstly a history of the increasingly complete revelation of God, but the Bible nevertheless shows this against an ever-darkening background, as mankind as a whole descends from an original perfection to depths of confusion and corruption which end with the Apocalypse. After this, a new world was said to begin, though the world-drama is one which is conceived as beginning and ending in eternity, and to this extent it could be called a cycle.

Such is the conception of historical time which is now felt to belong to ages of relative ignorance, partly because the eternal and the supernatural are so often taken to be merely means of filling gaps in one's knowledge of nature. But now that belief in progress is losing conviction, it should be possible to reconsider the merits of ancient and medieval ideas without too much conflict with prejudice. Modern research discovers natural explanations for almost everything except the modern world itself, because such explanations, even if they were forthcoming, would be too much on the same level as the thing explained to be of any use. Real explanation can only come by means of a method which gets conceptually outside the modern world, along with all particular eras, and the special merit of traditional ideas is that they do this very thing.

The biblical chronology can be shown to contain more specifically cyclic elements than the general idea referred to above, and this will be examined in a later chapter, along with its implications for the way in which we need to understand the Jewish and Christian traditions. A further general indication for the present is the fact that, in Greek, the word *aion* can mean either 'world' or 'age' equally, so as to form a dilemma for New Testament translations. The Hebrew word *olam* has the same double meaning, showing how far ancient thought was steeped in the idea of successive worlds.

THE NEED FOR A THEORY OF TIME

However, a proposed recovery of premodern ideas of time may be mistaken for a rationalization for a reactionary and negative outlook, which is typically the distortion made by those who reject the cyclic idea, ignoring the fact that the great achievements of the ancient civilizations were by no means spoiled or diminished by it. On the contrary, the element of pessimism in the ancient worldview acted so as to filter out false expectations and deceptive values, whereas the optimism of modern times allows anything to win influence and acceptance merely by being the latest thing to be produced. This belief that the new must be the best nearly always works in favor of the bad. Just as a frank acceptance of the fact that one's own body is subject to degenerative changes is the rational basis on which one can resort to the relevant measures of exercise and diet which can minimize the effects of such things, so the health of a civilization depends on a frank understanding of its degenerative processes. It is obvious enough that to refuse to contemplate such facts where they concern one's own health is simply neurotic, and tends in any case to allow maximum scope for the very evils which are not faced, but not everyone sees the danger in the equally neurotic reaction in regard to the health of a civilization, although the parallel is a close one. Besides this kind of reaction, there is another, which stems from the perception that a non-progressive theory of world history at this present time must reflect on the competence, or even the legitimacy, of those in positions of power and authority. This was not the case before the idea of progress was made current, of course, but since it has become so, it confers an added dignity on those who are in controlling positions, whether political, religious, or academic, and who are therefore liable to see the cyclic idea of time as subversive. It confronts them with the idea that the world over which they preside in the eyes of the public is really controlled by forces which are no more subject to their wills than to anyone else's. If, then, the ideas examined here should happen to be generally repressed by prejudice, fear, or entrenched self-interest, the reasons for that should be clear enough.

The progressive idea of time contains an element of truth which can nevertheless be comprehended within the cyclic idea, even though the latter cannot be contained in the former. Cyclic time allows full scope to both natural and supernatural realities without either confounding them or keeping them without relation. The central issue is an idea of time which transcends the categories of optimism and pessimism, or of progress and reaction, which result mainly from a projection of subjective attitudes onto the outside world. It is a study of the original reality out of which these notions arose through a long period of spiritual deviation, which has gone to such extremes that 'the end of the world' has under some aspect or other become an issue for many minds, and by no means only in a religious context.

A REASON FOR PESSIMISM?

In the natural world, cycles appear as life-cycles, where development peaks and then goes through an inevitable decline ending in death. The process of decline implicit in the cyclic conception is one which applies primarily on the cosmic level, while it may or may not control the interior lives of individual persons to some degree at the same time. It is most directly in opposition to the world-view based on the constant progress of science and technology, since the latter is a progress in things which are only ancillary to life's needs, not in what is essential to life. While there is no point in denying the reality of progress in numerous forms of human consciousness, where it works in specialized fields, as well as in industrial products, all such things serve only to mask a relentless loss of both a consciousness and of a spiritual energy of a far more essential kind.

The achievements of technical progress over the centuries are directly demonstrable and tangible, so that they can almost stifle any sense that something else may have been lost at the same time. Yet there is a widespread emotional dependence on the past which reveals an unspoken conviction that the passage of time is in fact marked by a relentless draining away of something irreplaceable. As to what this vanishing value may be, a relevant but misleading answer would be 'consciousness'. It could be misleading because on the one hand consciousness of the contents of the sensory world has hardly ever been so active or so fully developed as it is today; but on the other hand consciousness also extends into realms far beyond sense, and where these ramifications atrophy, the meaning and value even of sensory consciousness is threatened. To clarify this further, more will be said about the special nature of human consciousness in later chapters.

If there were a universal ebb tide of consciousness in the fullest sense of the word, it would have consequences which would cut across all arguments as to whether the fine arts are or are not in a state of decline, and whether traditional religion is in decline or merely changing. Regardless of the numbers of persons who practice a religion or engage in creative or interpretative arts, the real loss will be interior and nearly invisible, as the higher reaches of consciousness become closed or darkened. While this should undoubtedly give rise to outward signs of decline, therefore, the latter will be of interest only as symptoms of some more profound change. This kind of change is at too deep a level to be corrected by any possible increase in practical activities.

However, it is not only technical progress which shields modern man from a sense of inferiority or insecurity from such things, because he now is able to look back over more than twenty centuries of continuous recorded history and dozens of generations. He knows them, and in some ways more about them than they knew themselves, while they of course do not know him. This gives rise to a sense of superiority such as comes from the way that human beings know flora and fauna without being known by them. But the fact that such knowledge of the past is confined mostly to externals can only mean that such feelings of superiority are ill-founded.

Even if it is admitted that this points to the need for an alternative to the idea of universal progress, however, it may still be asked whether it can be justifiable to advance in its place such a seemingly negative idea as that of inevitable cosmic decline. Such a conception is clearly full of dangers for those who may see it only as a justification for a hopeless fatalism, or even as a rationale for new evils. In less abnormal times, this could be an adequate reason for making little mention of it, but at the present time there are in any case so many causes for such attitudes that the risks from adding to them are minimal.

The course of modern history can easily create the impression that the traditional beliefs and values under attack today must be devalued or even invalidated by the sheer scale of the historical forces ranged against them. In particular, this is shown by the position of the historical Christian churches, whose ritual and doctrinal influence on society has been in retreat for the past three hundred years. Even with temporary revivals, the trend remains relentlessly downward, with the perverse result that those who are intellectually mature enough to have a need for more than a blind faith are the ones who are under the most pressure toward unbelief, in proportion to this need.

The best answer to this is to make known the root cause of the evil in as much detail as possible, so that it can be seen to be neither more nor less than a subtle cosmic force which has no more bearing on truth than have the cruder forces of the elements. For this purpose it must be understood that spiritual truths are in no way dependent on the degree to which they are manifest in the world, and the more clearly this is seen, the closer one will be to the liberating discovery of what it is in us which can not only escape the cosmic process, but can actually reverse it, in the life of the individual at least. The effects of such a truth, when lived, can have far-reaching consequences in proportion to the extent to which truth and reality outweigh falsehood.

A further reason, related to the above, why the cyclic idea of time is relevant today is directly owing to modern science, which employs a time scale for the age of the universe which reckons not merely in millions, but in thousands of millions of years. For a long time the conviction that this is fact and not theory has subverted the historical position of revealed religion, since its history extends at most about four thousand years from the time of Abraham. There are immense psychological difficulties in seeing anything very meaningful about a period of four thousand years when it is appended to one of four thousand million, and similarly, the idea that the earth has been mainly the home of dinosaurs serves only to drive home the same problem in a more concrete way.

Under these conditions, a surer basis for a rational faith would be a combination of the orthodox idea of a created world occupying some thousands of years, with the perspective of innumerable other such creations, arising and falling in succession across a vast time scale like that of science. Such is the cyclic conception of time, and it thus forms a natural solution to the problem posed by the inhuman scale of the scientific universe, as to how humanly-meaningful eras can be integrated into the immensities which surround them.

MODERN AND ANCIENT SOURCES

A common fault with the usual accounts of modernity is that they have no foundation in metaphysical principles, and so cannot form part of a kind of knowledge related to reality as a whole. A notable exception to this rule is to be found in a book by René Guénon, written soon after World War II, translated as *The Reign of Quantity and the Signs of the Times*. In it, the cyclic idea of time is developed in all its ramifications. The modern world is judged in relation to a set of ideas which are all strictly part of traditional wisdom, in a way which challenges the modern belief that the ancients could not have had their own means of understanding all the ages of the world, including our own.

As the point of view taken in the following chapters will be similar to that of Guénon in some respects, I should make its points of divergence equally clear. No attempt will be made to pursue the theosophistic thinking which was always a major element in Guénon's work, because there is no reason to suppose that the present subject is not treatable by normal intellectual procedures, or that it should need quasi-mystical means of support.

A further reason is connected with the means by which Guénon's work was accepted as authentically traditional, among a readership with an interest in religious orthodoxy. The cyclic idea of successive worlds can evoke, subjectively at least, the reincarnationist idea of 'successive lives', this idea being a natural part of monistic doctrine. Subject to the belief that personality is a true reality, the idea of reincarnation, with its identification of persons who are by definition alive with other persons who are by definition dead is too incoherent for it to be either true or false. Outside this belief, on the other hand, reincarnation is a natural means of inculcating the idea that all finite beings are illusory and that only the Absolute is real. Despite its obvious logical connection with monistic doctrine, however, Guénon excluded all reference to reincarnation from his own works, except where he attacked it, while at the same time retaining most of the other essentials of theosophistic thought, regardless of consistency. By this means he avoided being identified with Theosophism, though how justifiably is far from clear.[1] Although there are associations between cyclic time and monistic pantheism, therefore, this seems only to be owing to their common inclusion in the writings of authors who have used ideas which were neglected by the academic world, and not to any logical connection between them.

---

1. Guénon's real attitude to Theosophism can be judged from a lengthy book, *Theosophy: History of a Pseudo-Religion*, which he wrote after breaking with theosophism. This book is given over almost entirely to the shortcomings of individual theosophists, and contains hardly any condemnation of theosophistic teachings as such.

It would in any case be unfortunate if this book were to be identified with the indiscriminately negative judgement of Guénon and his closest followers, because the implications of cyclic laws do not lend themselves to simplification. Oversimplified views of them can easily give rise to reactions of anger, hysteria, and fundamentalism, which could only cancel the advantages gained from metaphysical insight. While it is true that the traditional idea of time implies a grave judgement on the values of the modern world, there are some important compensating factors to be allowed for.

The spiritual superiority of the ancient traditions is limited in a way which is usually ignored by modern idealists. Pre-modern members of the traditions indeed held their beliefs with a purity of conviction which is rare in today's world, but there was a price to be paid for this. Traditional man for the most part held his religious beliefs simply out of acceptance of what his society saw as the most advanced state of knowledge as it then was. Thus religious beliefs were held as we, as members of modern society, believe that viruses and bacteria cause diseases and that the earth moves round the sun. As a result of this, the number of such people who lived out the truth of their beliefs as individuals may not have been so much greater in earlier times as is often supposed. By no means everyone realized the higher possibilities arising from God's greater manifestation at such times; all too often, it only made defiance of God more obstinate and more impassioned.

Be that as it may, the fact that traditional religion in recent centuries at least was not always tied to personal understanding and commitment shows why the loss of tradition is irreversible. Such religion is largely unconscious in just the same way that no one is conscious of being part of a modernist movement just because they believe that atoms can be split. Another reason why there can be no return to the original form of tradition lies in the development of scientific knowledge. The ancient traditions, for all their metaphysical depth, were nearly all wedded to pre-scientific cosmologies which not even the hardiest modern fundamentalist is able to believe. A Christian example of such things is the belief that everything in creation is there for the satisfaction of human needs. This belief lives on in the minds even of those who are 'post-Christian', and who make excessive demands on technology. This means that modern man has to determine what is truly of religion and what is not, whereas archaic man could confuse it with the theocratic culture which grew out of it. Any return to tradition must perforce be an act of conscious individual choice, therefore, and for this reason it differs necessarily from the original, even though its theological constituents may be the same. Another compensating factor with regard to traditional ages is the fact that it is really only a minor achievement to live spiritually in an age when spiritual values are established and expressed everywhere and the unspiritual is marginalized. This is related to the impersonal and collective way in which it was possible for many to practise a religion at such times. The true way is only fully realized when everything is more or less opposed to it. Such is the meaning of the Cross, as well as the purpose of ensoulment in the material world.

There is in practice no longer any clear dividing line between the traditions and the secular world, however separate they may be in theory. On the contrary, the need for a tradition to survive may cause it to take in even more of the spiritually deviant culture around it than would be accepted by many individuals relying only on their own judgement. Here is the contradiction of unqualified neo-traditionalism: if one grants absolute authority to a tradition as a denial of the point of view of modern secular culture, one is thus making an open-ended commitment to that very culture, as boundaries between tradition and anti-tradition dissolve. In this way, the normal function of tradition can actually be inverted under modern conditions, for the naive and the unaware, at least. For example, the three monotheistic religions have each grown increasingly absorbed by their historical social roles, so that it has become an exercise of awareness to relate to the spirit which they nevertheless embody. However, the very excessiveness of the trend against authentic spirituality in the modern world can also unmask itself inasmuch as every denial is an inverted affirmation of what is denied, for those who are willing to see this.

The relentless unfolding of a descending cosmic process should also be understood in relation to the soul and its world-representation, because cosmic change is part of the inner life of the soul as much as it is an external force acting on our physical existence. This conception excludes the supposition that the necessity of the cosmic process could have an equally necessary effect on the individual, because this process takes place by definition *within* the soul or self rather than to it. Thus there is no objective necessity for the will to follow the direction taken by the world in the soul's representation of that world. If it should in fact do so, it can only be owing to a failure to understand the way in which the self and the world are respectively in one another.

The theoretical treatment of what follows will be seen to depend to a large extent on Neoplatonic thought, though this is only because that philosophy is best supplied with the language and concepts involved, and not because of an aim to propagate a system for its own sake. Far from being another individualistic 'philosophy of life', this study seeks to surmount the barriers between the modern mind and a kind of knowledge which has always existed. It does not seek to perform some new and rather improbable feat of reasoning. Only to the extent that it is not essentially new, invented or subjective can this idea deserve to shape our view of the world. While the reality involved in this is anything but a pattern of personal spiritual evolution, its positive role is to give a fuller conception of the hostile forces which our response to the spirit must overcome.

2

PREHISTORICAL TO POSTHISTORICAL

HISTORY AND ABSOLUTE CHANGE

Cyclic processes always involve an element of regular repetition, like the hours of the day, or the rise and fall of the tides. The intervals between these repeated phenomena may be quite short by human reckoning at one extreme, or unimaginably long at the other, depending on the cyclic law in question. In every case, a process of change is counteracted by a return to its original state, and in this respect it contrasts with the idea of true change, where successive alterations made in the passage of time build upon one another so that each stage diverges further from the original in a way which would make any return to it ever less likely.

The world shows an abundance of evidence for both of these kinds of temporal process, and it is not easy to see how they could relate to one another, or how either could depend on the other. This issue arises in the question whether history repeats itself, and how much similarity between events could constitute repetition. Such repetitions are more easily seen in the general forms of eras than in particular events, and the cyclic pattern can be seen in the way in which a historical development leads to a state which manifests the essential features of the one it started from. For this purpose, some relevant examples can be drawn from the development of European civilization from the early Middle Ages to the present time.

Contrary to the usual practice, the term 'prehistorical' will be applied to the beginning of this period and the term 'posthistorical' to the present-day end of it. The reason for this choice of terms lies in the special meaning that the word 'history' itself has acquired in recent centuries. Thanks to a unique series of connected and cumulative changes, history has ceased to mean a mere heaping-up of chronicled events, and has come to mean a kind of universal and irreversible change comparable with the plot of a novel.[2]

Given this conception of history, it is doubtful whether some parts of the world could be said to have any 'history' at all, since tribes may hunt, migrate, grow and decline, and fight among one another for millennia, without there resulting the kind of cumulative change that this word now implies. But if there can be no real history of a primitive people living close to nature, it is scarcely more possible for there to be one of a traditional civilization where all values and objectives are prescribed, not by nature, but by a code of values and priorities fixed for all time. No matter how great a disruption may be suffered by such a civilization, it returns to its original pattern as soon as it is able. The ancient civilizations were all more or less of this type, and were to that extent ahistorical, as can be clearly seen in the case of ancient Egypt, which retained the same theocratic form for some five thousand years without any radical or irreversible change in its spiritual or social order. Now it is just because Medieval Europe shared in this traditional form, in however limited a way, that it cannot be counted as historical in the same way that post-Renaissance Europe can. There was nothing in the period from the ninth to the fourteenth centuries which need necessarily have led to anything essentially different after another five hundred years, whereas the pattern of changes from the fifteenth century onward was unmistakably cumulative.

SELF-NEUTRALIZING CHANGE

Such is the general character of our 'prehistorical' period, and on the same basis the present century can be called 'posthistorical'

2. This idea also appears in *The Arrogance of Humanism*, chap. 4, by David Ehrenfeld, quoting R. Seidenberg.

because the present period falls outside the historical period as defined above, just as much as do the Middle Ages, though for different reasons. Modernity can be called 'posthistorical' because it too offers no scope for radical change, even if this idea seems paradoxical at first sight. The present age is surely the Age of Change if there ever was one, but this must not obscure the fact that the flood of changes released in modern times consists mostly of changes that affect only matters of detail and technique, and for no great time at that. On all essentials modern civilization is now just as immobilistic as that of the early Middle Ages. It is designed for the production of endless minor changes in all manner of restricted realms, with all energies mobilized for this purpose under the headings of industry and bureaucracy, and hardly any deviations of effort are permitted from these priorities.

That unlimited change should turn out to be self-neutralizing results from the metaphysics of change itself, since change is only conceivable at all on the basis of a component which does not change, within and against which the change can be effected. It is thus dependent on its opposite, permanence, if it is to effect anything. The permanent, however, is not necessarily bound to any other condition, being self-sufficing by nature, and this puts it on a different level of reality from that of change. This is the real reason for the apparent paradox that a civilization cannot undergo real historical change unless it possesses a structure of permanent principles which impose limits on the possible scope for change. Should these limits be removed, the final result will be to make change so all-pervasive that every change will be countered by another one before it can make any difference, and the only permanent condition left will be just this condition where all forces cancel one another out.

Thus the positive principle of permanence is represented by the 'prehistorical' civilization, while change as such will be manifested in the 'historical' period starting approximately with the fifteenth century, and lastly the 'posthistorical' period manifests permanence again, not in its original principle, but in its lower reflection, a negative permanence of creative exhaustion and universal conflict. The state of 'total change' which is being approached by modern civilization is more deeply opposed to real historical change than is institutionalized permanence, since the permanent at least contains the potentiality of change, as the static traditional civilization contains the possibility of a historically changing one. Universal change, on the other hand, has no potentialities at all, since everything in it is actualized already, so that a final cessation is the only new frontier it could cross. The advance to some such finality is indicated by the fact that there is now scarcely any element in present-day culture which is not subject to more or less irrelevant pressures from innumerable others, so that the growth of anything truly new is practically ruled out. Culture is everywhere under state control, while the states themselves are tied to the same economic goals by their mutual dependence. If that were not enough, modern high-speed communications have abolished the regional privacies in which new identities could develop. In contrast to this permanence in sterility, the permanence of a traditional civilization appears as a store of energy, like that of water behind a dam, which was released in the creative processes of history, and which is now tending to exhaustion, as the original store of energy is dissipated.

RECURRENCE AND ACTUAL CHANGE

Here, then, is the correspondence between beginning and end which is the hallmark of the cyclic process. It is in fact a correspondence and not an identity, because the cyclic movement involved here has not so much completed a circle as one turn of a spiral, which is why it is not to be identified with the idea of perpetual recurrence. The historical movement has been from a state superior to change to one which is inferior to it, and as with all cyclic correspondences it entails an identity between the opposite extremes under at least one aspect. Both the opposition and the identity are equally real in their separate ways, and neither need be thought to contradict the other so long as the cycle is represented by one turn of a spiral. The aspect of identity or recurrence will be represented by the completion of a single turn, while that of opposition or resultant change will be represented by the vertical interval between the beginning and the end of this part of the curve. By means of this model, it can be shown that the aspects of identity and opposition also admit of degrees, since that of opposition can in any case be increased according to the number of turns of the spiral. These two realities can be seen in the circles of the Same and the Different, whose union underlies the cosmic order in Plato's *Timaeus*. A gross imbalance of either of them, it is thought, would make the continuation of the natural order inconceivable.

The modern world lies at an extreme of opposition to its origin because of the time for which the present creation has lasted, while its correspondences to its past are being steadily increased by rediscoveries and reconstructions based on archaeology, so that more is now known about some parts of antiquity than was known about them in their own times. This enlargement of historical recapitulation is also another indication that the 'historical' era of original developments is now over.

What has been said concerning the cyclic process and the historical phases that illustrate it is not intended to be a proof of the theory, so much as an illustration of it, drawn from generally-admitted facts. What has been said about the resistance to change which characterizes the 'pre-historical' and 'posthistorical' eras will be easier to understand if the difference between change and mere disturbance is borne in mind. Some of the major events of the twentieth century, such as World War II, have caused vast amounts of disorder and disruption without essentially changing anything beyond confirming and accelerating all the characteristics of this century which were fully present before the conflicts began. On this basis it could be said that the difference in historical meaning and value between human action and that of floods and earthquakes has practically vanished. This applies even more clearly to the innumerable violent events of today; no real change is involved, any more than if it were a matter of fights between primitive tribes.

This posthistorical situation has occurred innumerable times before at the latter stages of other civilizations, but what makes it different and doubly significant at the present time is the fact that it now embraces the whole human race and not just one part of it, as was the case in all earlier times. For the first time in recorded history there is no spiritually young and untried part of the human race by which history could be continued, as there are no peoples left which have never known any other kind of life except that of direct struggle with nature. This static condition is compensated by an ambience in which knowledge can be increased more easily than ever before, however, and the manifest unification of mankind is in itself a challenge to the understanding. If the advanced state of knowledge in modern times should turn out to be far from unique in universal time, it will in any case provide the richest resources for attempts to understand the meaning of such periodic rises and falls in the state of knowledge.

CIVILIZATION AND THE NATURAL ORDER

The solution to the enigmas of universal time requires a study of reality as a whole, and not merely of the aspects of it which are the province of the natural sciences. The outward appearances of the world, more or less as they appear to common sense, are as well suited to this purpose as are theoretical principles. The general appearance of the world at a given time is filled with a symbolic content which, *qua* symbolic, never seems to result from human intentions, even though it is as a whole the net outcome of countless human activities. This distinction answers to the way in which the world of appearance results from two systems of causality, the one being natural causality acting through the passage of time, and the other being archetypal causality acting from outside the natural forces so as to impose its eternal types upon their causal flow.

Outward appearances are in some sort the lowest point reached by the action of cosmic causality, but this aspect of triviality is compensated by a law of polarity according to which only the highest cause can extend to the lowest level of effects. This is expressed by Proclus on the basis that 'the higher principles both begin to operate before the lower and extend beyond them to things which the lower by remission of power are precluded from reaching.'[3]

3. Proclus, *Elements of Theology*, prop. 59.

The overall appearance of a world is therefore specially fitted to reveal something of the archetypal cause it is conditioned by at the time, and this appearance includes that of both nature and of civilization. The successive phases through which civilization has passed, from Classical Antiquity to post-Renaissance, along with the parallel changes in religion and in human aptitudes, are the result of social reactions to changing cosmic conditions which are sensed rather than understood. Innumerable small changes are made to the ways in which things are done, therefore, until these small changes result in a new form for the whole. Part of this process lies in the way in which minds are motivated by successively different paradigms, not least where there is no general agreement that this should happen.

This collective attachment to ruling paradigms has a force in it which is manifested by the fact that no innovation ever prevails unless it harmonizes with the complex set of conditions which has arisen from causes beyond individual human choice. For example, the attempts by philosophers like Bacon and Locke to establish their empiricist philosophy would have had little result were it not for the fact that the collective state of mind had for a long time been moved in this direction by subliminal changes.

The same could be said of the rise, or rather restoration, of natural science in the seventeenth century, since the discoveries then made public would have been hardly less physically possible in the Middle Ages or Classical Antiquity, where the operative factor in them was the kind of technical skills that craftsmen have always had. Thus there is no physical reason why the telescope and the microscope should not have been invented centuries earlier than they were, by Roger Bacon, for example, as legend suggests he did. But in fact these developments had to await the conditions under which they could meet with a receptive response.

The fate suffered by anachronisms illustrates the same point from the negative side. Where something is achieved which could change the prevailing mindset before it had run its course, it has to lie dormant until changing conditions favor it. Such was the case with the astronomical tables compiled in the Eleventh century under King

Alphonsus X, which were accurate enough to have prepared the way for the Copernican Revolution by showing that the Ptolemaic system did not fit the facts. In the event, their appearance had to wait until the late fifteenth century. The modern idea that man simply does as he pleases with his technical resources is in reality quite unfounded, except, of course in the twentieth century itself, and even this age of all-out technical liberation is part of a sequence over which the individual has no power.

This great upsurge in the sciences is not an altogether new thing, even though it is without precedent in historical times. Even in today's world, there is still evidence for the existence of advanced scientific knowledge in more remote antiquity. Such evidence includes the units of measure which have survived from ancient times, and which can be shown to be related to exact measurements of the earth and the solar system.[4] Such facts are usually ignored, because they are meaningless to the majority who adhere to a linear conception of time.

ABSTRACT AND CONCRETE TIME

As the form of civilization changes, its human and cosmic elements each prepare changes for one another in endless alternation. Each moment in time comprises a combination of cosmic influences which gives it the qualitative uniqueness peculiar to all different times. Cosmic influences are known to vary in a cyclical manner, but there is no repetition among the combinations they form, even though the latter will not change at random. This is the view of time which conflicts with the abstract idea of time which makes time immune from the properties of the changes which pervade it. Such an idea of time would make it an endless succession of empty intervals with no specific relation to their content. Its moments differ only numerically, therefore, so that they can be represented by equal intervals along the axis of a graph, as is required by physical science. It thereby receives continual experimental corroboration in

---

4. See John Michell, *Ancient Metrology.*

experiments where every phenomenon but one is either excluded or is under human control.

However, if this idea of time was any more than a practical simplification justified for short intervals, it would be impossible to see how there could be all the synchronisms and anachronisms referred to above, or how the passage of time could always bring irreversible changes with it. All changes would occur more or less at random, so that there would be no temporal patterns except those imposed by human contrivance. In reality, the abstract time of science is the result of a subtractive process which removes most of what is essential to it, leaving a lowest common factor which functions compatibly with other scientific entities-of-convenience such as bodies without extension or friction, and masses and extensions without color or sound.

In contrast to this, the concrete idea of time requires there to be a special relationship between the moment and its content, so that the distinction between them exists only for thought. If it is supposed that to complicate the idea of time in this way is to forego any chance of grasping the essence of time, such as might appear when all other realities were separated from it, the objection would only be valid on the grounds that time really was just an abstract quantity of extension, so that this could be a matter of question-begging. The reduction of time to an abstraction in fact makes it harder, not easier to define.

Where successive moments are successive changes in the qualitative condition pervading the world according to a law of some kind, the result is at least a conception which is testable against experience in realms which extend much further than the controlled conditions in a laboratory. Such time is an object of direct experience, whereas abstract time is never experienced as such at all, even though it is the chosen instrument of a science which claims to reduce everything to experience.

The disappearance of radical and consecutive change in the periods referred to above as 'posthistorical' goes in parallel with precisely the rise of a general belief in a qualitatively empty and abstract time, in a way which is not likely to be coincidental. The way the world appears to the majority of observers, and what those observers believe about it, react upon and reinforce one another because of the way in which minds both contain representations of the world and share their experiences both consciously and unconsciously. The practice of seeing only what one expects to see has obvious dangers for individuals, but insofar as it is done collectively, it does not seem to lead to any mishaps in the short term, at least.

FREEDOM AND COSMIC CONDITIONING

The distinction between concrete and abstract time corresponds to two different ideas as regards the relation between mankind and the cosmos. If the passage of time is a mathematical abstraction with no inherent direction or quality, the uses it serves will be likewise matters of human choice and convention, and therefore not grounded in the natural order. Such uses are necessarily based on the assumption that human actions, or a significant proportion of them at least, are free in relation to their cosmic conditions. Whether this is valid or not, the rules for activities of this kind are not relevant for a study of the structure of time which precedes all forms of manipulation. The latter conception of time was common to nearly all systems of pre-modern thought, as instanced in Plato's statement that 'time and the heaven came into being together,' and similarly in Chinese tradition according to Marcel Granet,[5] who says that in ancient China they chose to see time as a compound of 'eras, seasons, and epochs,' rather than as a succession of identical units passing at a uniform speed. Such a conception is well suited to embrace both human and non-human realities equally. There is a vast range of phenomena, both biological and astronomical, together with their interactions, which follow cyclic orders, to an extent that they could be said to exemplify nature's dominant pattern. The populations of different species, the ice ages, tides, rainfall, sunspots, growth rhythms of trees, the precession of the equinoxes, volcanic eruptions, and human affairs as they appear in

5. *La Pensée Chinoise*, chap. 1.

the volume of international trade, all reveal the same kind of regular rise-and-fall in quantity. In forms of thought where time is not abstracted from its content, therefore, the idea that time is cyclic in itself will follow naturally from the universality of this order.

The integration of mankind with the natural order, which is implicit in the way in which the cycles of human activity depend on those of cosmic origin, may invite comparison with similar views on man's cosmic condition expressed by evolutionist thinkers such as Teilhard de Chardin. For such thinkers, the human race integrates with the cosmos simply through being a part of the biosphere as a result of having been the product of solely biological processes.

On this basis, man cannot rationally be conceived as having any destiny outside the cycles of the biosphere, whatever mystical rhetoric may be used to neutralize the facts. No such reductionist aim is being pursued in the present use of the cosmic connection, however, because metaphysical principles can comprehend this relation without any need to take natural phenomena for its primal realities. On the contrary, they show the relation of man and cosmos as an element in his being which results from the way in which both physical human existence and nature as a whole are equally material instantiations from a single system of archetypes or formal causes, these being the timeless source of the temporal creation. According to this conception, the deep relation between the human race and its world has nothing to do with the idea of the one being physically produced by the other. It is established without any need for forced explanations of the human psycho-intellectual-corporeal complex by means of its material elements alone.

The primacy of consciousness and its cognitive functions over our experience of material realities implies that it is nothing less than our share in the reality from which the physical world originates. For all their superficial similarities, therefore, evolutionist thought and traditional metaphysics are poles apart concerning the relation between man and cosmos.

One consequence of the distinction between these two ideas of human origin is that in the one case, the cosmic relation means inescapable determination by natural forces, where only the material element is involved, while in the other, the determination is only conditional. This is because an origin from whence issues intelligible and psychical reality along with the physical, is one which cannot determine mankind exclusively by any one of these three, especially as the human state comprises all three. If there is a question of determination on the physical level at the expense of the other two, therefore, this must derive from a tendency rooted in the collective human condition, not from its First Cause. The alternative to determination of human activity by the cosmos is in fact a metaphysical causality of both human and cosmic powers by causes which transcend both of them.

Far from giving an account of the conditions under which human life may possibly be controlled by natural forces insofar as their role is not understood, evolutionist philosophies leave no grounds for thinking there is any alternative to cosmic determinism. Despite this, the doctrine of evolutionary materialism is popularly associated with optimism, while its counterpart is associated with pessimism, an inversion owing more to propaganda than to logic. In modern times, the way in which evolutionist thought inverts the metaphysical conception of man's relation to nature corresponds to the outlook of a large majority, though it is hardly possible to say whether this outlook results from materialist teachings or whether it is the other way round. In any case, they are mutually reinforcing. The fact that there is no reason why 'more evolved' should mean 'more desirable for most human beings' is lost on the popular consciousness to which such ideas are directed, because of the ease with which the 'ascending' aspect of evolution can be viewed with a kind of tunnel vision which takes it out of relation to other values.

The opposite conception to this one is that of the entropic increase which cyclic change reveals, which is as indifferent to individual reactions to it as the trend of evolution. Given two such opposed conceptions, one needs to be able to decide whether there is anything in the nature of things from which either kind of change would result necessarily. Neither cosmic tendency can be all-comprehensive, however, since the intelligence at very least must be extra-cosmic in its working and determined only by truth, or theories about cosmic change would be of no use. The mind which defines a set of conditions cannot itself be a part of them, on pain of absurdity. With this essential reservation, the laws of necessity may be illumined by those of reason, which has a necessity of a quite different kind.

3

The Principle of Plenitude

The Cause of Cosmic Descent

Besides the idea of regular repetition, it is necessary to account for the accompanying idea of a progressive devolution from an original cause or standard. These two aspects are inseparable because in the absence of an overall progressive change, the beginning and end of a cycle would not be distinguishable. If the prevailing quality was either constant, or if it varied at random, then there would be no basis on which cycles could be manifest as distinct entities. Even where this conception is not considered, the doctrine that the world was created with as great a perfection as was possible for it, and that it then became increasingly subject to the effects of the Fall, implies the same qualitatively declining aspect of the time process, with its progressive loss of relation to God.

Such a world could not spontaneously grow better than it was created, if it started by definition from its ideal state of being, and it could not remain constant in this original perfection without negating the ontological level to which it belongs; in other words, the material creation would, without change, be indistinguishable from the eternal Forms through which it was created. Time and change are inseparable from the divisibility of matter and its passivity to external forces, however, and the overall effect of this change can only be to tend away from the first state of creation for the reasons just given.

Such is the conclusion which follows from the creationist perspective, but the idea that every state of being necessarily gives rise to another more limited than itself is by no means dependent on creation, important as that idea is. The idea that the order of existence has a mathematical form which is in a sense prefigured in the natural number series, and which allows for all possibilities to be realized is part of a metaphysical tradition which has crossed the boundaries of the main religious traditions. Strangely enough, this principle was never given a specific name until modern times, when it was named as the Principle of Plenitude.[1] This is the principle to which Guénon is in fact appealing where he says:

> This gradual movement away from essential unity can be envisaged from a double point of view, that of simultaneity and that of succession; this means that it can be seen as simultaneous in the constitution of manifested beings, where its degrees determine for their constituent elements a sort of hierarchy; or alternatively as successive in the very movement of the whole of manifestation from the beginning to the end of a cycle.[2]

Thus the scale of creation down from the angels to the lowliest created things will also be manifest in the time dimension as a progression from the highest realities to the lowest, as space and time both manifest the same things, each according to its own principle. Of the two points of view, the static and the successive, the successive is clearly the one which is relevant here, while the Principle of Plenitude itself transcends the distinction between the temporal order of succession, and the hierarchical order of being. For Guénon, this principle is an assumption, and therefore he does not offer arguments for it. Nevertheless a deeper layer of theory exists, which will be approached when some classic accounts of Plenitude have been considered.

PLENITUDE UNDERSTOOD IN ANTIQUITY

Since this is the principle on which the present subject depends, it should be taken in as much detail as possible. It is to be found in

1. See A. O. Lovejoy, *The Great Chain of Being.*
2. *The Reign of Quantity,* chap. 7.

numerous places in the *Enneads*,[3] because for Plotinus it also appears as a primary reality, so that he chooses to elaborate on it:

> Something besides a unity there must be or all would be indiscernibly buried, shapeless within that unbroken whole: none of the real beings [of the Intellectual Cosmos] would exist if that unity remained at a halt within itself: the plurality of these beings, offspring of the unity, could not exist without their own next taking the outward path.... Every kind must produce its next... and so advance to its term in the varied forms of sense.[4]

Proclus renders the same conception[5] with his idea that the nature of the Good is to be productive, and that all beings participate in the Good to some degree, whence it must follow that all beings have causal powers which extend in an outward and downward process from greater causes to lesser. He also includes in this idea the Principle of Undiminished Giving, which is equally essential to Plotinus' understanding of the action of the Forms.

This is an idea of emanation for which every causal power acts beyond itself, so that nothing is ever subtracted from the cause itself in the things it gives rise to. This idea is implicit in the way in which Forms cause their instantiations, for which they are both causes and normative patterns. The productive process has an unbroken continuity according to the principle that 'every productive cause brings into existence things like to itself before the unlike.'[6]

Where these principles are expressed by the Neoplatonists, their application is not confined either to the hierarchy of being or to the temporal transformation of this structure in successive moments. They apply to the whole of being in a way which includes all possible orders of relation, including therein no doubt many more than the space and time to which our awareness is confined. In any case, their application to all temporal change is clear enough, and for Proclus the truth of Plenitude is found from his analysis of causality.

---

3. See *Person, Soul, and Identity*, by the same author, chap. 2, pp 88–92.
4. *Enn.* IV, 8, 6. See also *Enn.* III, 3, 3.
5. *E.T.* props. 25–30.
6. *E.T.* prop. 28.

The same principle is expressed equally clearly by Saint August-ine, for whom it is a means of reconciling the existence of evil in the world with the goodness of creation:

> Suppose someone should say that it was not difficult or laborious for an omnipotent God to see to it that everything He made should so maintain its proper place that no creature would come to the extremity of unhappiness; for being omnipotent, He could have done so, and, being good, He could not be envious. I will say in reply that the orderly arrangement of creatures extends all the way from the highest to the lowest according to certain just gradations in such a way that only envy could prompt a man to say that a creature should not exist, or that it should be different. For if he wants it to be the same as something higher, *then such a creature is already existing. . . .*[7] [author's italics]

While pursuing this idea at still greater length, Augustine stresses something in the above which is essential to the Plenitude idea, which is that a relatively inferior possibility is more fit to be realized than a superior one if the latter has been realized already, and so would only be repeated. The non-repetition of realized things and events is a consequence of the infinity of the Divine creative power, besides being more in keeping with the necessity for the material world to be wholly subject to change. (Identical repetitions of things would severely curtail the scope for change.)

This aspect of the idea is also taken up by Aquinas, who gives a new example to illustrate it, in the form of a question as to whether it would be more fitting for God to create two angels (assuming them to be very similar angels), or one such angel and a stone. He shows that the latter choice is the correct one, because it is irrelevant to object that a stone is so much inferior to an angel, when the nature of creation requires the greatest possible multiplication of different kinds of being.[8]

The fact that this implies a downward tendency does not matter, because the realization of the more superior possibilities has been

7. *The Free Choice of the Will*, Bk. III, chap. 9.
8. See A.O. Lovejoy, *The Great Chain of Being*, chap. 3

secured from the beginning. Insofar as the world is created for ends which do not lie in time but in eternity, the descent to lower or lesser grades of possibility does not mean any devaluation of the whole. Aquinas expresses the idea in a theological form as follows:

> God wills and loves His essence for its own sake. Now the divine essence cannot be increased or multiplied in itself, as it can be multiplied solely according to its likeness, which is participated by many. God, therefore, wills the multitude of things in willing and loving His own essence and perfection.[9]
> Furthermore, in willing Himself God wills all that is in Him. But all things in a certain manner pre-exist in Him through their proper models.... God, therefore, in willing Himself wills all other things.[10]

If God must needs will all that can be, this must comprise all levels of all possibilities, and the infinity of divine power must be reflected in an infinity in the content of the creation. Elsewhere, however, Aquinas says things which conflict with this because there are in fact two fundamentally different kinds of answer to the question as to what the purpose of creation is, and a *Summa* has to account for both. The first kind is the one already considered, namely the fullest realization of the plenitude of creation, while the second involves a process in the contrary direction, namely the assimilation of the creature, humanity, to the nature of its Creator. These are respectively the cosmological and the soteriological reasons for creation, and of the two, only the cosmological will be considered in this book, since it is devoted to the ultimate conditions under which the human race as a whole has to live. The other is not excluded, of course, since it is present at least implicitly in this context, in the way in which knowledge can penetrate the negations which are all-pervasive at a certain level.

There is in any case no question of either of these two kinds of answer being any 'more true' than the other. The one reflects the outflow of the cosmos from its source, and the other reflects the

9. SCG. 1, 75, 3.(9).
10. SCG. 1, 75, 5.(9).

returning movement from the creation to the Creator by which alone it can reach its proper perfection. They combine in the harmony of the whole in a way which can be compared to the way the upward-pointing and downward-pointing triangles make up a Star of David.

The spiritual assimilation of creature to Creator is also involved in the inequalities among creatures which Plenitude implies, in the 'all possible grades of goodness' comprised in it. As God is superior to all created beings, the superiority of one creature over another is therefore one more way in which the divine nature is manifest in creation, and so it is fit to serve as a symbolic reminder of God. An equality among beings would be more expressive of the chaos which preceded creation than of the providential order.

This value which Plenitude confers upon inequality merely balances the way in which it prescribes the realization of all kinds of beings. However, since it implies that the desirability of a thing's existence bears no relation to its degree of excellence, there can be no guarantee that a world-historical process governed by it will always tend in a direction agreeable to human desires and aspirations. This supra-human character no doubt accounts for much of the opposition to it, along with the related idea of entropy.

THE REAL AND THE POSSIBLE

More technical objections to Plenitude, based on the idea that, if true, it would necessitate a vastly greater range of species and varieties than we actually see, result from a confusion between the world we know in its limited portions of time and space, and the totality of all being. Plenitude implies only that every possibility is realized in some part of space and time, without this giving any reason to conclude that more than a limited number of them should exist at any one time in any one relative world.

Against this idea that all possibilities are realized sooner or later, Aristotle argues that 'it is possible for that which has a potency not to realize it, and that 'it is not necessary that everything that is possible should exist in actuality.'[11]

11. *Metaphysics*, 1071b, and 1003a.

Within certain limits, these are simply common sense judgements which do not conflict with what has been said above. Any number of things which are possible in principle can be impossible at a given place and time because of their incompatibility with other possibilities already realized. For example, an acorn which could possibly grow into an oak tree will never do so unless the right conditions are provided for it. In the general case, this means that there are many more potential causes than there are possible effects. Thus it is possible that any number of instances of a given possibility may never be realized, but on the other hand it is not possible for no instances of a given possibility ever to be realized.

To say that X is possible, but that on a certain planet, in a given society, in a given period of its history, it is never actualized is perfectly reasonable, but to say that X is possible but never becomes actual in the whole of space and time is quite different. The possible may be defined as whatever does not involve self-contradiction within the created order, in which case each possibility will comprise a set of logical compossibles which is itself compossible with at least one set of conditions. There is thus a group of closely-connected ideas, namely, logical consistency, possibility, and actuality. Here, the possible is the mediating idea between the logical and the ontological realms, and should there be any doubt about the reality of the connection, let it be supposed that there was something which was possible but which never became actual under any conditions. In this case it would be indistinguishable from things which are by definition impossible because self-contradictory. By the Identity of Indiscernibles, therefore, an unrealizable possibility would in fact be literally the same as an impossibility.

Granted only logical coherence, then, actuality will follow necessarily from possibility, as the Principle of Plenitude requires. This undoubtedly extends the range of realities to an incalculable extent, but this is as things should be, since the real problem would lie in an arbitrary limitation to the range of possibilities, if there could be such a thing. These ideas of limitation to the real survive mainly in mythical ideas such as that of the earth as a flat disc that one could fall off if one travelled to its edge.

The argument that the equivalence of the possible and the actual militates against free will can be shown to rest on the same mistake as does the objection already discussed, that we should perceive an unlimited range of different realities at a given time. This idea that actuality always follows possibility would imply that everything that can happen must happen, so that our choices would be just so many acceptances of the inevitable. This, however, applies to the whole of being throughout space, time, and all other modes of existence. But each relative world contains only a cross-section of the universal possibilities. This limitation to our actual world means that there must be voids among the possibilities proper to it. Such breaks in the continuum mean that the will can determine what is to be realized and what is not. If freedom is the power to realize potentialities, therefore, the Plenitude idea can form part of any philosophy of freedom.

The Finite and the Infinite

A specially significant example of the transition from possibility to actuality is to be found in the way in which instantiations result from Forms, as for example in the way combinations in twos and threes result from the Forms of duality and triplicity. Given a Form of, say, whiteness, the actualization of white objects in matter will follow automatically, even though the Form has no power over how many instances there may be. The Principle of Plenitude can shed additional light on this necessity with which the Forms become instantiated.

While the Form remains unaltered in itself, it nevertheless continually goes beyond itself in its self-projections in material substances, and this ontological going-beyond is essential both in regard to the Forms and in regard to Plenitude. Any deeper understanding of this principle should thus proceed from a deeper understanding as to how this 'going-beyond' is built into the nature of things. There is a property of the infinite which answers to precisely this condition. At first sight it seems that the finite must always be nothing in relation to the infinite, but it can be shown that this is only a relative nothing. Every finite quantity is in fact infinitely more than nothing, as one may illustrate from the way in which the equation $n \div \infty = 0$ gives rise to $\infty \times 0 = n$, where the finite quantity differs from zero by a factor of infinity. (This does not contradict the meaning of $n \div \infty = 0$ because this form of the equation establishes only the *relative* nullity of n, like that of a surface in relation to a volume, whether the surface and volume are both finite or both infinite.)

In all such cases, nullity in relation to a higher-order reality is all of a piece with the possession of a real degree of infinity. Because of this, there is a real sense in which the finite can add something to the infinite. This gives rise to the seeming paradox that the infinite as such is not after all the maximal conceivable quantity, because the real maximal quantity is rather the combination of the finite with the infinite: '*the true infinite* is the unity of finite and infinite,' with their distinction 'not simply abolished,' but 'retained within the unity.'[12]

Thus the essential nature of the infinite is one of an inherent passing-beyond itself, while the infinite is also a primal reality whose nature is participated in by all forms of being as much as they participate the finite. Here is the solution to the classic problem as to how the world of finite things could ever issue forth from the infinite. When the infinite is conceived solely as a simple unlimitedness, there never can be any answer to this question, but once its real nature is understood as infinite and finite, there is no longer any problem, because the finite as such is equiprimordial with the infinite. According to W. T. Stace,

> This doctrine of the infinite triumphantly solves the oldest and most formidable difficulty of philosophy and religion ... the true infinite has the finite within it ... there is no such thing as an infinite that is *first of all infinite*. ...[13]

The Hegelian conception of the role of the finite was anticipated to some extent by Proclus who saw the finite as an equal constituent of reality with the infinite: 'All true being is composed of limit and infinite.'[14] By 'limit' (το πέρας) Proclus means what has just been

---

12. W. T. Stace, *The Philosophy of Hegel*, pt. II, subsect. III, 'Quality', p148.
13. Ibid.
14. *Elements of Theology*, prop. 89.

termed the finite, only with the emphasis on its being the Finite Itself, which has the positive aspect of being the foundation of all intelligibility. The Form of Being has infinite power since it is instantiated in all that exists, whence it participates the infinite (το απειρον). It is also one and indivisible in its own nature, whence it participates the finite. Thus Being, and therefore all existence, results from the union of the finite and the infinite, where the term 'infinite' is used in its simple and unreconstructed sense. Proclus did not proceed to the idea that Being conceived in this way must be a fuller development of our idea of the infinite, because the infinite was thought of too much in connection with the indefinite for it to be a main interest for the Greek mind. Nevertheless, what he says in this connection is enough to show that the final dialectical development made by Hegel is not so much an innovation as the completion of a concept which was part of the Western intellectual tradition.

The self-extensive power of being, which is accounted for on the basis of the inherent movement of infinite and finite is deployed in the Principle of Plenitude and in the theory of Forms. From this, the cyclic order of time with its pattern of descent can be seen to follow as an application in the phenomenal world.

THE REALITY OF CREATED BEING

A further consequence of the way in which the Infinite inherently issues in the finite would be that it rules out the kind of relation between God and the world which exists for monistic systems, which confine all reality to God. Instead of a totally real divinity and a completely unreal world somehow lying alongside one another, we have here a conception which results in an infinitude of different degrees of reality proceeding through all levels from God in whom the true infinite resides with all other archetypal realities, down to the most evanescent residues of creation. This continuum does not make God into the highest part of the scale of creation, moreover, any more than a Form can be a member of its own range of instantiations, but rather it means that there is a continuous gradation from the part of creation with the fullest participation of the divine down to that which has least. This delegation of real being involves an incomparably greater creative act than would be involved in the production of an illusory world which was merely a distorted reflection of its creator. For this reason alone, Plenitude has a special role in Theistic doctrine which it cannot have in doctrines which deny creation, besides which it is the assumption behind rational proofs for the existence of God. Consequently, there is no logical reason why one of its implications, the cyclic law, should be any less a part of Western tradition than it is of Oriental tradition.

The diffusion of real being is nevertheless compatible with a 'cosmic illusion', as I have argued elsewhere,[15] only with the reservation that this illusion does not result specifically from the world as such, but essentially from the way in which human faculties grasp it when their activity is incomplete. The contraction of awareness which occurs with the descending tendency of the world means a worsening of this condition, and thus an increase in the extent to which the world is a *de facto* illusion for the majority of mankind. Although for many the end of the illusion will no doubt not come about without the end of the world, the more positive way in which it can be overcome lies in understanding its causes.

If there is any question as to whether it is justifiable to conceive of God as an agent imparting being to an endless sequence of creatures, so as to realize the greatest number of possibilities, the rationality of this might imply an anthropomorphic view of God. However, it should be realized that the opposite idea of God acting in arbitrary ways, withholding existence as much as imparting it, could also be anthropomorphic for different reasons. Any mode of personal agency by God can give rise to such problems, if that is what one wishes to find.

Insofar as it can be, the divine agency is normally conceived to be as rational as possible, since reason is recognized as sufficient for a knowledge of God. A suitable image of this rationality can be seen in the natural number series, especially in the way in which every number comprises all the other numbers lower than itself, so that it embodies the permanent possibility of separate existence for each

15. See *The Logic of Spiritual Values*, chap. 14.

one of them. Thus ten comprises nine, nine comprises eight, and so on. In general, any given number n must also give $(n-1)$, $(n-2)$ ... 3, 2, 1, i.e., all the numbers below itself. In this connection we may take number as a pattern for all realities, as it was for the Pythagoreans, in such a way that the continuous downward extension of number reflects the development of creation throughout time, in its simplest aspect. In reality, this development is complicated by many lesser cycles, each of which manifests the overall pattern in its own realm, and this is enough to disguise the universal tendency, which never simply follows a one-way course.[16]

This is not to say that number causes the sequence of being, but rather that the sequence of being and the law of number both manifest the same principle. The Principle of Plenitude connects all levels of being in order, and does so in an 'upward' or in a 'downward' direction, depending on one's point of view. If we can say that every higher and greater possibility must give rise to a lower and lesser one, then by the same principle, lower forms of being will be bound to the higher ones, and creation will reveal its Creator. If Plenitude were not valid, therefore, there would be no reason to suppose that any experience could establish a belief in God, and theology would be deprived of its status as a science. The life of religious faith includes a continuous exercise of the metaphysical intuition expressed as Plenitude.

16. See chapter 16, where this is shown in more detail.

4

FROM FORM
TO MATTER

THE FUNCTION OF DUALITY

What has been said of the cosmic process indicates that physical change must embody an inherent cause of deterioration, which leads to the question as to how this deterioration is manifest, and how the theoretical account of it relates to the appearance of the world. The world is in one sense a unity, and without this unity change would not be knowable as change, since change can only be known within a system where the overall structure gives the means of measuring it. However, unity is *per se* exclusive of change, since all forms of dynamism require at least two distinct elements in juxtaposition. Consequently, the most universal dichotomy that can be made in regard to the phenomenal world will be implicitly the most universal basis for change.

There is no need to invent such a conception, because the changes and transformations that make up the cosmic process have always been treated philosophically as the interaction of a pair of opposites, called Heaven and Earth, or *yin* and *yang* in the Far East, *Purusha* and *Prakriti* in Indian doctrine, and Form (ειδος) and Matter (υλη) in Western thought. (Here 'Form' is a collective term which includes all Forms or archetypal realities, while υλη denotes an undetermined matter known also as *materia prima*.) In each instance the pair consists of an active, unified, informing principle of fixed identity, and a passive, receptive, mutable and multiform principle. The latter is activated by the former and is the medium of its multiplication in many transient forms, propagating the archetypal identities without having the power of originating or of conserving any of them unalterably. For the present purpose I shall use the terms Form and Matter for them. These are the two opposite poles of existence between which the whole pageant of the visible world may be seen to unfold.

Being the principal causes of all things perceptible by sense, they cannot themselves appear among them; they are both outside the world of perception, Form because its perfection and permanence of being places it in a sense 'above' the world, and Matter because its essential emptiness and instability place it 'beneath' it. Besides being the causes underlying the relative reality of the world, Form and Matter are also the archetypes of all the endless dualities, polarities, and complementarisms in which natural life so largely consists. Some of these are body and soul, subject and object, male and female, cause and effect, quality and quantity, acid and alkali, light and dark, positive and negative, active and passive, interior and exterior, substance and attribute. Some of these pairs occur in the table of opposites drawn up by the Pythagoreans, who sought the ones which should have the greatest cosmological importance.

All things are thus conceivable as combinations of the two universal causes in one guise or another, though the necessity for these combinations is far from guaranteeing a balance between them in any given case. From the definitions, it could be said that the greatest predominance of the Formal principle will bring the greatest degree of stability and unity, whereas the predominance of the Material principle would imply just the opposite, mere confusion, and emptiness, with constant and inconsequential changes affecting such realities as remained. The phenomena of change, speed, matter and quantity are all bound up inextricably with one another, as can be seen from the most casual observation of present-day civilization which is replete with the material attributes of endless mutability and of receiving everything while retaining nothing.

It is remarkable that the relation of Form and Matter, which has been a familiar part of philosophy for millennia insofar as it relates to the static unions between them manifest in objects of sense, should be so little known in its dynamic relation. The difference between the two cases is like the difference between a knowledge of the parts which make up a machine, and a knowledge of the function the machine performs. That philosophy should have ignored the dynamic relation is even stranger in modern times, when science has established the principle of entropy, whereby all physical changes result in an irreversible loss of order. While the metaphysical idea of change does not depend on scientific findings, it is certainly not at variance with them either, and in fact they have parallels which will be examined later.

FORM AND MATTER IN PROCESS

The instability of matter is necessary for existence as we know it, however, because the material world can only manifest the fullness of the Formal principle fragmentarily, in a serial manner, where one thing has to be effaced so that another may be realized. When, therefore, the whole range of things subject to change is narrowed down to the minimal two, the only way in which change can take place is by way of an increasing predominance of either one over the other. This increase and decrease will not affect Form and Matter as they are in themselves, but only the realm of perceptible things in which they are instanced. The march of historical time would therefore mean an overall increase in either the spiritual or the material principle in the life of mankind.

An increase in the spiritual principle has been excluded before, on the grounds that what results from creation cannot be exceeded at its own level. For this reason, long-term cosmic change involves a continual reduction of the Formal principle, no matter how much this may be masked by a march of progress in the production of substitutes for its direct action. However, a constant change of this kind in one direction only cannot go on for ever, and neither can it develop in a uniformly predictable manner, or it would lack the power to deceive which is in fact necessary for it to be able to act unopposed.

It may seem possible that the relation between Form and Matter in the world might simply follow an endless ebb-and-flow movement with no fundamental change ever arising. But on this basis, the material world would exist for ever; in other words it would be unlimited in duration when it is by definition finite and relative in all ways. While there is indeed some such ebb-and-flow, the overall tendency of it is therefore always toward the material extreme. There is of course a permanent equilibrium between these two principles in their unmanifest or principial state, but this state cannot be manifest in time except indirectly by the reversals made by the beginning of new world cycles. This account of the working of the relation between Form and Matter does not include the creation, the establishment of the Formal principle in the world at its beginning, because this does not form part of the normal 'downstream' movement of nature, but is rather the cause of it. While the process subsequent to it is temporal, the emergence of the original state is not, which is another reason why it does not belong to a study of this kind.

What has been said about the twin causes of the cosmic process, and about the cosmic position of humanity, offers a direct explanation of the relentless onset of materialism in modern times, whether it be as a theoretical account of the world or whether as a form of popular common sense. Materialism is much more than a subject of human choice; it is the counterpart in the human microcosm to the relative increase in the material component in the macrocosm.

The advance of materiality in the one and the other is the same thing in parallel realities, according as the world is represented in individual minds. Materialism in human life and thought is thus man's imitative response to the universal process when individuals fail to separate their own identities from it. As a theoretical account of the world, its conclusions are, ironically enough, in broad agreement with the ones developed here, except in the vital question of meaning and value. For one side of the issue, the materialization of reality represents the advance to the fullness of truth and reality, while for metaphysical understanding it means a descent into the final residues of a world which has nearly run its course. Once the true nature of the material principle is understood, any state in which it reaches a culmination can only be one in which the formative realities of intelligence, order, permanence, and unity are all reduced to the lowest degree.

Consequently, the advance to the material extreme inevitably means a loss of distinction between things and a trend toward equalization,[1] and in human beings, a corresponding loss of understanding as to the meaning of the things that still escape this process. Equality could never have become the center of concern it is today without there having been first an extreme diminution of all the realities concerned. This diminution or dissipation is also evident in the breaking down of all spheres of activity into portions too small for any creative genius or cultural leadership to have any scope, even where it still exists. This deficiency is supposedly made good by wholesale borrowings from cultures of earlier times, and from other parts of the world, as though there was a void to be filled which no contemporary resources were equal to. There results a state of ever-deepening dependence upon the lights of the past, while modern minds stay rooted in the belief that the ancient civilizations have all been superseded by the march of progress, without anyone sensing the obvious contradiction in this. Such things indicate a general mentality which is incapable of objectivity about its true situation.

Another example of the effect on human life of cyclic change is to be found in its destructive effect on the practice of religious belief, whether or not this is masked by political and cultural motivations. A process has been slowly gaining momentum for centuries now, one which marks a decline both in the depth of belief and in the number of those who consciously profess it, which in vulgar perception means the same as a denial of its truth. Confusions result from this situation because many minds see the idea of a general loss of relation to God as a claim that some such failure must be theirs also, in which case it can be speciously denied. Nevertheless, this is no answer to the possibility that traditional religion may convert ever fewer persons, even where it is unchanged in itself. Numbers are a superficial indication, it is true, but when that indication is consistent in one direction over a long period, it cannot be ignored.

1. See chapter 10.

The revelation of a religion is a special case of the entry into the world of a universal Form-principle, one which is a paradigm of all that can counteract in the human realm the fatal run-down of history. In theory, the liberation which it brings from 'the course of the world' could postpone the end of the world-cycle indefinitely, so that there is something like the supposed conflict between irresistible force and immovable object involved here, represented by the downrush of the cycle and the truth which is impervious to it. Religious values and practices imply a detachment from the realm of process and a state of attachment to a reality which is ontologically 'before' the world, so that they reconnect the world with its origin through the believer.

In this connection there are widespread traditional beliefs to the effect that the continued existence of a world depends on the correct performance of rites, a belief which need not be seen as superstitious if man's centrality in creation is taken into account. As an epitome of creation, he is metaphysically in contact with its whole range of content, whether he wills it or not. For this reason, each person is an agent whose words, thoughts and deeds give rise to effects in parts of the universe far more remote than the things to which they ostensibly relate. What seems trivial in its immediate context may be anything but trivial in the whole sum of being, therefore. Where the influence of religion and spiritual values weakens, there follows a corresponding weakening in the realms of intellectual and creative endeavor, since the higher values are too closely connected for them to be able to decline or develop independently. The issue then is the paradox of the decline of something which is the very negation of decline and corruptibility. But its effect on this world depends on the extent to which it is realized in each generation. Man's falling short of his destiny allows cosmic necessity to outflank the spiritual power, if not to defeat it, in accordance with a general movement which takes its origin from the Fall.

THREE LEVELS OF CHANGE

One of the main factors which masks the descent from Form to Matter is something inherent in the nature of cyclic change itself, which never shows itself in anything like as simple a form as that of a wheel rolling downhill. This factor is one whose outward effects we have already referred to in chapter one, where historical extremes correspond in a certain manner. This meeting of extremes results from a property of causality according to which 'whatever is simple in its being may be either superior to composite things or inferior to them.'[2]

The highest realities both consist in and result from very few causes, while the number of causes in operation steadily increases up to the intermediate level, only to start to decrease again as the lower extreme is approached. As with Plenitude, this process can be envisaged in relation to the order of creation as a static hierarchy, or as a temporal series of related states, and again, the latter is relevant for the present purpose. The passage of time between certain pairs of limits should therefore exhibit a transition from a simplicity of potentiality to a simplicity of exhaustion, passing through a maximum wealth of complexity during the period between them. Proclus gives this as a logical deduction from the fact that the highest cause acts on all the beings subsequent to it, down to the very last, while the next highest causes act on all the intermediate levels except the lowest, and so on, while the causes closest to the mean position do not act beyond themselves very far at all. This property of causes will be illustrated later by a corresponding property of the natural number series, which will show its significance among the archetypal patterns.

The symmetry between highest and lowest, second-highest and second-lowest, third-highest and third-lowest, is the basis of the three-fold division of a cycle which may be manifest in a nation, a civilization, or in the development of the arts, and it is a factor which confuses our perception of the cyclic order itself. The mysterious significance of the number three is thus able to imprint itself on the form of historical eras, as is indicated by the fact that the earliest parts of most eras of civilization hardly ever seem to have been the golden ages they should have been according to the theory, even if this should be due only to a scarcity of records or artifacts. The

2. *Elements of Proclus*, prop. 59.

times of greatest achievement generally displayed by civilizations would seem to lie roughly half-way between their earliest and latest ages, not at the beginning. But if tangible evidence for the existence of a higher state of being at the origin is wanting, this should not be confused with an actual absence of the reality of which all physical evidence is only the shells and rinds, so to speak, whether it be in the form of writings, arts, crafts, or sciences. Modern thought usually equates the absence of such tangible traces of intelligence in remote ages with the state of emptiness and barbarism it would mean in modern times, ignoring the very possibility that the world could have undergone profound changes since antiquity which would obliterate the most significant traces of the past.

What is a process of descent by absolute standards will therefore appear as one of ascent on a relative level up to a certain point, beyond which it reverses and begins to mirror the absolute tendency. Within some historical periods it can be shown that visible and tangible forms created by art to eternalize the spirituality of the age are as much a symptom of decline as of fulfilment. For example, Christianity in Apostolic times had no need of cathedrals to impress its message on mankind, because at that time one was still close to the historical origin of the faith. The building of the cathedrals only became necessary when the early vision began to be lost; it therefore cannot mark the high point of faith in the Christian Era. Great achievements in the arts are more realistically to be seen as the disclosure at the sensory level of some spiritual experience which can only be preserved by being objectivized.

The closer in time mankind is to the origin, the less need there is for conceptual and aesthetic forms to represent it and to awaken its influence in minds which might never have known it directly. However, even the greatest achievements of this kind are only temporary barriers against the downward movement because a point is always reached at which minds are too materialized in their orientation to be able to respond even to these secondary sources. There still has to be some spiritual energy to sustain a sense of what was lost and to attempt to regenerate the original vision. Where even this is lacking, spiritual realities simply get identified with the means used to transmit them and they are effectively made into idols, if they are still regarded at all, as the finger pointing to the moon is mistaken for the moon.

This is evidenced in a general way by the history of art in the West since the early Middle Ages. Typically, neither modern nor Medieval art has the direct aim of depicting nature, but rather certain realities manifest through it, though their spiritual orientations are utterly different. Between these periods there is the art of the period from the sixteenth to the nineteenth centuries, which is primarily naturalistic. These three broad categories represent three basic relations to natural forms, ranging from a perspective superior to them because relating to their origin, to one beneath them, because it is concerned only with their impact on the mind of one individual, who as a rule is not qualified to perceive any spiritual reality in them.

Evils from Cosmic Necessity

From this stage onward, art and symbolism deviate further and further from their original purpose until they end with an inversion of it. With the passage of time, the scope of this deviation takes in an increasing number of activities until, in the final extreme, it comprises the whole civilization. This may be understood in an alternative manner from the point of view of equilibrium. When created forms and structures are used to exert an action of just one kind, benign and spiritual though it be, the result is an increasing disequilibrium, since created or instantiated forms are *per se* spiritually neutral. This can only be remedied by the intelligibility of the same forms. Regardless of the intentions with which these things were first brought into being, their effect eventually becomes anti-spiritual for increasing numbers of persons who read their meaning at the wrong level.

This is a dominant issue toward the end of a cycle, because a cycle cannot end without a balancing of all the disequilibria which have come into being since it began. This follows from the nature of a cycle as a self-contained whole of connected events. Any disequilibrium remaining at its end would be the immediate basis of a corresponding action which would give the subsequent events a measure of continuity with the past cycle. In other words, the cycle would not truly have ended. But, being finite in all respects, it must end, and therefore in full equilibrium, even though this means ending amid evils which counteract the good it has realized at earlier times, on the cosmic level at least.

There are thus two related reasons for the evils which arise at the end of a world-cycle, firstly the overall removal from the origin, and secondly the necessity for its residual conflicts to be counterbalanced in a way which will leave no basis for any new beginning at its end. This is not to say that there will not be a new beginning, only that this beginning must be causally independent of previous time series. The function of discontinuity is equally important with that of continuity in the passage of time, for reasons which will be considered in the next chapter.

The spiritual energy dissipated in the cyclic descent is to some extent recovered by being converted into forms, whether conceptual, artistic, or institutional. But *qua* finite creations, these things are as it were a two-edged weapon. While they serve up to a certain time to protect and propagate the truth they embody, they ultimately become the means whereby it is attacked. Truths and values which are beyond the reach of attack by their very nature thus become capable of being defeated insofar as they are equated with the forms given them. Spiritual creative achievements are, because of their finitude, a kind of coagulation, and what has coagulated is always liable to dissolution. This ambivalence and instability inherent in created beings can also be understood from their origin in the union of Form and Matter ($\upsilon\lambda\eta$, *materia prima*) which is a union between fullness and emptiness, or between order and chaos.

From this there results the spiritual neutrality of created things already referred to, through which they can serve the 'upward' or 'downward' tendencies equally. They are in any case the content of the outgoing movement of creation, which is on the one hand a manifestation of God in its essential nature, and on the other, an obscuration of God inasmuch as it results from a 'downward' or 'outward' movement in relation to God. In the course of a world-cycle, all possibilities pertaining to it will be realized in order of compatibility with their origin, and this means that a creation which is good in itself will increasingly cast its shadow as the end of the cycle is approached. The end is as obscure as the beginning, though for fundamentally different reasons.

CYCLIC LAW REFLECTED IN NUMBER

The cyclic law of passage through the three levels of complexity, where there is a symmetry between the first and the third, can be seen from the properties of the natural number series when it is set out in a triangular pattern. While this is in no sense a mathematical proof of the idea, it does show how the realm of number recapitulates the universal order according to its own laws. The cyclic law in question prescribes a pattern of complexity which could be described as diamond-shaped, the greatest amplitude being at the center.

The first state of a cycle is a cause in relation to all those that follow it, so that it could be shown below as Cause 1, or more simply, C_1. Each state that comes after it is an effect in relation to those before it, while being a cause in relation to those that come after it, in the causal chain $C_1 C_2 C_3 \ldots C_n$. The last one, C_n is an effect only, not a cause, while all the others except C_1 are both at once. The first cause in the order, C_1, is the simplest of them and is solely a cause, which is shown below by its position above all the others, where the increasing complexity of the subsequent ranks of causes is represented by the increasing numbers of causes in each:

Number in Rank (= Complexity)

$$C_1 \ldots \ldots 1$$

$$C_2 \quad C_3 \ldots \ldots 2$$

$$C_4 \quad C_5 \quad C_6 \ldots \ldots 3$$

$$C_7 \quad C_8 \quad C_9 \quad C_{10} \ldots \ldots 4$$

$$C_{11} \quad C_{12} \quad C_{13} \quad C_{14} \quad C_{15} \ldots \ldots 5$$

In this way, however, the degree of complexity can only keep on increasing; it will never rise to a maximum and then decline, as the theory would indicate. Things would be just the opposite if the complexity of a given rank was proportional to the number of effects which came *after* it. In this case, C_1 in the above would have a complexity factor 14, as it is followed by fourteen others, while the second rank, C_2 C_3 would have a complexity factor of 12, as there are twelve more after it. The lowest level, number 5 in rank, would have zero complexity, because no more follow it. However many ranks of causes are taken, this method results only in a constantly declining complexity, again with no maximum at the center, although both the number of causes operating at a given level and the number subsequent to them are equally relevant for the present purpose.

The solution to this problem lies in taking the *product* of these two factors of complexity as follows: (number of causes in rank n) x (number of effects following rank n) = complexity of rank n.

In the previous example, this would mean that the complexity of C_1 would be $1 \times (15-1) = 14$. That of rank 2, containing C_2 and C_3 would be $2 \times (15-3) = 24$. For rank 4, it would be $4 \times (15-10) = 20$.

On this basis, symmetry between higher and lower ranks results from the fact that the complexity embodied in a small number of powerful causes with many effects will be the same as for a large number of weaker causes with few effects. For Rank 5, being defined as the last, the complexity factor will have to be: $5 \times 0 = 0$, though this is not symmetrical with rank 1, which does not have zero complexity, though it is one of the lowest.

If C_1 were to be preceded by a 'zero' cause, C_0, its complexity value would indeed remain zero as a product of zero with all the causes in the system, but what could such a cause mean? All the causes numbered from C_1 onward belong by definition to the created world, and so share the same mode of being, no matter how much they differ in other ways. This means that the Creator, whose transcendent causality never exists as such among the created, has not yet been represented. When the symbol C_0 is inserted for this purpose, its non-cosmic nature is shown by its being placed above and outside the triangular structure already employed:

$$C_0$$

$$C_1$$

$$C_2 \quad C_3$$

$$C_4 \quad C_5 \quad C_6$$

With this addition, a fully symmetrical causal pattern can be set out, using an odd number of ranks (after C_0) so that maximum complexity will appear clearly in one term:

No. Causes x No. Effects = Complexity

$$C_0 \ldots 0 \text{ x } 28 = 0$$

$$C_1 \ldots \ldots 1 \text{ x } 27 = 27$$

$$C_2 \quad C_3 \ldots \ldots 2 \text{ x } 25 = 50$$

$$C_4 \quad C_5 \quad C_6 \ldots \ldots 3 \text{ x } 22 = 66$$

$$C_7 \quad C_8 \quad C_9 \quad C_{10} \ldots \ldots 4 \text{ x } 18 = 72$$

$$C_{11} \quad C \quad C \quad C \quad C_{15} \ldots \ldots 5 \text{ x } 13 = 65$$

$$C_{16} \quad C \quad C \quad C \quad C \quad C_{21} \ldots \ldots 6 \text{ x } 7 = 42$$

$$C_{22} \quad C \quad C \quad C \quad C \quad C \quad C_{28} \ldots \ldots 7 \text{ x } 0 = 0$$

Only with the inclusion of the transcendent Cause, which is numerically zero to show its unique position, is it possible to make a product with the whole number of causes in the structure, in this case 28, and obtain a zero result corresponding to the last. The complexity of the causal process in the above array is clearly at a maximum in rank 4. The pattern appears even more clearly in larger systems of 45, 55, or more, which space does not allow here. For completeness, the last rank should be detached from the main structure to show that it, like the transcendent Cause, is not part of the visible order.

A MANICHEAN IDEA OF EVIL

What has been argued as to the nature of the cyclic movement creates an association between the ideas of 'descent,' 'matter', and 'evil,' which can perhaps be mistaken for the Manichean and gnostic idea that the material world as such is evil. There is a source of constant confusion here for those who fail to distinguish between matter (υλη) and *material things*. When understood in the light of the ideas used here, material things are by no means mere matter, but are instantiations of Form (ειδος) in matter, where matter is understood as a universal quasi-reality which is below the threshold of anything perceptible by the senses.

Matter so conceived is the condition for the formation of material things and is therefore devoid of qualities, including those which are habitually called 'material'. Insofar as evil is deprivation, therefore, matter so understood is rightly associated inevitably with evil, even though this matter is also the condition for the good which is realized in the material creation. For the same reason, the progressive removal of Form from matter can only be evil, and indeed it could not be so-called if the material world were not good; the idea of evil makes no sense without a primary good to undergo its destructive action. It is also significant that the conceptions of matter and evil employed here derive from Neoplatonism, which at its origin arose in opposition to Manichean ideas. The intelligibility of the world is necessarily a part of its goodness, and without this intelligibility, there is no metaphysical knowledge.

5

THE RHYTHMS OF TIME

TIME'S UNION OF OPPOSITES

The title of this chapter refers to the other principal property of cycles, their discontinuity and repetitive pattern. Rhythms result from breaks in the temporal flow which appear as breaks in the continuity of sensory phenomena at one level or another. Time is to be identified with the flow of phenomena because the idea of an absolute time which would continue to elapse even if nothing existed only makes it harder to understand while giving no new insight, and seems in any case to rest on nothing more than an unsupported assertion. The content of the temporal flow consists of the instantiations of Forms which do not as such have any part in it, since they are not subject to any kind of corruptive or destructive change. The content of time is wholly subject to change, while its causes are eternal.

Here then is the first pair of opposites involved in time, namely, the eternal and the ephemeral. The material world cannot separate from its formal cause, but neither can the two be combined directly. Complete separation could only mean dissolution for the world, and a lesser degree of it would give change such a dominance that created beings would cease to exist as soon as they began to do so. Given direct union, on the other hand, the world would again perish, but this time by absorption. One way, and possibly the only way, in which an intermediate nature between the changing and the changeless can be formed is in a kind of change which continually progresses through the same stages and returns to the same starting-point. The most obvious instance of this is to be seen in circular motion. Insofar as the natural order is dominated by motion of this kind, then, it will participate in the changelessness of its origin, but in a way which will allow change to remain itself.

Though it is not part of the argument, the cosmic background to this could hardly be more comprehensive: every planet and star revolves about its axis; every moon about every planet; every planet about its star; and every star about the center of its galaxy. All these motions are more or less circular. Time, motion, and rotation seem to be inseparable, as was observed in antiquity:

> Proclus remarks that time revolves as the first among things that are moved; by its revolution all things are brought round in a circle. He says explicitly that the advance of Time is not like a single straight line of unlimited extent in both directions, but limited and circumscribed. He understands Plato's phrase 'throughout *all time*' (36e) as meaning the Great Year, the 'single period of the whole,' which embraces all the periods of the planets and contains all Time, 'for this period has as its measure the entire extent and evolution of Time, than which there can be no greater extent, *save by its recurring again and again*; for it is in this way that Time is unlimited.' (II, 289) 'The motion of Time joins the end to the beginning, and this an infinite number of times.[1]

A motion which always returns upon itself is also a pattern for other forms of change, like the life-cycles of living beings, which are able to conserve the species which are subject to change, keeping the destructive powers of change within bounds. Just as it is clear that cyclic time unites the unchanging with a world of change, so it is clear that the abstract idea of rectilinear time does not. The latter belongs to a materialistic philosophy for which the universe is self - existent as though it were another God. It has no place for causes operating outside time, or for the intrinsic patterns of time.

The irreversibility of time or of natural processes comprises another reason for the cyclic structure of time, one which connects with what was ascribed to it in the last chapter. The dissipation of Form from the world and the reduction to matter obviously cannot go on indefinitely, since this must bring about the cessation of the

---

1. F.M. Cornford, *Plato's Cosmology*, 37c–38c, pp104–105.

very conditions within which any further change could take place. This points to two alternatives, namely, that there is one world, finite in duration, before which and after which there is nothing, or that there is a series of such worlds, all developing according to the same basic pattern of alternate restoration and deterioration. The former possibility requires the assumption that the created world adds nothing to God, not just relatively, but absolutely. But in this case, creation could only be a play of illusions, like that of *Maya*. If this were true, one could consistently believe the world to be finite in all respects and without either predecessors or successors. However, if God has created real spiritual and physical beings, there must be a sense in which God and creation are more than God alone. In this case, an absolute cessation of the world would imply a negative change in God and in the archetypal causes. This is why an indefinite succession of worlds is consistent with a real creation in a way that a 'flash between two long nights' is not.

Consequently, 'the world' can be a collective term for an indefinite series of worlds which are physically independent of one another, though all belonging to the same order of space, time, and matter. This requires three premises, (a) that each successive world is finite in duration, (b) that the relation of Form and matter in each world develops qualitatively in one sense only, that is, at the expense of Form or quality, and (c) that the cosmic time-process as a whole can have no inherent limits to its extent.

The beginnings and endings of cycles, and especially of those which comprehend the existence of whole worlds, are necessarily the discontinuous aspect of time, which is just as necessary as the continuous. These two realities form another pair of opposites which the passage of time must unite in its own process. Continuity and discontinuity are woven equally into the structure of all cosmic conditions, and they are comprehended in what Plato meant by the circles of the Same and the Different, which signify more universal realities than the Celestial Equator and the Ecliptic, which are really only symbols. If continuity prevailed alone, distinct beings and events would be impossible, and there could be no world. But if there were only discontinuity, no order or development would be possible, because there could be no elements common to all beings, and therefore no basis for the relations that form a world. If we can say that X has changed, there must be some part of X which has not changed, or there would be nothing in regard to which the change could have taken place, and consequently there could have been no change, but just different things at different times.

The temporal flow, not being separate from the entities which compose it, therefore unites the two conditions of continuity and discontinuity, and the manifestation of this union is the cyclic order. Rectilinear time differs from this by comprising only the continuous aspect, which is another factor which shows it to be an abstraction. From the nature of a cycle it results that the longer the cycle, the greater is the discontinuity involved in its beginning and ending, and the greater the rupture that results, balancing the extent of its erstwhile continuity. At the same time, its repetitive property mediates between change and non-change, and in this way eternity and change, and continuity and discontinuity are all combined in a dynamic structure.

No Eternal Recurrence

The recurring property of cycles is always liable to cause confusion between the repetition of the general forms of events and of the beings engaged in them, and the exact repetition of those beings and events themselves. In the latter case, the implication would be the eternal recurrence of everyone and everything, albeit at enormous intervals of time. A widespread and instinctive feeling that this is physically impossible, even if possible mathematically, is often used as a means of discrediting the idea of cyclic time itself. The question as to whether there can be any such thing can be considered either on the basis of a materialist cosmology, or on a creationist one.

Beginning with the materialist hypothesis that the world consists in a finite quantity of matter in finite space which exists in infinite time, it would seem that in this case matter must always return to the same combinations, as all its possibilities of combination must be worked out. Let it be supposed that one thousand million years must elapse before any given person, event, or thing is identically repeated by the random combinations of atoms. But where random changes are involved, this period of time can only be an average. If recurrences really were possible on this basis, therefore, a tiny proportion of them should occur within the time-span of a human lifetime. There is even no reason why the recurrence should not be contemporaneous with its original in one or two cases, nor is there any reason why two or three recurrences should not also occur together in a short period of time. In reality, identical repetitions of persons and historical events are never experienced, and the fact that they do not occur on quite short time-scales implies that they do not occur on the longest, either.

However, it might be argued that the universe may end and be succeeded by another one, identical with it. This hypothesis involves the question of creation, however, because the end of the universe on any material basis must exclude the possibility of anything else after it. Once ended, only God could bring another universe into being, and this would cancel the present hypothesis. Only an endless, continuous existence of the same universe meets the materialist criterion. There could not therefore be any random recurrences if they depended on new universes, subject to the materialist model. It might well be that the recurrence of any one individual could not really be possible without the recurrence of everything else at the same time, but as this requires a series of new universes, the whole idea must depend on creation and not on natural causes alone, if it is to be realized.

Moreover, the idea of randomly formed (not created) recurrences does not take account of the fact that every person and event is the outcome of an individual history, which involved a passage through innumerable combinations of place and time. Now even if phenomena of a very similar nature could be made to recur in all those same places, there is no question but that they must be at very different times. All place-time combinations are necessarily unique. Recurrences could therefore only occur if moments of time differed *solo numero*, although this is a hypothesis for which there is no evidence, however useful it may be for simplifying calculations. The passage of time is rather experienced as a flow of qualitative change. Closely connected with this is the question of ever-rising entropy, which conflicts with any possibility of recurrence in one and the same universe. Random recurrence is in any case dependent on the assumption that space and the quantity of matter are both finite, while time is infinite, although reason would either take all three as finite or all three as infinite, given that there seems to be no way of proving that they differ in this way.

If the creationist conception of the world is taken as a possible basis for eternal recurrence, the consequences only differ from the above by being even more clearly negative. For God, or indeed any being in eternity, recurrence can have no meaning. What is possessed there is possessed always, and to think otherwise is to conceive the Creator as another temporal entity such as ourselves. Secondly, if the creation of an identical recurrence was proposed as an option for God, it would appear that this could come about for one of only two reasons: that He wished to create something different but was not able, or that He was able but chose instead to withhold it and prevent any new extension of the good in that sphere. The former case conflicts with omnipotence, and the latter with goodness. So little is repetition or recurrence compatible with the action of an infinite and all-powerful Creator that we never even see it where it might be supposed not to matter—every blade of grass, every leaf on every tree, every snowflake, is a unique formation. Although eternal recurrence attaches to the cyclic idea of time like a kind of shadow, it has no share in the validity of the latter. It is in fact one of the most incoherent notions to infect the human mind, whatever stimulation it may afford the imagination as a nightmare scenario.

THE LAW OF CYCLIC ANALOGY

The objection that recurrence is never manifest in everyday instances is by no means transposable to the cyclic conception itself. It is in everyday examples that constant manifestations of it occur. The passage of time in cycles of the very greatest scale is reflected in the cycles of day and night, and then in the lunar cycle, and then in that of the four seasons. The existence of these minor natural cycles does not prove the existence of world-cycles, but they are nevertheless what one should expect to find in accordance with the principle that the Whole is always liable to appear in the part. Every concrete experience of time is perforce a part of the cyclic series referred to above, so that we could reasonably conclude that cyclicity pertains to the essence of time in the absence of proof to the contrary.

When one starts from the cycles of days and seasons, the imagination has no difficulty in envisaging ever greater cycles built out of them, as minutes enfold seconds, hours enfold minutes, and so on, and this can account for the belief in cyclic time which was common in pre-modern times. Until modern times the association between time and the celestial phenomena which measured it impressed itself on nearly all minds, so that time and the rotation of the firmament were taken to be practically the same thing. This identity appears in Plato's cosmology:

> Time 'moves according to number,' being measured by a plurality of recurrent 'parts', the periods called day, month, year. Nothing that we can call time can exist without these units which both measure and constitute its substance. These in turn cannot exist without the regular revolutions of the heavenly bodies, the motions of the celestial clock. Time is accordingly said to 'come into being with the Heaven,' in the sense that neither can exist without the other.[2]

By treating time in this manner in his cosmology, Plato was continuing a tradition which had long been typical of antiquity, and Aristotle expressed it no less clearly:

> Neither alteration nor increase nor coming into being can be regular, but locomotion can be. This is why time is thought to be the movement of the sphere: it is because the other kinds of change are measured by locomotion and Time by this (circular) movement. This also explains the common saying that human affairs form a circle, and that there is a cycle of all other things that have a natural movement and come into being and pass away. This is

2. F.M. Cornford, *Plato's Cosmology*, re 37c–38c.

because all these things are discriminated by Time and have their beginning and end as though in a certain period; for *even time itself is thought of as a sort of circle* [author's italics]. The reason, again, is that Time is the measure of this locomotion and is itself measured by it; so that to say that many things which come into being form a cycle is to say that there is a circle of Time, which means that it is measured by the circular movement.[3]

Circular motion is declared to be a reality basic to the physical world, while this philosophy excludes the idea that any of its primal realities exists as an object of sense. In other words the manifest circular motion is also the instantiation of a Form, like any other reality of sense. The operative principle is the archetype of the cosmic circular motion rather than the circular motion alone, and this has an additional significance owing to the way in which this Form coincides with the soul's power of self-motion. The circulation of the cosmos would on this model be primarily the instantiation of the self-motive power of the universal Soul, and secondarily that of all the souls in whose representation the world is manifest. The world has an existence independent of its representation in human awareness, but this independent existence results from its affiliation to the universal Soul, of which it is the instantiation. What I have indicated already about the mediating function of the cycle between the Forms and the world of change is neither more nor less than the analogue of the function of the soul, which is to unite these two orders of reality in an interior manner, enabling it to conceive the realities of intellect and model temporal things on them. The cosmic movement is thus both the content of the soul's representation and the sensible realization of the soul's universal operation.

The division of the cosmic process into cycles which are themselves composed of lesser cycles is an expression of the way in which the whole is manifest in the part. This results from a property of causality itself, according to Proclus:

It [the cause] is not in part everywhere and in some other part nowhere; for thus it would be dismembered and disparted from

3. Ibid.

itself...it is entire everywhere and likewise nowhere. Whatso-
ever can participate it at all attains it in its entirety and finds it
present as a whole....[4]

The first cosmic cause is the revolution of the All-Soul, and the
greater cyclic periods are causes of the lesser, not vice-versa, and so
the primary revolution is recapitulated on successively smaller
scales. In this way theoretical principles point to a system of analo-
gies which was once grasped intuitively.

TIME, CREATION, AND CAUSAL TRANSMISSION

Some of the most far-reaching implications of causality apply to
the transmission of a world-order through all its different levels of
being, and not in ways that present problems for common sense.
The causal powers behind the cosmic process can be understood on
two different levels, namely, that of the archetypal causes which
both act in and transcend what is caused by them, forming no part
thereof, and the relative, whereby the state of the world at any given
moment is the cause of its state at a later moment. However, it will
be seen that there are general theorems on causality which apply to
it on both levels equally:

Whatever is complete proceeds to generate those things which it
is capable of producing, imparting in its turn the one original
principle of the universe,[5] [and] every producing cause brings
into existence things like to itself before the unlike.[6]

Here is expressed in the most direct manner the necessity for a
causal basis for the self-propagation of the cosmic process and the
necessity for this cause to excel in power whatever follows from it.
That no productive power can produce anything greater than itself
or equal to itself is thus the basis of the idea that the beginning of a
world-cycle is also its most perfect state or 'golden age'. The first age

4. Proclus, *Elements of Theology*, prop. 98.
5. Ibid., prop. 25.
6. Ibid., prop. 28.

is closer by nature to the eternal prototype of the world as a whole than is any subsequent age, each successive time being the cause of another which deviates further from the norm, in essentials at least, in comparison with those before it. This is an application of the principle that 'something does not come out of nothing,' which excludes the idea that a richer and more complex state of the world could be produced by one which was less so.

The principles of cause and effect related to this show that the cyclic order of time is not so much an addition to the creationist doctrine as a rigorous consequence of it. It is even clearer that this idea of causality and cyclic time are inseparable, since any productive cause logically implies a series of sub-causes through which its activity is distributed in so many downward steps. This aspect is expressed by Proclus as follows:

> The originative cause of each series communicates its distinctive property to the entire series; and what the cause is primitively, the series is by remission.[7]

The examples of this principle that most easily come to mind lie more in the personal realm than the cosmic. It is specially significant for theories of personal development, for which personality is shaped by events in early childhood, the early happiness or trauma being the 'originative cause' and all the subsequent times of the person's life being the 'series'. Nevertheless, the scope of this conception is universal. By means of it we can see the reason for the irreversibility of time, when time is not abstracted from its content. It is at one with the irreversibility of cause and effect, which is itself based on the necessity for a productive cause to produce only what is subordinate by nature to itself.

If the series is 'by remission' what the cause is 'primitively', the same distinction will be reproduced between successive members of the series, producing a uniform pattern and direction of change. This continues until the originative cause is hardly discernible at all in its last consequences. In this way, every degree and modality of the original will have been realized as an object or action. Apart

7. Ibid., prop.97.

from the very first and very last members of the series, each of its members is both an effect in relation to the one before it and a cause in relation to the one after it, albeit subject to the restriction that these relations are understood as causes more or less in the scientific sense of the word, and not as Form to instantiation.

There are many examples to illustrate this action of causality in the way natural forces spread their effects. The power of an explosion or an earthquake is experienced at its true level at its center, not some miles away; the heat of a fire is most like the thing itself at close quarters, not at a distance; things which deteriorate with use work best when new or newly restored; the ageing of the body results from its having repeatedly to make copies of copies of its DNA pattern, which grow less true with the passage of time.

The way in which I have ascribed causal power to the state of the world at one time in relation to its state at subsequent times agrees with the common sense idea of causality, and partially with the scientific, in spite of the fact that the latter recognizes only efficient causality. The action of the Forms produces effects, but not in the same way as this, and in order that they too can be included in the causal category the idea of cause is best enlarged after the manner of Aristotle. Applied to the example of the potter and the clay, four different kinds of cause can be found for the finished product, these being (a) the Formal Cause, which is the design of the vessel in the potter's mind, (b) the Material Cause, which is the clay it is made of, (c) the Efficient Cause, which is the manual skill and activity of the potter, and (d) the Final Cause, which is the purpose for which the completed vessel is intended.

Subject to this analysis, it can be seen that cause-and-effect relations between earlier and later events in time all belong in category (c), that of Efficient Causality. Formal causality is, however, required in this connection as well, because the things brought into being through temporal change owe their being just as much to the ideas or Forms they embody as to the physical activity involved. Similar remarks could be made for the other two kinds of cause, but they are outside the limits of the present purpose, for which it is enough to concentrate on the way in which the prime force of causality takes precedence in time. Most of what follows in the later chapters will be a detailing of the consequences of this and its associated causal principles.

CAUSALITY THEORY AND THEOLOGY

The cyclic conception thus derives on the one hand from a study of the nature of causality, such as that of Proclus, and on the other from a universal analogy with days and seasons together with innumerable natural processes. The latter more empirical approach is the more effective insofar as time is not conceived as an abstraction apart from the phenomenal flow of nature. Taken together, these two approaches make a combination of the *a priori* and the empirical which places the subject in a region where philosophy and science cover similar ground. In its relation to theology, it shows how belief in creation is the key to a cosmology with a rigorous causal principle. One part of the cyclic idea, that of ontological descent, follows directly from this, while that of periodic reascent does so more indirectly.

This conception of the world avoids making it the closed-in mechanism it is for Deism, since it is animated throughout by the continual self-extension of the first act of creation, and at the same time it avoids the identification of Creator with creation made by Pantheism. In relation to this form of the cyclic idea, both Pantheism and Deism can be seen to be extreme positions which equally distort the truth from opposite points of view. If the resulting idea of the cosmic process is nevertheless impersonal and predetermined, that is simply the condition for there being a cosmos. As such, it is the 'ground-level' of reality upon which more personal and more spiritual modes of existence may or may not be developed. The determined cosmic movement is in reality no worse than neutral in regard to the spiritual aspirations of human beings, though this fact is often obscured by the way in which the cosmos impresses itself on some minds to a degree which stifles their own sense of identity. The sentiments, common among both materialists and fundamentalists, according to which cosmic necessity must be surrendered to or utterly denied are in either case merely results of an immaturity which is itself part of a failure to develop one's awareness in the different realms open to it. Thus there result two contrary reactions to the same deluded over-estimation of a physical reality.

In any case, doctrinal suspicions are inconsistent in this realm, as can be seen where the natural sciences construct a world of physical necessity without any necessary denial of man's spiritual nature. Even more basically, the universal necessity upon human life to be born, physically mature, reproduce, and die is never made grounds for the kind of objections as are sometimes raised against the cyclic law, though with as little consistency here as in the previous example. If in fact any life were to comprise no more than its physical minima, that could not be blamed on the universe, and the same remark applies to all the other physical aspects of human life, even including its cosmic setting and temporal infrastructure.

6

COSMIC DESCENT IN WESTERN TRADITION

THE FOUR MYTHICAL AGES

Possibly from an analogy with the four seasons, there is a universal myth which teaches that the world began with a golden age, which was followed by ages of silver, bronze or brass, and iron. The qualities of these metals were understood as symbols of the prevailing qualities of the four ages, and have no connection with the bronze and iron ages of archaeology, which simply result from the periods when these metals came into general use. The sequence of ages involves the idea of a certain constant deterioration of the world which man cannot prevent, at least on the collective scale. The golden age is said to owe its quality to that of the beginning of the world when nature and the supernatural were still in harmony, and all things had the fullest degree of perfection possible for them. Among its sources in Greek literature, it appears in the poetry of Hesiod, who wrote in the eighth century BC. A fifth, or heroic age, is added by him to the four, between the ages of bronze and iron, but it does not alter the picture of decline from the original state of the world:

First of all, the deathless gods who dwell on Olympus made a golden race of mortal men who lived in the time of Cronos when he was reigning in heaven. And they lived like gods without sorrow of heart, remote and free from toil and grief: miserable age rested not on them; but with arms and legs never failing they made merry with feasting beyond the reach of all evils.

The ages following this one end with that of 'the race of iron', when 'men never rest from labor and sorrow by day, and from perishing by night':

> The father will not agree with his children, nor the children with the father, nor guest with his host, nor comrade with comrade; nor will brother be dear to brother as aforetime. They will not repay their aged parents the cost of their nurture, for might shall be their right: and one man will sack another's city.
> Strength will be right and reverence will cease to be; and the wicked will hurt the worthy man ... and bitter sorrows will be left for mortal men, and there will be no help against evil.[1]

It is said in the same place that 'the race of iron' will so degenerate that even the new-born will bear the marks of old age, until finally Zeus destroys it. Aidos and Nemesis are said to take leave of the world, representing the loss of any sense of shame at wrong-doing and of any righteous indignation at wickedness. Far from being peculiar to the Greeks, this is in full agreement with other traditions, not least with biblical tradition, but before that, I will compare the above with a later development in Greek thought which has connections with it.

A PLATONIC VIEW OF UNIVERSAL TIME

The full extent of the ever-recurrent course of cycles appears in the view of the world contained in Plato's dialogues. It is to be taken as a myth, but it must nevertheless be a myth about realities for which we cannot have historical knowledge, owing to the totally disruptive character of the changes involved:

> When the time allotted to these events was fulfilled ... the helmsman of the world, abandoning the rudder, so to speak, withdrew to his lookout post, while the universe was turned back in the opposite direction by its destiny and natural tendency. All the local deities, who assisted the supreme divinity in his rule,

---

1. *Works and Days*, 109–115 and 182–201.

recognizing at once what was happening, likewise abandoned the parts of the world entrusted to their care. Turning this somersault, which involved a complete reversal of its direction, the world produced within itself a mighty upheaval, which once again destroyed animals of every kind. Later on, after the passage of sufficient time, when this cataclysmic upheaval had ceased, the universe followed its normal and appointed course, watching over and controlling both itself and all that it contained, remembering as best it could the instructions of its author and father. At first it managed to carry out those instructions exactly; but toward the end its fallibility gradually increased owing to the corporeal principles of its constitution and to the inherited characteristics of its primitive nature, which included a large element of disorder before attaining the present cosmic order. From its maker it received all that it has of beauty; but all the ills and evils of the world flow from its former state, whence it receives them and whereby it produces them in living beings. Insofar, therefore, as it enjoyed the aid of its helmsman in nourishing the living creatures it contains, it engendered (with few exceptions) nothing but great good. Once separated from him, on the other hand, it begins by still doing all for the best; but as time goes on and it becomes subject to forgetfulness, so do the remnants of its primitive chaos gradually regain control, until at length confusion bursts into full flower. Then indeed benefits are few and far between, and so numerous are the evils of which it is compounded that it is in danger of destroying itself together with all it contains. Wherefore the god who organized it, seeing its perilous situation, begins to fear lest it break up amid the waves that buffet it, and sink in the bottomless ocean of dissemblance. So he takes his place once more at the helm: regrouping the parts that have been damaged or dislodged in the cycle just completed, he puts it in order and restores it in such a way as to render it immortal and imperishable.[2]

---

2. *Statesman*, 272e–273e.

This account endorses both the ideas of alternating decline and restoration and indefinite repetition of the general order of universal change. It appears that Plato thinks of each cycle as divided symmetrically into two halves, one of making and the other of unmaking, each being of 36,000 years. The immortality he attributes to the universe is owing to the way in which it always rises to new life after every decline to death, owing to the action of the demiurge, although with the difference that it is a living creature with a consciousness of its own by which it can collaborate with the periodic transformations. It has also been observed[3] that there is more than a hint of these cosmic reversals in Hesiod's idea that the signs of old age appear at the start of life when the world itself is nearing the end of its cycle.

The substance of the material world is at bottom a thing of chaos, but while it is conceived to be under God's direct control it is mastered by the informing and ordering principle. However, this never means that this chaos is abolished, but on the contrary, as soon as the creative power is relaxed it begins to break loose again and reveal its presence ever more widely, in a manner already referred to in the change from Form to matter. This shows how Plato understood the meaning of what is known today as rising entropy, millennia before it was scientifically formulated. The descent into chaos or ever-greater randomness can only be reversed while natural forces are acted on by a spiritual reality; nature by itself can only deteriorate.

One aspect of this which can only be mentioned in passing is that the cosmic reversal from a positive to a negative circulation is, according to Plato, also manifest in an inverse manner in the life of an individual person. The birth of a human being throws the revolution of his soul's motion into a negative, disorderly direction, while the process of growth and the acquisition of wisdom reverses it again and brings back its true order. In this connection, what Plato says in the above should be closely compared with what he says about the 'circles of the soul' in the *Timaeus*. This is one respect in which the microcosm reflects the macrocosm in reverse, because an

---

3. See James Adam, *The Nuptial Number of Plato*, pt. 2, sect. 6.

autonomous tendency of self-motion is a necessary condition for the self-individuation of spiritual substances, which can be said to consist in a specific flow of volition, as I have explained elsewhere.[4] This opposing tendency which arises from the soul's self-motion is also linked to what was said in chapter 2 about the returning movement which balances the outgoing movement of creation. While the full realization of this opposing order of motion is anything but automatic in the individual life, it serves to underline the point that the cosmic deterioration cannot *necessarily* inflict itself on the individual. Insofar as the downward cosmic movement does replicate itself in human life, however, the signs which manifest it are known universally, as can be seen in what follows.

THE END TIME IN BIBLICAL HISTORY

The biblical account of world history corresponds to the cyclic one inasmuch as this history begins with the earthly paradise of Eden and is followed by ages corresponding to those of silver, bronze and iron, each marked by successively shorter lifespans ascribed to mankind. The earliest patriarchs after the Fall are said to have lived for over nine hundred years, and although these figures may not be intended as literal, they convey the idea that cosmic conditions were profoundly different at that time.

The same conception is apparent in the vision of world history in the book of Daniel[5] in the form of Nebuchadnezzar's dream. The figure seen in this dream symbolized the succession of ruling empires, and was made of all four of the symbolic metals, having a head of gold, breast and arms of silver, belly and thighs of brass, legs of iron, and feet of iron and clay. This prefigured the empires of Babylon, Persia, Greece, and Rome, with a final prolongation added to the latter, adding a fifth element to the basic four. The last of these four is presented as the most evil of them, symbolized by its iron quality, and this is matched by the fourth and most destructive

4. *Person, Soul and Identity*, chap. 2, sects. v–vii.
5. Dan. 2.

of the four apocalyptic beasts which appear in a later vision,[6] where they also correspond to four empires.

This not only illustrates the universality of the four metals as symbols of the world order throughout time, it also shows that the pattern of change governing the world as a whole is continually recapitulated on a smaller scale, since the empires represented by the four main parts of the figure occupy only the period from about 600 BC to 400 AD. The 'golden age' of this vision, equated as it was with the period of the Babylonian Empire, comes nowhere near the Edenic or original golden age of this world, but it follows from what has been said of the cyclic law that it should recur on varying scales of magnitude within the same universal cycle. While this concept has a clear biblical basis up to a point, doctrine has mostly limited it to the perspective of one universal cycle, and has not considered the idea of its being a member of a succession of worlds or re-creations.

There was some practical justification for this position in times before the idea of other worlds contemporaneous with this one became current, because a belief in the uniqueness of this life can give an added urgency to the question of its meaning and purpose, though this is not supported by modern cosmology. The idea of worlds or creations multiplied in time is in fact no more than the natural correlate of their being multiplied in space. What has been said already about infinity and finitude is equally applicable to time and space, so they should not be treated separately. The orthodox view of universal history takes it as beginning and ending in eternity, and this union between beginning and ending is enough to accommodate it to the cyclic order.

What is said about the last times of this world is broadly similar in both Old and New Testaments and the Apocrypha, as I shall try to show. The prophecy against Gog[7] presents a picture of evil as in the form of a world power expanding to an unprecedented degree before bringing about its own destruction. A similar vision is rendered in Daniel, and some of its features reappear in Revelations. In

6. Ibid., 7.
7. Ezek. 38 and 39.

the Apocrypha, the same tradition is taught in the book of Esdras:

> Nevertheless, as concerning the tokens, behold the days shall
> come, that they which dwell upon earth shall be taken in a great
> number, and the way of truth shall be hidden, and the land shall
> be barren of faith.
>
> But iniquity shall be increased above that which now thou seest,
> or that thou hast heard long ago.
>
> And all friends shall destroy one another; then shall wit hide
> itself, and understanding withdraw itself into his secret chamber,
> and shall be sought of many, and yet not be found: then shall
> unrighteousness and incontinency be multiplied on earth. . . .
> At the same time men shall hope, but nothing obtain: they shall
> labor, but their ways shall not prosper.[8]

The progressive detachment of religion from tradition, combined
with a belittlement and incomprehension of it, and a consequent
spread of moral anarchy characterize the end time according to the
New Testament as well. The fate of religion reveals in high profile
the latent collective condition, while the relentless contraction in
the general mental horizon means that life is robbed of many vital
realities. The involution of a world and the involution of the faculties by which that world is known are equally part of the same
invariable pattern. Early Christians who thought they were living at
the end of the world were not mistaken in the general nature of the
'signs of the times' they read, therefore, even if they were so in the
application of them:

> But understand this, that in the last days there will come times of
> stress. For men will be lovers of self, lovers of money, proud,
> arrogant, abusive, disobedient to their parents, ungrateful, un-
> holy, inhuman, implacable, slanderers, profligates, and fierce
> haters of good.[9]

---

8. II Esd. 5:1–2, 9–10, 12 (*The Apocrypha*, Authorized Version).
9. II Tim. 3:1–4 (R.S.V., Catholic Edition).

For the time is coming when people will not endure sound teaching, but having itching ears they will accumulate for them-selves teachers to suit their own likings, and will turn away from listening to the truth and wander into myths.[10]

Now the Spirit expressly says that in later times some will depart from the faith by giving heed to deceitful spirits and doctrines of demons, through the pretensions of liars whose consciences are seared.[11]

For that day will not come, unless the rebellion comes first, and the man of lawlessness is revealed, the son of perdition, who opposes and exalts himself against every so-called God or object of worship . . . proclaiming himself to be God. . . . Therefore God sends upon them strong delusion. . . .[12]

The Gospels confirm these indications and link them to a corre-sponding disorder in nature as well, according to the constant rela-tion of inward and outward realities:

For many will come in my name, saying, 'I am the Christ,' and they will lead many astray. . . . For nation will rise against nation, and kingdom against kingdom, and there will be famines and earthquakes in various places. And many false prophets will arise and lead many astray.[13]

For then there will be great tribulation, such as has not been from the beginning of the world until now, no, and never will be. And if those days had not been shortened, no human being would be saved. For false Christs and false prophets will arise and show great signs and wonders. . . . Immediately after the tribula-tion of those days the sun will be darkened, and the moon will not give its light, and the stars will fall from heaven, and the powers of the heavens will be shaken.[14]

10. II Tim. 4:3–4.
11. I Tim. 4:1–3.
12. II Thess. 2:3–12.
13. Matt. 24:5–7, 11.
14. Matt. 24:21–24, 29.

The rest of mankind, who were not killed by these plagues, did not repent of the works of their hands nor give up worshipping demons and idols of gold and silver and bronze and stone and wood . . . nor did they repent of their murders or their sorceries or their immorality or their thefts.[15]

No change in the moral disposition of mankind is brought about by the first cosmic irruptions, and the process of dissolution then continues to its limit:

But by the same word the heavens and earth that now exist have been stored up for fire, being kept until the day of judgement and destruction of ungodly men. . . . But the day of the Lord will come like a thief, and then the heavens will pass away with a loud noise, and the elements will be dissolved with fire, and the earth and the works that are upon it will be burned up. . . . But according to his promise we wait for new heavens and a new earth in which righteousness dwells.[16]

The last verse anticipates both Heaven and the renewal of nature that is to follow the end of the present world-cycle, and this theme is continued in the book of the Apocalypse:

And I saw a new heaven and a new earth; for the first heaven and the first earth had passed away, and the sea was no more. And I saw the holy city, new Jerusalem, coming down out of heaven from God, prepared as a bride adorned for her husband.[17]

There is no accident in the association between man-made and natural evils which scripture emphasizes, since the appearance of the world and the mental state in which the majority of mankind perceive it influence one another reciprocally. The real world is the sum total of the objective world and the combination of all individual representations of it, in a way which recalls the derivation of the true infinite from the union of infinite and finite in chapter two.

15. Rev. 9:20–21.
16. II Pet. 3:7, 10, 13.
17. Rev. 21:1–2 (R.S.V., Catholic Edition).

Minds or souls have, moreover, the power of choice by which they create their own scales of value and priority in the world they experience, and these priorities may or may not be an adequate reflection of the order of realities as it is in itself. The world comprises material, psychical, and intellective realities which differ markedly among themselves in meaning and value, and if the scales of value in individuals differ extremely from this, there will result a deformation of the world which, if widespread enough, would result in a breakdown of the perceptible structure of the cosmos.

One of the passages quoted speaks of the stars falling from the heaven, a text which has been regarded from the earliest times as one not to be taken literally. However, if the natural order in itself is not capable of any such thing, the same cannot be said of its manifestation in the collective human consciousness. If it is legitimate to think of the world in human minds as a kind of conditional prolongation of the world in itself, there is no reason in principle why an extreme collective derangement of mankind's moral, intellectual, and spiritual condition should not result in the collapse of the world as it is humanly comprehended. The fact that there is an objective world known to science would not then be an adequate objection to this, since the world of science is a logical deduction from some parts of experience, and is never itself experienced. For this reason, the close connections made in some texts between cosmic and human realities have a meaning which is in no way reducible to pre-scientific speculation. The conception of the world as representation shows how scientism and fundamentalism are not merely a false opposition, but that they are really just two opposed postures of the same one-dimensional outlook.

THE HERMETIC APOCALYPSE

The parallelism between interior and exterior goods and evils in traditional writings is no less a feature of the *Hermetica*, or writings of Hermes Trismegistus, the ancient Greek version of an Egyptian wisdom tradition. I include it last in order of time as its relatively late date of composition (second or third centuries A D) is so much insisted on by modern scholarship. Here again is a vision of universal descent and universal restoration:

> For she, the Holy [Land], and once deservedly the most beloved of God, by reason of her pious service of the Gods on earth—she, the sole colony of holiness, and teacher of religion [on the earth], shall be the type of all that is most barbarous.

> And then, out of our loathing for mankind, the World will seem no more worthy of our wonder and our praise.

> All this good thing—than which there has been fairer naught that can be seen, nor is there anything, nor will there ever be—will be in jeopardy.

> And it will prove a burden unto men; and on account of this they will despise and cease to love this Cosmos as a whole—the changeless work of God; the glorious construction of the Good, comprised of multifold variety of forms: the engine of God's Will, supporting His own work ungrudgingly: the multitudinous whole massed in a unity of all, that should be reverenced, praised and loved—by them at least who have eyes to see. For darkness will be set before the Light, and Death will be thought preferable to Life. No one will raise his eyes to Heaven; the pious man will be considered mad, and the impious a sage; the frenzied held as strong, the worst as best.

> For soul, and all concerning it—whereby it doth presume that either it hath been born deathless, or that it will attain unto deathlessness, according to the argument I have set forth for you [all this] will be considered not only food for sport, but even vanity.

> Nay, [if ye will] believe me, the penalty of death shall be decreed to him who shall devote himself to the Religion of the Mind.

> New statutes shall come into force, a novel law; naught (that is) sacred, nothing pious, naught that is worthy of the Heaven, or Gods in Heaven, shall [e'er] be heard or [even] mentally believed.

The sorrowful departure of the Gods from men takes place: bad angels only stay, who mingled with humanity will lay their hands on them, and drive the wretched folk to every ill of recklessness to wars, and robberies, deceits, and all those things that are opposed to the soul's nature. Then shall the earth no longer hold together; the sea no longer shall be sailed upon; nor shall the Heaven continue with the courses of the Stars, nor the Starcourse in Heaven. The voice of every God shall cease in the great Silence that no one can break; the fruits of the earth shall rot; nay, Earth no longer shall bring forth; and Air itself shall faint in that sad listlessness.

This, when it comes, shall be the World's old age, impiety—irregularity, and lack of rationality in all good things.

And when these things all come to pass, Asclepius,—then He, [our] Lord and Sire, God First in power, and Ruler of the One God [Visible], in check of crime, and calling error back from the corruption of all things unto good manners and to deeds spontaneous with His Will [that is to say God's Goodness]—ending all ill, by either washing it away with water-flood, or burning it away with fire, or by the means of pestilent diseases, spread throughout all hostile lands—God will recall the Cosmos to its ancient form: so that the world itself shall seem meet to be worshipped and admired: and God, the Maker and Restorer of so vast a work, be sung by the humanity who shall be then, with ceaseless heraldings of praise and [hymns of] blessing.

For this [Re-]birth of Cosmos is the making new of all good things, and the most holy and pious bringing-back again of Nature's self, by means of a set course of time—of Nature, which was without beginning, and which is without end. For that God's Will hath no beginning; in that 'tis the same and as it is, it is without an end.[18]

---

18. *Thrice-Greatest Hermes*, G.R.S. Mead Edition, vol. 2, 'The Perfect Sermon', XXV–XXVI.

This text has been quoted at some length, not only for its beauty and for its agreement with the cyclic conception, but for its parallels with biblical texts, some of which have already been quoted, for example, the time of wars, persecutions, famines and earthquakes. It may also be relevant to compare 'the great Silence that no one can break' with Rev. 8:1, 'there was silence in heaven for about half an hour.' There is besides a similarity between 'nor shall the Heaven continue with the courses of the Stars' and Rev. 8:12, 'and a third of the sun was struck, and a third of the moon, and a third of the stars.'

The statement that 'the sea shall no more be sailed upon' compares with another text from the Apocalypse, this time concerning the fall of the great Babylon, Rev.18:17–19, 'and all shipmasters and seafaring men, sailors and all whose trade is on the sea, stood far off and cried out as they saw the smoke of her burning.' They, along with kings and merchants are said to be left desolate by the downfall of the great city, as though a similar breakdown in civilization was prophesied by both texts.

The Hermetic text differs from the New Testament texts inasmuch as the former ends with an affirmation that the restoration of nature by God is all part of a cosmic life which goes on without end, on account of its being willed by God's eternal will. The same position was declared in the Platonic text, and the fact that it does not appear explicitly in the New Testament may nevertheless not rule out its presence there. The 'new heaven and new earth' are certainly an indication that this is the case. To examine this more fully, and to determine whether the whole of time could exist in a single world-cycle without successor or predecessor will form part of a consideration of time and infinity later on.[19]

DISORDER A CONDITION FOR NEW ORDER

From the texts quoted, it appears that the decline of civilizations is closely associated with a spread of moral corruption and a corruption of religious beliefs. But while this can be verified, moral corruption is as much an effect of as a cause of the process as a

19. See chapter 12.

whole, which points to the existence of yet other causes of corruption in the realm of consciousness. There are other tendencies in human nature which, though apparently reasonable, are no less fatal in the long run. They spring from a flaw in the quest for self-realization.

In connection with the realization of all possibilities, I have indicated the way in which this gives rise to the uniqueness of the individual, not merely in persons, but even down to such things as pebbles and blades of grass. In conscious beings, moreover, uniqueness is not held passively, but is rather the pattern of a potentiality waiting to be lived out and fully achieved. In the extreme, this is taken to mean that the individual must seek only goals, criteria, and activities peculiar to himself and his generation, and so reject those of previous generations. Anything else would be a denial of something essential to personal identity, and this is the ontological root of the passion for originality. When human beings act in this way, they unwittingly act in accordance with the Principle of Plenitude, realizing possibilities mainly because they were hitherto unrealized in this world. When this is done, the choice of a new development will be determined more by the fact of its being untried than by the extent to which it connects with the higher values. Thus with the passage of time, the possibilities realized will become generally 'lower', that is, less conducive to the full intellectual, moral and aesthetic development of the individual, when the only alternative would be to continue the 'higher' ones which were already realized elsewhere.

It may be observed that the purpose of spirituality is largely that of realizing personal uniqueness in ways which do not require it to be exclusive, so that the present analysis may be taking too low a view of human nature. However, spirituality is not a majority occupation, and it is the behavior of majorities which is decisive from the cosmological point of view. The statistically normal tendency is to see the uniqueness of the person on the level of physical fact alone, with the consequence that it must primarily be realized in externals.

The constant selection of new alternatives which have ever less scope for universal values leads back to the question of moral corruption, and the element of punishment implicit in the downfall of civilizations, and of separate parts of civilizations. To bring together the different kinds of criteria used so far, their negative meaning can be summed up as *loss of analogy*, the loss of analogy between the world of sense and its archetypal cause and pattern. The religious ritual, social hierarchies, arts and sciences, which have been inherited from past ages were, among other things, humanly-devised and socially functional forms of analogy between natural life and the realm of Forms or archetypes. Ontological analogy is the only mode of connection between the eternal and the temporal, and by means of it society has a way of participating in the stability of supra-temporal reality. Nature, on the other hand, possesses this cosmic analogy as part of its very being, so that it is inherently open to God in a way that the human world is not. The secularization of civilization and the destruction of natural environments therefore work together for the suppression of analogical order in both human and non-human realms equally, as though it were decided that nothing was to be able to escape the final conditions of this age.

However, the sustaining analogical forms which attach the human world to its Formal causes are by no means confined to visible practices, symbols and organizations, because the most essential realm of cosmic analogy is the human soul, wherever it fulfils its role in transcending the natural conditions of life. By living according to its own principle, the inner being lives so as to be assimilated to the inner law of nature, a law of which all its particular laws are dependent derivations. It is for the furtherance of this growth of the soul into a membership of the formative realities of the world that all the more or less exterior analogical or symbolical forms are maintained.

Insofar as this part of the human vocation ceases to be understood, the world will be deprived of the elements by which it can continue to form a distinct reality. At the lower limit of this change, the deprivation of in-forming realities can no longer be remedied from within, and the result of this is not a cessation of being, but rather an 'implosion' of the Formal cause into the world which finally reverses its decline. History has shown how this has happened in relative ways where a decayed civilization is taken over by one which is still vital, but this kind of change is in principle capable of happening on a much more universal scale. With the reduction of the qualitative principle, the state of the world approximates to that of matter in the absolute sense of the word, and matter has by definition no power to prevent the entry of Forms and of entities which instance Forms to a special degree. The reduction toward matter is in reality a removal of Form which prepares the way for a new influx of it, so that the word 'implosion' is suited to what happens; disorder is ultimately self-correcting. In this connection, the common saying that 'nature abhors a vacuum' shows how widely Plenitude is at least partly understood. Mankind is situated between the natural and the supernatural, and so is at the center of the universal decline and restitution described in the Platonic, Biblical, and Hermetic sources, which express the human aspect of these changes.

7

'THE GREAT WORLD DECAYS IN THE LITTLE'

THE HISTORICAL POSITION OF THE THEORY

The last chapter may prompt the question as to whether the texts quoted were ever given an importance sufficient for them to dominate the official ideas of world history. The simplest way of answering this is to refer to the debates on the meaning of world history during the transition to modern times. The title of this chapter is quoted in a book devoted to a seventeenth century controversy between an Anglican bishop, Godfrey Goodman, and an Aristotelian philosopher and archdeacon, George Hakewill, who debated the question as to whether the world had been in a state of ongoing decline ever since the Fall.[1]

Part of my reason for introducing this subject is to show that the idea of cosmic decline had been an assumption of Christian orthodoxy until the second half of the seventeenth century. This may well be surprising to many minds which are so steeped in the idea of progress and of the accommodation of religious belief to it that they are unaware of the part played in the history of thought by the ideas in the above book. The psychological effect of an unquestioned belief in progress is all too evident in the author of *All Coherence Gone* himself, where he says:

---

1. Victor Harris, *All Coherence Gone*, The University of Chicago Press, 1949.

the scientists ultimately rejected the belief in decay not only because of the empirical evidence against it, but because it was based on a teleological view of the universe.[2]

This is said as though science knew nothing of the Second Law of Thermodynamics, which requires that an irreversible 'decay' must result from every physical operation of nature, and it shows how progressive ideologies can result not merely in a distortion, but in an actual inversion of the scientific principles involved. Moreover, Harris' conviction that Hakewill is in the right in denying the cosmic decline is not disturbed by the fact that nearly all of Hakewill's arguments depend on the Aristotelian belief that the heavens were made of an incorruptible substance quite different from terrestrial matter, a belief which was even then being exploded by Galileo's experiments. Goodman's arguments, on the other hand, will be seen to be of a kind that are not dependent on changes in scientific theory.

Concerning the earlier history of belief in the continuing corruption of the world, Harris quotes from a book by Polydore Vergil dating from 1499, to the effect that 'an ende by putrifaction' is the conventional Christian position.[3]

The fact that this idea was defended by bishop Goodman is in any case a good indication of its traditional position, because the Reformers were not religious innovators in any creative way, but differed from Catholic tradition only in what they rejected. However one may explain the way it came about, therefore, the long-term decline of the natural order is an ancient belief, one which appears in the Patristic writers, notably in the writings of Saint Cyprian. Its establishment may have owed much to the effect of the barbarian invasions on Saint Augustine's idea of history, and to the effect of the Dark Ages on many other influential minds. Be that as it may, it is a logical setting, maybe the only fully logical one, for a religion which is concerned above all with salvation. The progressivist philosophy cannot provide any such setting, and in a religious context

2. Ibid., chap. 1, p5.
3. Ibid., chap. 4.

it can only be a popularized form of the belief that man can save himself by his own efforts alone. So seductive to human nature is this belief that the combined forces of reason and constant experience can hardly dislodge it.

THE MICROCOSM AND THE MACROCOSM

The 'little world' or microcosm in relation to the 'great world' plays an important part in the cosmological controversy, besides which it is specially relevant to its wider issues treated here, not least because it has a decisive effect on our relation to the vast quantities peculiar to time and space. Instead of feeling dwarfed or threatened by such immensities, one may on this basis see them as component though peripheral parts of one's own being when that being is understood as microcosmic by nature. Thus the experienced immensity would be a property of the soul or self in which the universe is reflected. Without this property of the human state, moreover, the problem of knowledge must remain insoluble, and the question of man's place in the universe will not be understandable in a way that could be humanly realistic. This truth is expressed by Nicolas Berdyaev who fully realized its importance:

> Man is a small universe—that is the basic truth for knowing man, and the basic truth which precedes the very possibility of knowing. The universe may enter into man, be assimilated by him, be attained and known by him only because in man there is the whole component of the universe, all its qualities and forces—because man is not a fractional part of the universe but an entire small universe himself.... Man and the cosmos measure their forces against each other, as equals. Knowing is a conflict between equal forces, rather than between a dwarf and a giant.[4]

Because this conception is so often not understood, with its implication that the humanly experienced world is a private representation in each soul, the unimaginable quantities of the universe can

4. *The Meaning of the Creative Act*, chap. 2.

appear as a threat to the significance and even to the reality of the individual. The endlessness of outer space in which the earth is but a point, the aeons of time, and the incalculable number of souls that have had embodied lives may astound the imagination, but for all that these quantitative magnitudes are logical inferences and are never directly experienced or even experienceable.

The individual human state is at the center of all these macrocosmic realities in a much more profound sense than that of spatial centrality. The metaphysical truth in this was once conveyed to mankind by Ptolemaic astronomy with its geocentric description of the universe, and it stood for something much more profound than a supposed need to enhance human feelings of self esteem. In the Copernican revolution, this was replaced by a technically more effective model, but one which obscured the truth of man's relation to his world. But regardless of the prevailing theory, the quantities proper to the spatial and temporal world are present in each consciousness in a mode that makes them intelligible to us.

The relation of macrocosm and microcosm, like all dualities, points the way to a third reality which creates equilibrium between them. In this case, the third reality would be a greater macrocosm or 'metacosm' which would comprise the macrocosm and the grand total of all the representations of it realized in individual beings. On this basis, the real world would then be in effect a community of spirits, rather as Leibniz conceived it. Such an enlarged and spiritualized idea of the macrocosm makes it easier to understand the mutually corrupting (and conversely, mutually regenerating) roles ascribed to microcosm and macrocosm in the Goodman-Hakewill controversy. Some such interaction is also indicated by Berdyaev where he says that 'the destinies of the microcosm and macrocosm are inseparable—they rise or fall together. The condition of the one is imprinted upon the other; they mutually penetrate each other.'[5]

Because of the mutual interpenetration of the great and the little worlds, the corruption of man has its effects on the physical processes of his world, so that much more is involved than questions of

5. Ibid., chap. 2, p72.

personal and social value. In the biblical account of the Fall, the earth is said to be cursed because of Adam, so that it loses much of its fertility. This in turn requires of Adam a different relation to the world as painful work with its attendant discomforts becomes necessary. In the life of the rational soul, therefore, the macrocosm may be either spiritualized by being joined to the will of God through the mediation of the human soul, or corrupted by being separated from it. When it is said that the microcosm 'reflects' the macrocosm, this does not mean that it has a purely passive function like that of a mirror. On the contrary, the formation of the reflection or representation results from the soul's constant flow of volition. But although the soul is essentially activity, the direction of this activity is liable to vary in the manner of the symbolic circles or circulations described by Plato in the *Timaeus* and in the passage quoted in the previous chapter. This comparison with clockwise and anti-clockwise motion highlights the idea that the microcosm's creative energies can be deployed either in harmony or disharmony with the normative cosmic motion.

In theory, these considerations would allow no more scope for the degeneration of the world than for its regeneration, since the mutual influence for good or ill by the great and little worlds need not imply an excess of one influence over the other. The miraculous powers attributed to saints manifest the positive potential of this possibility, and in them the macrocosm is raised to its highest potentiality in anticipation of its ultimate redemption. But while the regenerative process never actually ceases, the balance of forces tells increasingly against it over the greater part of history, simply because numbers are not on the side of those who follow the regenerative way.

The idea of the human soul as a microcosm is implicit in all biblical and traditional teachings which link natural disasters and disorders to corresponding moral and spiritual disorders in individuals and in societies. Once the theoretical reasons for this are appreciated, there is no need to see such teachings as merely the work of pre-scientific minds which failed to understand causality. The main barrier against such insights is the near-universal belief that the human mind relates to its world only in the way of a piece of photographic film to its objects. This belief is a result of ignorance of the creative power of the human state, and of the fact that even the simplest perception does not arise without the application of a mental act to it similar to that of reading a word or decoding a symbol. The world of experience results from the activity of the individual mind in concert with all other human minds together, and while the world in itself is not created by the individual mind, nor even by the sum total of them, it is nevertheless conditioned by the latter to such a degree that the moral, intellectual and aesthetic development of mankind as a whole has a cosmic significance.

On this basis, there is a close parallel between the relationships between man and God and between nature and man, and a given change in the one relation automatically produces a corresponding change in the other. If human minds grow increasingly closed against God, nature will grow increasingly closed and hostile toward humanity, as appears in the fact that ever greater ingenuity is needed to keep the world inhabitable. The microcosm concept is also relevant to this inasmuch as the positive role of the microcosm in relation to the macrocosm is unrealizable except where the divine law is acknowledged. The will of God coincides with the realization of this cosmic role.

The Traditional Arguments

When we consider the arguments used to justify the belief in the world's decay as they were used in the sixteenth and seventeenth centuries, they evidently assume an experience which is not shared by modern minds. It is as though up till about three hundred years ago mankind still shared a race memory of a higher state which had been lost, a memory which could be awakened by natural evils which followed upon that loss. For this reason, the arguments deriving from such sources will not be relied upon for the present purpose *qua* arguments; rather it is the *existence* of such arguments and their widespread acceptance prior to the eighteenth century which is the main issue.

Harris observes that there was a belief that all the different forms of corruption that result from the Fall had the effect of suppressing two distinctions, one of them between the Fall itself and the continuing decay of the world, and the other one between the decay of the macrocosm and that of the human microcosm. These distinctions were of course insisted on by those who, like Hakewill, argued against the world's decay. But a corruption confined solely to man would refute man's place in nature, and a Fall without ongoing consequences would be reduced to a mere historical incident.

In the course of the controversy, it was only possible for Hakewill to deny the orthodox position, breaking the dependence between microcosm and macrocosm, on the grounds that the visible heavens were made of an incorruptible matter. In that case, the macrocosm would be safe against the unhindered spread of decay in a way that man was not. While the scientific discoveries made at this time disposed of this belief that the heavens were incorruptible, the simultaneous discovery of increasing numbers of scientific laws was to give rise to a belief in a permanent world-order based on the unchanging truth of equations like the laws of motion. The philosophical impact of these laws was in effect a resurrection of Aristotle's incorruptible crystal spheres in a more sophisticated form, but the assurance they gave about the stability of the world was equally specious. The fact that it is unchangingly true that the acceleration of a body is proportional to the force applied to it cannot communicate even the tiniest bit of its absoluteness to that body itself. The eternity of natural laws reveals only the patterns of creation as they are in the mind of God, while no such eternity is imparted to the material world. To think otherwise would be like supposing that Socrates must be immortal because it is eternally true to say that Socrates is mortal. But this did not deter the new vision.

Goodman's motive in arguing for the world's decay was to teach the folly of relying on nature, so that one would see the need to seek God instead, and in this he was only saying what orthodoxy has always said. Signs of nature's corruption were besides to be used to put mankind in mind of the end of the world:

Any denial of the decay was an un-Christian denial that the world would end. Churchmen of all denominations were eager to defend the world's mortality against the Aristotelian doctrine of its eternity; and this desire, together with the popular expectation that the end would come soon, did much to bring converts to the belief in decay.[6]

The arguments for the decay of nature proceeded as though the doctrine could be confirmed by simple observation. The increasing loss of fertility in the soil, and the way in which only useless and harmful plant growth could still flourish in it, was taken as an outward sign of the inner condition of mankind, as also was the fact that most of the world was not inhabitable for one reason or another. Such signs included things as diverse as the preponderance of evil over good in the world, enmity between mankind and the animals, the necessity for tilling the soil (it was believed to have been so fertile at one time that this was not necessary), the humiliating conditions of birth and death, and the preponderance of trouble and sorrow over happiness. Even the arts and sciences were said to exist as a result of the need to repair some of the ruination caused by the Fall. As man was the center of creation his corruption made it rotten at the core and so much the more able to spread the evil, as one man with the plague could infect a whole city. The fact that man suffered the effects of corruption to a greater extent than the irrational creation simply reflected the divine justice.

The continuing decay was manifest in the extinction of species and in a weakening of the life-giving influences of the heavens. Much use was made of the Aristotelian idea of privation, the idea that the number of Forms instantiated in matter was always much less than it could have been, so that matter unmastered by Form could so much the more easily revert to chaos. The dominance of evil was said to appear in the fact that it was always much easier to destroy than to build or create; likewise the difficulty of learning and the ease of forgetting; wealth is gathered with so much labor, but so easily lost; for how much of life man was weak either through

6. *All Coherence Gone*, chap. 1, p3.

immaturity or old age; there was but one way to be born, but innumerable ways led to death.

Nature's corruption was hastened by an increase of privation, which meant that the relation of matter and Form was diluted by a real nothing. This not-being supposedly mingled with the things that were, and showed in a weakness, slackness, and instability in all things. Thus they were more vulnerable to the violent alternations of contrary forces which hastened nature back toward the nothing from whence it was created. Man's physical weakness and susceptibility to pain and sickness were said to be greater than ever before, and his intellectual powers appeared to decline in a similar manner. Only man suffered from idiocy and insanity, which was said to be a condign punishment for the sin of curiosity which was instrumental in causing the Fall. It was part of the same punishment that the desire for knowledge was nearly always frustrated, and that man was ignorant of what he most needed to know, his own soul. While sorrow was real, joy was said to be mainly illusory because it was so largely involved with recollection and anticipation rather than with the present, besides which happiness and pleasures took much time to reach, but were very soon over when reached. The future, whether in this life or the next, was a source of constant anxiety which spoiled much of the peace and happiness one could have at any given time.

Most of these evils were said to be rooted in the conflict between the body and the soul which had arisen since the Fall. The Fall had resulted in the body's becoming corruptible, whereas the soul was not so affected, and this was what produced a profound disharmony between them:

The spiritual soul, 'exempted from any elementarie composition,' must nevertheless be coupled with the base body. It is no wonder that neither part of man understands the other. The two belong to different worlds, 'and therefore in reason should not admit any fellowship or societie betweene themselves, much lesse be the members of one and the same corporation.' The understanding is betrayed by the body, so that sense rather than intelligence dominates man, whose concern is thus with particulars instead of generals and whose actions are guided by his passions instead of by his rational soul.[7]

Man was created with sovereignty over all creation, and now all that was left of that was his sovereignty over woman, and even she was turning rebellious. Heresies, and confusion and disputes about religion were increasing, while a decline in the practice of religion was continuing as it had done since ancient times, and Goodman's fear was that the whole world would finally turn infidel in its last dotage. But material and spiritual things always declined equally, and so there was a diminution of wealth in the world, while the goods that money could buy became both more scarce and poorer in quality. He observes the improvements in man's methods for controlling natural forces and for deriving benefits from them, but these things showed only how feeble nature had become, that it had to be submitted to human action in order to be capable of any good. Greater efforts were always needed for the same results.

This kind of thinking relies on a sense of the potentialities in man and the world which belong more to their archetypal causes than to them, and it makes the contrast between the ideal and the actual the more painful in proportion to this perception. Intelligence in earlier centuries was more developed on the intellectual than on the rational plane, and so could reach the essence of things when its rational arguments could not convince modern minds which have developed rationality almost to the exclusion of the intellect. But what matters here is that the declining world-order was always a part of orthodox thinking until quite recent times, and was expressed in a huge literature. Traditional thought was guided by the image of the microcosm which summed up the Christian idea of the whole organism, uniting in man the corrupt and the incorruptible, the elemental and the celestial, and intelligence and sensory perception. Man's seven ages are linked to the seven planets, in a way that heaven and earth, stars and elements are all in some sort in man:

Even in the body of man, you may turne to the whole world; This body is an illustration of all Nature; Gods recapitulation of all

7. Ibid., chap. 2, VI, p 40.

that he had said before, in his *Fiat lux*, and *Fiat firmamentum*, and in all the rest, said or done, in all six dayes.[8]

COSMIC PESSIMISM AND THE MODERN REACTION

For all its negative implications for the material world, the old cosmology was far from negative in its effect on human minds and wills. Belief in the world's decay was held with increased conviction during the century before it began to be abandoned in the later seventeenth century, so that it was the dominant idea of history throughout the period of the Renaissance. This fact is significant for any understanding of the meaning of cosmic pessimism. It clearly did nothing to inhibit creative inspiration in any field, and may rather have stimulated it. The same observation applies to Classical Antiquity, which was even more devoid of any idea of progress. The world's decay evidently confronts man with the alternatives of either combating it or of becoming part of it. The belief in progress which displaced it appears in contrast as a consoling sedative which allows the higher potentialities to rest and sleep. This does not mean it does not stimulate desires, since it undoubtedly creates greater expectations of financial and material improvement. But the energies it stimulates are almost entirely industrial and economic, so that its purpose could almost be defined as that of the channelling of human energies into economically-related activities.

Authors advocating the idea of progress began as a small and obscure minority in the sixteenth century and grew in numbers and influence during the seventeenth and eighteenth centuries. Their arguments were nearly all empirical, and did not dispute against metaphysics so much as ignore it. Material improvements already achieved were examined and set up as patterns for more of the same in the future. Later on the accumulation of advances in the production of wealth were thought to have gone on long enough for material progress to be an actual law of history.

It could be said that the idea of progress was talked into existence by a long succession of thinkers, the great majority of whom were

8. Ibid., chap. 5, IV.

French, according to the account given by J. B. Bury.[9] One of the earliest such thinkers was the historian Jean Bodin who asserted the uniformity of nature's powers and rejected the idea of universal degeneration. About the same time Francis Bacon published his ideas for the domination of nature through scientific discoveries. The new idea very early found itself in conflict with the doctrine of Providence, which taught that events were ordered by God for the sake of the Church and the salvation of individuals. This belief had to be discredited if progress was to be the ruling principle of explanation, and events could be reinterpreted as human means to economic ends, and not divine means to spiritual ends. The newly discovered natural laws played a part in this change, because they at least appeared to imply that God could not act directly, so that Providence would have to wait on the operation of physical laws if it were active at all. This is not to say that there is any *logical* conflict between natural laws and Providence, but that the new concentration of minds on the details of short-range natural causality created a mindset which was not open to the wider perspective of Providential ordering. In reality, God's dispositions of things come from outside the time series just as much as do the natural laws themselves.

The central role of French thought during the seventeenth, eighteenth and nineteenth centuries in bringing the idea of progress from obscurity to worldwide dominance is illustrated by the names of the thinkers whose work is reviewed by J. B. Bury. Following Bodin, they include Fontenelle, the Abbé de Saint Pierre, Montesquieu, Voltaire, Turgot, Diderot, Condillac, Helvetius, Condorcet, Chastellux, Auguste Comte, Guizot, Fourier, Saint-Simon, and Renan, to name the principal ones. Despite the contribution made by Bacon and Hobbes and other non-French thinkers, the strange fact remains that the amount of materialistic and atheistic works of French origin exceeded that of all the rest of Europe put together during those three centuries. Their success can be attributed largely to the fact that they told the public something it naturally wanted to believe, and substituted an idea which demanded only a certain amount of energy for one which contained a moral challenge as

9. *The Idea of Progress.*

well. It was in this connection that Guénon applied the aphorism that *vulgus vult decipi*,[10] which is the more appropriate in that the modern spirit of rational criticism is notably inactive in relation to modern culture as such, where it might do some good and expose the negative motives behind the trends of modernity.

The eventual abandonment of the traditional cosmology by Christian thought in the wake of its rejection by secular thought was a change in the form of belief which was wholly owing to cultural, historical and economic pressures, not to any new discovery in theology or metaphysics. It has been observed that Christian thought had hitherto retained the idea of the world's decay but not that of world-cycles, and it will later have to be considered whether the abandonment of the latter was also brought about by human contingencies, or whether by a deeper insight into the nature of time.

10. 'The multitude is willing to be deceived.'

8

THE *KALI-YUGA*

THE FOUR AGES IN INDIAN TRADITION

The mythical and metaphysical character of universal time in Western tradition has clear parallels in Oriental tradition, particularly that of ancient India, with the advantage that many numerical data pertaining to it are preserved. The four ages of Gold, Silver, Bronze and Iron appear here as the *Krita-Yuga*, the *Tretā-Yuga*, the *Dvāpara-Yuga*, and the *Kali-Yuga*. These four are said to make up the total cycle of the present human race from its creation to the end of its world, the whole being called a *Manvantara* or 'era of Manu'. Manu is the name of the half-mythical lawgiver at the inauguration of the era. The four *Yugas* are said to have lengths of 1,728,000, 1,296,000, 864,000, and 432,000 years respectively, their lengths thus declining in the ratios 4:3:2:1. The construction of these numbers shows them to be symbolic and not historical, although historical figures are also given, as will be shown.

The four *Yugas* follow a declining order of spiritual quality, as is consistent with the idea of creation, but the metaphysical background to this form of the teaching differs from what has been considered so far. The division of qualities here is based on an analogy with the way space is divided by its three dimensions. All states of being are thought to be intersected by a vertical axis which is divided into upper and lower halves by a plane intersecting it centrally. The upper and lower halves of this axis and the central plane represent three universal qualities in Hindu teachings called the three *gunas*, which are called *sattva*, *rajas*, and *tamas* respectively. The first includes everything of an ascending tendency, and is manifest as light, peace and order, while in man it appears as an attraction to truth and virtue. The second of them, *rajas*, includes everything which involves an active development in the world, and is manifest in an energy which is expansive, constructive and morally neutral. The third, *tamas*, opposes darkness and confusion to the light and order of *sattva*, and inertia and destruction to *rajas*. From these three basic tendencies, which are moral and cosmic equally, result four, not three, world ages. Again, this follows from the analogy with spatial dimensions. As space can be seen to result from a doubling of each of the three dimensions in opposite directions in a three-dimensional cross, so the four principal ages are derived from duple combinations among the three *gunas*. The *Krita-Yuga* is qualified by a duplication of *sattva*, so that its dominant tendency is wholly ascending. The second in order, the *Tretā-Yuga*, is characterized by a combination of *sattva* and *rajas*, so that the upward tendency is mixed with one which is dynamic in a mundane manner. The next such combination is that of *rajas* and *tamas* for the third age, or *Dvāpara-Yuga*, in which the dominant tendencies are both neutrally mundane and mingled with the downward or anti-spiritual. The ruling tendency of the fourth age, the *Kali-Yuga* or 'dark age' results from a duplication of the lowest principle, *tamas*, symmetrically with that of the first.

In this way, the four *Yugas* possess their leading qualities, the things which appear in the greatest number of human beings who live during them. If it is not a question of an absolute elimination of good with the passage of time, it means at very least a progressively deeper concealment of it and an increasing deprivation of personal influence from it. While the truth has a power which secretly sustains the world through those in whom it still prevails, even during the worst times of disorder, it is always the conditions which are uppermost in the majority of human lives which are the central issue for cosmological teachings.

CHARACTERISTICS OF SUCCESSIVE AGES

The traditional teachings describe the four ages of humanity in considerable detail, starting from the condition of things in the world's springtime:

In the *Krita-Yuga*, the Dharma [or spiritual duty, symbolized here by the bull] shall walk on four feet and the people of this age shall reverence it. The feet of the powerful bull are Truth, Mercy, Restraint, and Generosity, O King.

The men of this age are mostly happy, full of compassion and benevolence, with senses tamed and at ease. They are patient, and find their well-being in themselves, regarding all things in an equal manner.

Men are then peaceful, ignorant of hatred, affectionate, of even temper, and glorify God by their asceticism, their inward calm, and in refraining from passions.[1]

It is made clear that this is the age in which man also possessed the fullness of knowledge, and it invites comparison with the state of Adam and Eve before the Fall, although it could also be the earliest time after it, since the Fall is not part of Hindu Tradition, which never adequately separates it from the creation. In this primal state it would not really be contradictory to say that human beings were spiritual 'naturally' since nature and the supernatural were then in the closest union.

The development of the next cycle is marked by the rise of the passional element in man and nature, albeit beginning with its least ignoble aspects:

In the *Treta-Yuga*, the fourth part of the feet of the Dharma gradually disappears under the [four] feet of injustice, which are deceit, misdeeds, insatiability and plunder.

During this period, the castes, following that of the Brahmins, are devoted to works [sacrifices] and to asceticism. Men are neither very wicked nor very sensual. They are attached to the threefold objective of human action [i.e., pleasure, profit, and virtue], and make a lifelong practice of the Triple Veda.

---

1. *Bhagavata Purana*, Bk. XII, chap. 3.

When human beings concern themselves with their duties, interests and pleasures, then, O Sage, know that it is the *Tretā-Yuga*, when Passion [*rajas*] reigns.[2]

The appearance of this cycle, or silver age, is marked by the rise of instability symbolized by the bull standing on only three feet. It is hard to tell whether the beginnings of corruption involved here made the men of this age truly morally worse or better than those who came later because, on the one hand, their deviation offended against a greater manifestation of the truth than was ever generally known at later times, while on the other hand their lives were objectively better than those which came after, if only because of their position in the cycle. This would reduce the moral responsibility to be ascribed to later generations in comparison with the earlier, and it is a compensating factor which applies at all levels of the cycle as well. The continuation of time into the *Dvāpara-Yuga* is represented by the same symbol, but standing on only two feet, to show a further loss of stability:

When greed, insatiability, pride, imposture and envy reign amidst works and sacrifices attached to self-interest, it is then the *Dvāpara-Yuga*, which is dominated by passion and darkness. [i.e., *rajas* and *tamas*.]

The more positive attributes of this cycle are not passed over, but they too contain the seeds of future ills:

During this age men of caste have a love of glory and magnificence. They take pleasure in the study of the Vedas; heads of families are luxurious and joyful. Kshatriyas and Brahmins are always at the head.[3]

THE BEGINNING OF THE DARK AGE

That these changes in mankind are believed to be historical and not only mythical appears in a text which Thomas Taylor[4] quotes

2. Ibid., Bk. XII.
3. Ibid.
4. Taylor (1758–1836), who was a Neoplatonist by religion, translated all the works of Plato, Plotinus, and Proclus with the support of patrons.

concerning the *Kali-Yuga*, the fourth and last of these cycles, this being the present age of the world. The figures quoted show no lack of precision:

> The beginning of the Kaly Youg, or present age, is reckoned from 2 hours, 27 minutes, and 30 seconds of the morning of the 16th of February 3,102 years before the Christian era; but the time for which their astronomical tables are constructed is 2 days, 3 hours, 32 minutes and 30 seconds after that on the 18th of February, about six in the morning. They say there was then a conjunction of the planets, and their tables show that conjunction. Monsieur Bailly observes that by calculation it appears that Jupiter and Mercury were then in the same degree of the ecliptic; that Mars was distant about 8 degrees and Saturn 17; and it results from thence that at the time of the date given by the Brahmans to the commencement of the Kaly Youg they saw those four planets successively disengage themselves from the rays of the sun. . . .[5]

According to Aryabhata the observations were made at Ujjain in central India, when there was also an eclipse. But if the period of 432,000 assigned to this era was also a historical figure, we should still be very near the beginning of it. However, the days, months, and years in the ancient chronologies often had symbolic meanings rather than our more literal meanings. A method for their reduction to a historical period will be explained in chapter 16.

Once the last age begins, neither of the two superior *gunas* is able to counteract the dark and destructive *tamas*. It is called the dark age with good reason if we judge by the next account, which will be longer than the others, not only because it concerns our own age, but because evil is always more multifarious than good; happiness and truth are said to have no history. This time, all but the last foot of the Dharma, or law of spiritual duty, is lost:

5. *Taurus, On the Eternity of the World*, additional notes and translations by Taylor, p81.

During the *Kali-Yuga*, the fourth and last part of the basis of Dharma diminishes in the face of injustice; in the end it disappears completely.

During this period men are greedy, unruly, pitiless, causelessly hostile, wretched and insatiable; Sūdras [the lowest caste] and sinners take the highest places.

When trickery, lying, inertia, slumber, misdeeds, vexation, consternation, trouble, fear, and sorrow reign, it will be called the *Kali-Yuga*, which is wholly dark.

During this age, men are short-sighted [have limited intelligence], have little resourcefulness, are gluttonous, libidinous, and indigent; women are lustful and wicked.

Fields are ravaged by robbers; the Vedas corrupted by heretics; peoples are oppressed by kings; Brahmins are given over to luxury and indulgence.

Young Brahmins do not keep the least part of their vows, nor practise purity; the heads of households receive alms instead of giving them; ascetics desert their retreats to live in society, and religious who have vowed renunciation are avid for wealth.

Women are diminutive, gluttonous, excessively fertile, without shame, gossiping endlessly, thieves, cheats, and insolent.

Trade will be in the hands of wretched merchants, hired liars; their ill-reputed profession will be accepted beyond the bounds of necessity.

Servants will leave their masters, even the best of them, when they become poor, and masters will dismiss aged servants of their family if they grow infirm, as with cattle which no longer yield milk.

Abandoning father, brothers, friends, and parents, devoted to luxury and illicit affections, wretched and debauched, those who live in the *Kali-Yuga* shall have criminal relationships between brothers- and sisters-in-law.

Sūdras attired as ascetics shall live by this imposture, appropriating gifts; those who know nothing but injustice shall interpret justice and take the highest places.

Souls shall be ever afflicted; tormented by famine and poverty; dread caused by the dryness of the land shall make them sick, in a land without rice, O King.

Without clothing, without food or water, without bed, strangers to pleasure, to baths, to luxury, people will be like Pisacas [outcastes] during the *Kali-Yuga*.

During the *Kali-Yuga* they will reject their own friends for a small sum of money; they will sacrifice life itself, and turn parricide.

People will no longer protect their aged parents, or their sons, regardless of their situation, for they shall be given up to luxury and intemperance in their abjectness.

Cuka said: from day to day, Duty, Truth, Purity, Patience, Compassion, Vision, Strength, and Memory will then perish by the power of time, O Prince.

In the *Kali-Yuga*, wealth will by its advantage replace nobility of origin, virtue and merit in mankind; right and rule will be settled by force.

In marriage they will seek only pleasure [prevent offspring]; in business only deceit; persons of either sex will be sought only for enjoyment; the Brahmin only for his mark of rank.

The different social orders will be separated only by external signs, facilitating passage from one to the other; if a man is poor his rights will not be respected; knowledge will be replaced by verbiage.

Poverty will be a sufficient cause for wickedness; hypocrisy will suffice for repute of virtue; cohabitation will be accepted as marriage; bathing will be only a cleansing [and not a sacred rite].
A distant lake will alone be considered sanctifying [and no

longer the Ganges]; beauty will consist in the style of the hair; the ruling aim of all will be to fill their stomach; insolence will replace freedom.

The bodies of all living things will perish on account of the crimes of the *Kali-Yuga*; men belonging to the castes and to orders will no longer know the way marked out by the Vedas.

The law of heretics will prevail; kings shall conduct themselves like brigands, men shall devote themselves to theft, lying, to futile murders, and to all manner of shameful practices.

All castes will be like that of the Sūdras; cows will appear like goats, hermitages like secular dwellings; parents will be no more than associates.[6]

INTERPRETATIONS OF THE CYCLIC CHANGES

The picture of the last times presented here corresponds as fully as possible to the prophecies of Western tradition. Although it is obviously intended primarily for the Indian peoples, the adaptation of it to our own civilization is mostly quite clear. Social changes such as the rise to dominance by the lower castes has its parallels in societies with no caste systems. The general mingling of all hereditary social groups is a universal feature of today's world, where it is taken to affirm the value and the freedom of the individual; it passes unnoticed that freedom means nothing without the variety of possibilities which is suppressed by trends toward social uniformity.

Even more generally, there is the reductionist outlook which deprives many things of their meanings and confines them to their basically physical functions. Such reductions are brought about by a mentality for which truth and reality are somehow bound to be simple and crude, as though the transcendent simplicity of God were being sought in the opposite direction, that of matter. At any rate, the less God is believed in, the more the sovereign simplicity is sought in the only realm which is still humanly accessible, and

6. *The Bhagavata Purana*, Bk. XII, chap. 3.

where it has of course no place. Such reductionism is also an attempt to make a matter of principle out of what is really an involution of human awareness which works like another law of gravity.

There is one apparent inconsistency where the text speaks equally of the misery, indigence, and starvation suffered by those who live in the dark age, and of their hedonism, luxury, and sensuality. While there is certainly something contradictory in this, it is a contradiction which is always a part of the world as we know it, and emphasis is laid on it in the above because it is seen to increase in proportion as the end of the cycle is approached. It seems to be a typical part of the disequilibrium of the present age that everything should run to extremes, as though the suppression of natural and legitimate differences in society causes a compensating cosmic reaction in the formation of differences as inhuman in their own way as is the prevailing equalization. Sameness and difference are realities whose essence is beyond human control; man can only choose the forms they are to take.

At the same time, the physical wasting away of plant, animal and human life is said to develop in parallel with a general loss of the moral and intellectual qualities. Where it is said that knowledge is replaced with verbiage, the knowledge in question can best be understood as metaphysical knowledge. In the modern world genuine metaphysical knowledge has long since ceased to have any foothold in the prevailing culture, and the void it has left is filled with semi-fictional notions drawn from popularized science. The atrophy indicated is so extreme that it could not develop to the full except toward the end of the *Kali-Yuga*, or the continuity of life would have been broken long before now, however clearly manifest this change was in its earliest stages.

Another significant aspect of the mingling of the different castes and its production of an increasingly large group with no caste, is that the latter corresponds at a lower extreme to the primordial humanity or *Hamsa* which existed as a social unity before the division into castes took place. The aim of life is closely bound up with the union between individual personality and a universal eidetic reality. This was to the fullest degree realized by the primordial humanity, but with the passage of time there comes a decline in man's capacity to take the measure of such a reality, with the result that Forms of lesser degrees of universality are substituted for the original, these lesser Forms being comprised in the various identities contained in the caste system. Finally, human limitations increase to a point where even identification with a relative ideal ceases to be possible and the individual nature remains within its particularity and with no connection to universality. It is possible to see in this historical transition from one kind of unity to another a clear instance of the three-phase law. The unities in question owe their quality to quite different causes, however. On the one hand, the unifying factor is a great spiritual potential which exceeds the possibilities of outward expression, and on the other it is simply an absence of potentialities.

THE COUNTERFEITING OF SPIRITUALITY

These two quotations emphasize a point already raised in connection with the transition from the state where men were above caste to one where they are nearly all beneath it. In a time when spiritual values are deformed or ignored altogether, the resulting confusion will be such that many will be able to believe they have 'reached perfection' without any experience appearing to contradict them. Here is another meeting of two extremes which are both characterized by freedom, though in the one case it is objectively real while in the other it is purely subjective and is sustained only by a confused race memory of the lost state it is mistaken for. There is thus a danger from the fact that the universal spiritual realities are integral to human nature: since man cannot cease to be aware of them as somehow part of his very being, he can easily mistake their presence as mere potentialities for their full actuality. The fact that man is spiritual by nature or 'theomorphic', cannot by itself give anyone the right to attribute an actual spirituality to himself because this state is connatural with us, just as one cannot claim to be a musician simply because one has inherited a good ear for music. This mistake is the basis of a confusion in spiritual matters which has reached epidemic proportions in today's world. It is aggravated by the near-elimination of metaphysical thought from the general culture, so that there is no insight into the correspondence between lowest and highest, and the way in which the lower state imitates the higher, as for example, where certain pathological conditions resemble mystical consciousness. Much of the problem arises from the pursuit of spiritual ideals outside any of the ancient traditions. The latter nearly always put difficulties and complications of their own in the way of such development, besides encouraging it, and this ensures that it is objectively real and joined to the work of Revelation, and not just a matter of the imagination, as may well be the case where enlightenment is made too easy.

Throughout these texts on the *Kali-Yuga*, the unifying factor is the relentless contraction in the range of human consciousness, which worsens with the passage of time. This relates to the number of distinct realities which one can be aware of and relate to at a given time. Since the need for physical survival demands attention to material needs and functions, this contraction of consciousness tends to eliminate everything but these functions, before it finally erodes even them. It may seem strange to speak of the mind as though it were a thing having a physical size, but it undoubtedly has its own analogue of spatial capacity. The variations which affect this have no corresponding effect on the success with which the mind comprehends or works with the things that still remain within its reach; on the contrary, there is often a compensating increase in its acuteness to balance its loss of scope. But clarity of this kind can easily be another source of illusion, because to grasp one part of reality brilliantly while being oblivious of the other things that human minds are capable of can be more opposed to the truth than perceiving all things equally dimly.

As for the question as to why there should be this continual contraction in the average size or capacity of the mind, the answer has been outlined in chapter 4, in connection with causal transmission. Any given generation is a cause in relation to the one which comes after it, and the property of natural causality is that the effect always falls short of the cause, failing which nature would be self-creating and self-perpetuating. Once again, the fact that there is more in mankind than can be comprehended by natural causality, and the fact that the causal contraction can be reversed in any given individual does not outweigh the social effect of the greater numbers of those in whom such possibilities are not realized. The agreement between Eastern and Western teachings on this subject is not unconnected with the fact that the Principle of Plenitude applies as much, and more, in Eastern doctrine. This appears in the freedom with which the latter delineates the endless succession of world cycles, in accordance with the idea that creation should have a temporal endlessness corresponding to the eternity of its Creator. This also results from a doctrine which is open to pantheism, however. The closer God and the world are drawn together, the more inevitable it is that there must be a correspondence between them, and it may well be a fear of a drift into pantheism which has inclined Christian doctrine to treat the world as being wholly finite. Nevertheless, the law of constantly diminishing effects in every causal series that time is made up of exemplifies the order implied by Plenitude. Because this affects the human mind, it suffices to explain the dilutions, distortions and inversions which corrode man's relations to God, nature, and society equally.

9
RISING ENTROPY
& EVOLUTION

THE COSMIC PROCESS ACCORDING TO SCIENCE

Modern minds are hardly ever uninfluenced by the theory of evolution, and to many of them it may appear that the traditional cosmology gives a picture of the world which is the very opposite of the evolutionary kind. They may therefore suppose that the cosmic process explained here is merely pre-scientific or even anti-scientific, which would be unfortunate, as the truth is very different. It can be shown that the real conflict is not with science itself so much as with certain ideological uses made of it. But before the question of the compatibility between the present subject and evolution can be considered, it will be necessary to put it in a scientific context through its relation to another law which is more universal and more important to science than evolution.

Science contains first principles which are coherent with cyclic law and a serious problem for evolutionary theory. Foremost among these are the two laws of thermodynamics, the First Law being that the total quantity of matter and energy in the world is a fixed quantity which can only be redistributed but not created or destroyed. The second Law of Thermodynamics states that every physical process involves an irreversible net increase of disorder or entropy, no matter whether the process appears to be destructive or not. This law was originally developed by Carnot and Clausius as part of a theory to explain why heat engines were able to do useful work. The direct implication of the second Law, that the fixed quantity of matter and energy is constantly breaking down into smaller and less usable quantities may more briefly be called the Entropy Law. So essential is it to science that it is one part of classical physics which remains valid for both classical physics and for the quantum and relativity physics of the present century. For this reason, what was said about it by Eddington in the nineteen-thirties is as relevant as ever today, making a notable exception in a subject where ideas get out of date more rapidly than in most others. At that time the law in question had already held its position for the greater part of a century:

> The law that entropy always increases—the second law of thermodynamics—holds, I think, the supreme position among the laws of Nature .... If your theory is found to be against the second law of thermodynamics I can give you no hope; there is nothing for it but to collapse in deepest humiliation.... The chain of deductions from this simple law has been almost illimitable.[1]

The scope of this law is both scientific and metaphysical equally, which adds more to its special nature. It has also been called the law of Morpholysis, from μορφη (morphe), 'form', and λυω (luo), 'I lose'. All scientific explanations require that apparent exceptions to this law be shown to be in reality instances of it. Until this conception was generally understood, scientific investigation could not even begin, because many natural phenomena were not felt to be in need of explanation. For example, it was supposed that insects were spontaneously generated from mud and decaying matter, until Pasteur proved by his sterilization experiments that this could not happen. Fossils, flint tools and axe-heads were collected and examined for centuries before it was realized that the forms of these things could not have resulted from the mere flow of the elements. To non-scientific minds, things 'just happened', whether they manifested order or not. But given the law that natural forces alone can only dissipate order, all ordered structures have to be the result either of intelligent agency or the exposure of some pre-existing form. On the basis of the Entropy Law, therefore, science agrees to a large

1. A.S. Eddington, *The Nature of the Physical World*, chap. 4.

extent with what has been previously argued from first principles. Consequently, there are no grounds for taking the ancient wisdom to be opposed to science, or for assuming that science must always support materialistic thinking. Its compatibility with what follows from the Principle of Plenitude is undeniable, no doubt because this principle has an essential role in scientific thought as well.

ONLY PHYSICAL DISORDER IS PROBABLE

The increase in entropy which accompanies all physical changes always develops toward the state which is statistically the most probable, this being the one in which differentiation between its parts is at a minimum. If it is not always clear why order and differentiation between component parts should be relatively improbable while disorder and lack of differentiation should be to the same extent probable, one need only refer to the example of two quantities of a gas separated by a partition, where the gas is at a high temperature on one side and at a low temperature on the other. Once the partition is removed the two quantities of gas will mingle until the whole is at the same temperature mid-way between the two initial temperatures. The typical experience that heat always moves from hotter bodies to cooler ones is likewise a question of probability; the reverse process would be inconceivably improbable, and it illustrates the tendency of everything in the universe to reach a single level of energy, one at which energy can no longer move because it can only do so where energy is at different concentrations. This state is that of maximum entropy, whether in the universe as a whole or in some smaller system. That the rise in entropy is irreversible appears from what would happen if one did try to reverse the above experiment and divide the gas into two halves again, and heat one half by the same amount above the other. The energy necessary for this could only be obtained by the dissipation of more energy from elsewhere, which will inevitably be greater than the amount which one succeeds in imparting to the gas. Because of this 'one-way' property of nature implied by rising entropy, which Eddington referred to as 'time's arrow,' nature cannot have existed in its present form over endless time without new order having been somehow imparted to it from outside. In a manner recalling the account given by Plato in chapter 5, Eddington has made this into an argument for the belief that God must at a certain time have caused the world to exist with a maximum amount of ordered matter and concentrated energy:

> Traveling backward into the past we find a world with more and more organization. If there is no barrier to stop us earlier we must reach a moment when the energy of the world was wholly organized with none of the random element in it. . . . The organization we are concerned with is exactly definable, and there is a limit at which it becomes perfect.[2]

The appearance of such a perfectly organized initial state, left at the mercy of random dispersal ever since, indicates a major discontinuity in God's creation, but that does not make it impossible, and it could be one of an endless series. Steady-state theories of the universe, which offered an alternative to this conception, have turned out to be untenable, because no exception to the Entropy Law has ever been found. This applies despite the fact that there are a great many natural processes which are theoretically reversible. These include all cases where objects can be treated as mere units or point-masses, as with colliding bodies, projectiles, pendulums, and orbiting planets and satellites. But these things are really abstractions which produce exact results only in idealized systems, so that they can only serve as descriptive models within certain limits. There is always the fact that the energy imparted to point-masses is not all converted to momentum, but is dissipated in other ways such as heat or noise.

Where chemistry is concerned, similar considerations apply. Every reaction of chemical substances is more or less reversible, but always at the price of an input of heat energy from combustion, so that the net loss of chemical energy and ordered molecules does not cease to increase. In experiments where it appears that chance alone can produce order in the form of more complex compounds, it is necessary that such things be isolated by human intervention if they

2. Ibid., chap. 4, p 84.

are to be preserved, failing which the same forces that produced them will reduce them back to disorder. 'Time's arrow' still moves forward, even when we put physical processes into reverse.

THE ENTROPY LAW AND BIOLOGY

The fact that this law so clearly applies in chemistry and physics has led some to believe that living creatures should be able to form an exception to it. Nevertheless its working is just as certain here, albeit behind a screen of appearances which can deceive casual, but not scientific, observation. Biology is concerned with the growth of plant and animal life and the huge range of forms of emergent order which that entails, but this continual apparent rise of new structures still results from the same breakdown of ordered matter and available energy:

> The Entropy Law applies only to completely isolated systems, whereas a living organism, being an open system, exchanges both matter and energy with its environment. There is thus no contradiction to the Entropy Law as long as the increase in the entropy of the environment more than compensates for the decrease in the entropy of the organism.[3]

The new order which arises in the tissues of growing animals and plants never equals the amount of order which is lost in the substances they feed on. The transition from the nutrient material to the organism is extremely wasteful, but the increased order or lowered entropy of the growing organism is clearly visible, whereas the consequent rise in the entropy of its surroundings, being scattered over time and space, is less obvious. If the growth of a certain organism realizes a kind of order which is of special interest from a human point of view, perhaps because it is like a step in the direction of human life, this does not release it from being part of the universal downgrading process. Since individual growth takes place by lowering one's entropy by what one takes from the surroundings, so it is conceivable that evolution could also take place through a

3. Jeremy Rifkin, *Entropy, A New World View*, 1980, Afterword.

comparable process of waste and dissipation. But this would mean that the most evolution could achieve would be small and localized instances of low entropy. There is no question of its being able to increase the amount of order in the world as a whole.

Where breeding and heredity are concerned, biology can supply a wealth of material which is supportive of the traditional cosmology, and in ways which are intelligible to everyone. The main rule of animal breeding is that only the best specimens of each generation should be used to breed the next one, not necessarily to improve the strain, but just to enable it to remain at the same standard. A similar result obtains for creatures in the wild state, either by a high general mortality or by a restriction of breeding to the dominant members of the pack or herd. Here again, the result is not a continual improvement of the species, but just the maintenance of a certain level of health, strength, speed, and so forth. This shows that the causal transmission as it appears in the reproduction of species always involves a certain deterioration, or deviation from the norm, in many or even most cases. Each generation contains a few specimens which are superior to the average of the previous generation, and a larger number which are inferior to it, so that if all bred equally the species as a whole would lose its competitive qualities and die out. The numerical preponderance of those below a given standard in relation to those above it is itself an illustration of the idea that matter is never fully mastered by Form, just as it also shows that the entropy of living species constantly rises just as much as in non-living systems. From the evolutionary point of view it is unfortunate that the one form of evolution which can always be observed directly is that of degeneration, as where animals lose their natural instincts in captivity. This point cannot be relativized away by making it purely a matter of definition, from the fact that every evolutionary change will necessarily be degeneration from the point of view of what existed at its beginning, and will be just as necessarily progress from the point of view of what exists at the end of it. Such thinking ignores the objective factor that a species has a set of potentialities which it can realize more or less completely in relation to a given environment. Experience shows that basic changes in heredity can only be deviations from an optimum condition.

The law of Entropy, or Morpholysis, parallels in its action what has been said of the descending cyclic pattern, with its irreversible downgrading of order on the physical level. However, this correspondence does not extend to the relative reversals and restorations which appear in cyclic processes, since the tendency of entropy is uniformly downward. As the imagery of the Four Ages shows, historical time manifests relative golden ages which to some degree recapitulate a much higher state. Since the human state is rooted in the material world, it must in a general way be subject to the laws of matter, but the presence of mind and spirit in man results in deviations from the uniform direction of these laws. Entropy is strictly applicable to physical processes, while the laws of mind are independent of it. Thus mind can intervene in nature both individually and collectively. The rise-and-fall pattern which this superimposes on the entropic descent exists both on the large scale and on the small, according as cycles of widely differing amplitudes develop concurrently. There results from this a very complicated order of descent and relative reascent, as befits a being whose nature embraces the whole range of realities through the material, psychical, and spiritual. Although mind as such is not subject to entropy, its psycho-physical operations can be, and its freedom in this regard varies on the collective scale according to certain time-periods.

THE RELATION TO EVOLUTION

What has been said about the Entropy Law creates the setting in which we can consider the way the traditional theory of time relates to evolution. The main difficulty in generalizing about evolution is that it takes a number of different forms, some of which are more or less compatible with creation. For simplicity's sake, I will divide it into two categories which could be called 'weak' and 'strong' evolution respectively. In its weak form, it may include the idea that the different species and their roles in nature embody pre-existent 'goals' of evolution, so that evolutionary changes will be teleologically ordered toward them. It also gives an account of the ways in which environmental pressures suppress some hereditary features of species and accentuate others, producing changes in their outward forms with the passage of time, and not necessarily irreversibly. In regard to the human race, it is accepted that both body and soul are involved in the changes which take place. Changes which the human physique may have undergone over millions of years would gradually allow differing degrees of freedom to the soul's higher faculties and possibly a greater self-awareness.

There is a clear analogy between this idea of evolution and the development of the adult from the child. In either case, it is a question of latent possibilities being worked out according to a universal plan. Evolution of this kind is what one refers to when it is held that religious beliefs are compatible with evolution, and its truth or falsity could not be a serious issue in the present context, although its psychological effects are far from harmless: it can only support the conviction that whatever is latest must be best and truest, no matter whether the facts will support this nor not.

The Entropy Law is the basis of the separation between the 'strong' and the 'weak' forms of evolution, because the latter is concerned with changes in the structure of species at certain times which are compatible with entropy. Such modifications to existing forms do not require any greater increase of order than is required by the natural growth of organisms from their conception. In its strong form, however, evolution would require an absolute increase in order and complexity of form, arising spontaneously in a way which could only be called creation without a creator. This conception of evolution consists in the formation of ever-increasingly complex organic molecules by random changes. At any given time everything in living creatures would be a result of this increasing organic complexity. Whether or not they acquire souls in the process would not be an issue because everything is determined by the physical constitution, including the very state of being alive. Unlike the weak form of evolution, this kind is not one where physical forms develop in conjunction with psychical or spiritual ones. Advantages resulting from random molecular changes would account for what we call our interior life as much as for our bodies.

This theory cannot be passed over, because it asserts that more complex structures continually arise from less complex ones, in a manner exactly opposite to what the Entropy Law and the cyclic cosmology would lead one to expect. Another, less obvious, but no less important reason lies in the implications that evolution must have for theoretical knowledge, whether it be metaphysical or scientific. In either of these realms, one must assume the adequacy of the human mind to the cosmic realities it wishes to explain. This adequacy for all purposes of knowledge, which formed a Scholastic definition of truth as *adaequatio rei et intellectus*, is all of a piece with the idea of the soul as a microcosm or epitome of all that it relates to in its world. Man the knower and his world could be said to be related like a key to its lock, therefore, which may be expected on the understanding that everything was specially created, whereas it must be extremely improbable if mankind were a product of evolution.

The adequacy in question is not affected by the degree to which its potentialities are currently realized; once it exists, it need only continue to exist in order to be developed to any degree whatever, no further evolution of man as such being necessary for this. The microcosm constitutes a natural perfection beyond which no other could have any purpose, and if it did result from evolution, that evolution must therefore have stopped. The very question of metaphysical knowledge, moreover, implies something of a transcendent nature in man, since knowledge of this kind is not dependent on sense, but comprehends phenomena without belonging among them. Nevertheless, evolution would require us to believe that this could result as an emergent reality from antecedents consisting entirely of natural phenomena, not in the way in which maturation brings a young person's mind to maturity, but rather in the way that history produces novel events.

THE FUNDAMENTAL PROBLEM OF EVOLUTION

Defenders of the theory of evolution claim that to deny it is to deny the possibility of a scientific explanation of mankind's origin, and that of other species besides. If we had to look to some action outside nature for this purpose, a line would be drawn against any further scientific discovery in that direction, and, worse, the world would be divided into two exclusive categories, the natural and the supernatural. It would be far more elegant and more economical if everything could be accounted for solely in terms of the natural, it is thought, but only because it is mistakenly believed that no more than the natural is involved in the scientific knowledge we possess already. In reality, the division between the natural and the supernatural invariably exists at the heart of scientific knowledge, for reasons which are next to be considered.

Both science and metaphysics have a common interest in a realm of intelligible realities, Forms, or paradigms, as they are named, depending on the context. Objective intelligible realities include whole theories as well as the elements of every theory and formula, and they are inherent in both the universe and in the human mind. For this reason, the discovery of each hitherto unknown paradigm is an acquisition for all minds alike, and is regulative for the mental processes of all minds as well. These conceptions are so inbuilt into human thought that no one knows how to relinquish them, even when they profess theories which logically require them to do so. For this reason, hypotheses which would reduce all knowledge to nothing are accepted and operated on the intellectual basis they negate.

Thus the theory of evolution is commonly believed to be a paradigmatic reality, although this can only be as a result of a confusion when the theory is taken in full rigor. If evolution were the whole truth about man's origin and formation, *there could be no paradigms*, not even the most universal, such as truth, goodness, beauty, or meaning. Everything in us, including our ideas as to what the truth consists in, would be solely the result of molecular interactions, and if these chance events had happened differently, we should have assigned truth and moral right and wrong to things quite different from what are actually so treated. Unlike paradigms or Forms, physical processes are non-referential, that is, they cannot be 'about' anything. Given that they accounted for our whole being, this would mean that what one person took for a true idea need have no such meaning or relevance for any other person, not least where the idea in question is that of evolution. The biochemistry which caused one person to think this theory to be true could not be in any way 'more true' or 'more real' than the biochemistry which caused another person to think it to be untrue. *Qua* physical changes, these biochemical effects could have no more relation to truth than have the movements of wind, sand, or water.

In this case, the belief that evolution was true, in even the most highly-trained mind, would have to be the outcome of the same causal system which had also determined his favorite varieties of music, food, and sport. There could be no difference in kind between the causes of the latter and the causes of his supposedly higher or intellectual activities. Since 'strong' evolution negates the common world of objective ideas, the beliefs of other persons could have no relevance for one's own ideas in this regard, and the rational deductions on which this theory is based for the expert would be in the same category with the physical peculiarities of the person concerned.

This is the typical *impasse* of materialistic systems. The supposed truth of the theory takes away all rational grounds for believing it to be true. The development and continuation of the theory of evolution clearly depends on reasoning processes whose validity requires that they be unaffected by natural causes, let alone produced by them, and this is something to which 'strong' evolution allows no meaning. Every theory, whether it be scientific or metaphysical, presupposes that the human mind can grasp the phenomenal world as a whole from a position which transcends it, and this is why all attempts to make that transcending intelligence a product of the phenomena it encloses are a waste of time. They fall into a self-contradiction from which there is no escape.

Unlike evolution in its 'strong' sense, the cyclic concept and the Entropy Law do not dictate any theory of human origins and formation. They involve only relations of phenomena within the field of consciousness, and do not require that consciousness be in itself invalidated or otherwise affected in its essence by the operation of their laws. For that reason, they are true laws. I have prolonged the treatment of evolution to try to make it clear that any conflict between these laws and evolutionary explanations of the world must be to the detriment of evolution. Not only does it demand an excessively improbable defiance of the universal rise in disorder, it deprives us of any coherent knowledge of the world when held in any more than the 'weak' sense in which it governs modifications to components of species which already exist. Although the implicit conclusion that our claim to knowledge should be given up is only too obviously self-refuting, theories which radically subvert knowledge are still accepted because the enormity of their consequences is not taken in. Besides, most minds are reluctant to face the hard alternatives of either rejecting fashionable notions or of giving up any right to absolute truth, and so they take refuge in a belief that the issue can be settled by compromise. However, the choice should be made easier by the fact that what needs to be discarded is only pseudo-scientific thinking, and not essential scientific theory. The cyclic cosmology is compatible with the latter, and not with the former.

10

THE SUBMERGENCE
OF DISTINCTIONS

VISIBLE SIGNS OF ENTROPY

The relationship which has been indicated between rising entropy and the cyclic law is a close one despite some important differences, and their combined effects are visible in human affairs at all levels from the most intellectual to the most simply practical. If the time necessary for the whole universe to reach maximum entropy is unimaginably long, the same cannot be said for small systems such as civilizations. They advance to their maximum entropy much more rapidly, roughly in proportion to their size in relation to that of the universe. As this final state is by definition one of non-differentiation and exhaustion of possibilities, the advance toward it will be marked by a reduction in the distinctive qualities of both persons and things, though this advance may develop slowly and almost invisibly most of the time. It is difficult to argue that such changes are always the dominant ones when one's presuppositions are not widely shared, as the Goodman-Hakewill controversy showed. Where the argument depends on evidence, and therefore on the range of one person's experiences and the number of comparisons that can be made among them, its objectivity cannot be ensured.

Fortunately, this difficulty can be overcome by the fact that the subtle and progressive changes in question give rise to effects of a kind which are a matter of common knowledge, whatever doubts there may be as to their causes. Just as roofs collapse when their timbers have rotted by a sufficient amount, so the reduction of quality and the consequent rise in the importance of quantity, cannot go beyond a certain point without finally putting an end to the special status or even the very existence of the entities concerned. This kind of change is constantly manifest in the cessations, amalgamations, and redefinitions of status affecting nations, institutions, professions, industrial products, and in a comparable sense, the lives of individuals.

Common sense mostly thinks in terms of things only either existing or not existing, but this is too simple a point of view. Existence also admits of degrees, and whatever difficulties may be found in the idea that things can 'exist more' or 'exist less', there is as much necessity for being and not-being to be related on a continuous basis as on the more obvious discontinuous one. The passing into or out of existence, however sudden, is always the culmination of many small changes, and so equally are the upheavals and revolutions that affect society. The distinctions between beings are an essential part of their reason for existing, since actual identity between two or more existents is a limit never actually reached. If they could differ *solo numero* they could not even be separate things in any case, according to the identity of indiscernibles. If this is borne in mind, it will not be hard to see why the degree of differentiation between beings is bound up with their share in existence, and conversely that the decrease in the qualities of things should become a threat to their continued existence.

Quality, identity, and stability in existence are all closely related; they increase and decrease together. Their reduction results in the optimum conditions for invasive change, and because of the belief that change means progress, the loss of qualitative identity is by no means always regretted. The diminution of quality brings with it an equivalent rise in the effect of quantity, as Guénon showed, and the constant technical calculations required as a result of that become the basis of an alternative culture, as with the takeover of many activities by computerization. This produces the paradox that the evacuation of quality and identity can itself be turned into a new collective identity. The intellectual procedures of perceiving the essences of things thus get replaced by the technical procedures for relating factual information. And the theoretical reasons for this qualitative reduction have already been given in terms of a cosmic movement away from the primal source of being and reality.

Personal Effects of Depleted Identity

One of the best known revolutions resulting from a depletion of distinction is that of the equalization of the social roles of women with those of men. But for all the attention it receives, its true causes are never explained because metaphysical principles are not applied. This lack of understanding makes it easy to ignore the fact that the process it forms part of has in any case too much power behind it for human approval or disapproval to have much effect. For this reason, no deeper problem is seen in this than the question of what activities people are capable of without too much emotional discomfort.

The question of either sex having a specific nature which might dictate their vocations is no longer arguable because the qualities which make up masculine and feminine identity have been for so long a time undergoing a gradual diminution. The result is that the old social order is made almost incomprehensible to those who are caught up in this process. The confusion caused by loss of identity is such that men themselves have failed to understand the reasons for their own traditional status. At the same time, the fact that women can find a vital interest in adopting many formerly masculine activities indicates a previous weakening of specific identity in them also. (I say 'specific' identity because a sense of identity may exist even though it never develops into a specifically masculine or feminine nature.) Like all the related changes, this one is in principle destructive because it derives from a process which of its very nature diminishes existence, making for a more disordered world. The only positive potential in this comes from the fact that the loss of a norm can in some cases open the possibility of living above it instead of beneath it.

The rise in human entropy which tends to equalize men and women brings about the erosion of other distinctions along with it. One of these distinctions is that between childhood and adulthood. In proportion as women do not have a way of life separate from that of men, it follows that children will not have a way of life separate from that of adults. The modern adolescent is usually fated to be an incarnation of this lost distinction, as adolescence becomes less a time of transition and more a mode of existence in its own right. Closely related to this is the weakening of the distinction between the married and the unmarried, insofar as both partners have the same way of life, whether married or not. What makes marriage now seem a questionable value is precisely the tendency toward a very similar kind of life for both men and women. Although such things result from a rise in human entropy and the related loss of essence or quality in individuals, they are also a means of accelerating the process.

The convergence of Man and Woman, Child and Adult, toward a being who would be effectively none of them points to a limit beyond which the human race would have to either cease to exist on this earth or turn into something quite different. It may be argued that such a change does not make the human spirit any less real, and that with the aid of science the future of the new race could be ensured. The problem with this is that the norms of Man, Woman, Child, and Adult belong among the archetypal realities, the realization of which never ceases to be a basic condition for existence. In proportion as these universal archetypes fail to be realized, life can easily be experienced as a continuous low-intensity mental torture which can produce life-threatening cumulative effects, owing to the maladjustment and interpersonal conflicts fostered by it.

Realizing significant archetypal realities in oneself, having a sense of identity, and finding happiness, are inseparable, because the archetype or Form is the ultimate object of self-knowledge, without which the self is not knowable even to itself. Only in proportion as one knows what one is can one consistently act in a manner coherent with one's own nature and find fulfilment. Consequently, the fact that human life may be technically sustainable apart from these conditions will be irrelevant if human beings cannot be made happy by it or find it worthwhile. This is in any case becoming an issue already, as can be seen by the increasing numbers of persons whose lives are in crisis for a multitude of reasons which all reduce to a failure to know their own identities. This is the issue in which the cosmic decline of the qualitative principle finally comes to a head and defies attempts to ignore it.[1] It reveals in the midst of human life the connection which was made theoretically at the beginning of this chapter between the *differentiae* of individuals and their ability to exist, so that the loss of the one entails the loss of the other.

EROSION OF SOCIAL BARRIERS

The failure of identity has its consequences in other realms as well, as can be seen from the confusion and dissipation of social classes, the very reason for which has ceased to be understood. As in other examples, the collapse of the barriers between the classes has come only after prolonged inner changes by which people lost consciousness of much that was essential to their natures. Modern minds are unable to see any meaning in classes or castes other than the reservation of privileges for a minority who are supposed to be favored without justification. Yet when the class system existed by the general will, it was found as satisfying to be able to distinguish oneself from a class above one's own in the social order as from a class below it. This fact shows the original class structure to have been an effect of a degree of self-knowledge, and once that knowledge began to fail, one's position in a given class could only be experienced as an injustice inflicted by society's prejudices.

A class or caste always defines itself around a given set of values and interests, like those of merchants or craftsmen, simply because the human mind cannot cope with an unrestricted range of values and options, and from this it follows that when these social organisms cease to exist, human beings are faced with the alternatives of either supporting an open-ended range of values or, more probably, of relinquishing the majority of them. The effects, on the one hand, of a sure sense of identity, or on the other the lack of it, on sexual

---

1. While it is a condition for which spiritual religion can provide the remedy, this remedy nearly always involves some kind of self-limitation, which to the modern mind is anathema. With a strong sense of identity, the freedom to experiment with an unlimited range of unrelated possibilities may not be very harmful, but without it, the result is to make the problem insoluble.

behavior are too well understood to need commentary, but most of the other consequences of human entropy are involved in this realm of human behavior. There is no reason to believe that the cessation of class and caste comes from a more open and more Christian attitude, because no such thing can be seen in the classless society, where human relations have become more, not less, adversarial than they were in former times. This is not surprising in view of the fact that the ability to relate in a positive way to others cannot go any further than the ability to relate to one's own identity.

In the extreme case, lack of self-identity is a typical part of insanity, and the relevance of this to the present subject can be seen from the fact that insanity typically leads to the adoption of totally alien identities as though they were one's own. This problem with identity means that it is more than usually difficult to judge which social class a given person comes from if they suffer from a mental derangement. For this reason the decline of the qualitative element in the world and the resulting loss of intelligible identities points to the possibility of some form of insanity eventually becoming so widespread that hardly anyone would be able to escape it. Such a condition is already partially acknowledged in the increasing difficulty in classifying many persons as insane under modern conditions, and in the spread of criminal behavior in cases where moral responsibility has to be minimized or even excluded.

An unrealized self is always a vulnerable self, and therefore very prone to fear, which compensates itself with outbursts of hate. This appears in the insane hatreds which flare up between different racial and religious groups all over the world. While differences of religion and culture are nominally to blame for such things, the real problem is above all that of the psychological vulnerability which comes with the loss of real selfhood, leaving a vacuum which can be filled with an invented identity. This situation also has implications for the moral codes of the traditional religions, which tend to become unworkable because they were devised for 'normal' humans who at least exemplified a type recognizable to itself and to others, but which make no sense amid the social and cultural chaos arising from confusions of vocation and gender.

Even though these changes are not human in their origin, the terms 'good' and 'evil' are still applicable to them, and it is inevitable that the movement toward equalization should be allied chiefly to evil, because good is fated, so to speak, to distinguish itself insofar as it is realized at all; it must surpass itself in order to be itself. Obviously the confusion of distinctions cannot avoid negating this tendency. The resulting uniformity can only benefit whatever is bad, since this obscurity means it will not be identified as such, while good has nothing to gain for the same reason. Equalization, moral corruption, and a darkening of the intellect are all closely related in this process. The effacement of individuality is in no way the same as the self-effacement which is often the way of those whose lives have a spiritual direction, despite some appearances. Such individuals are in any case unalterably 'distinguished' in their own way, so that their self-effacement cannot be a literal or absolute one, but obtains only in relation to human activities which would not be a suitable means of expressing their main purpose in life.

If, however, the human effects of rising entropy are on the whole evil, and if it is indeed the cause of a vast amount of mental suffering and maladjustment, it would seem reasonable to expect that attempts to counteract it would be thought welcome. But all such attempts founder on the fact that one part of this scenario at least is strongly willed by the majority. This consists in an over-simplified belief in freedom which is current in a conviction that everyone is free to become anything they may want to be. The flattery of this belief is so seductive that no one will take any notice of the fact that it is nonsense, or of the fact that it loosens everyone's hold on reality. It is as though the many centuries during which mankind was obliged to accept the austere belief that it was in a fallen state had to be compensated by a carnival of self-gratifying alternatives which are really far more misleading, for all that they are occasioned by a centuries-long exaggeration of the doctrine of the Fall which prevailed at the popular level.

Another aspect of this shaking off of traditional restraints is the great increase in the importance of sexuality as a value in its own right, as though it too had to be avenged for the ill effects of belief in the Fall. This typically modern development also follows directly from the continual dilution of personal identity along with other qualitative realities. This is because sexuality always gains strength from a failure to see the other person as a whole person, that is, from an unawareness of the problems, commitments, tastes, fears, practical needs, and so forth which make up the true person. From this it results that the process which erodes the qualitative core of personality will inevitably increase the strength and importance of sexuality in thought and behavior. The more there is a widespread failure to be fully a person, therefore, the more there will be a cult of sexuality for its own sake, even though this may have its roots in a spiritual poverty which lies beyond the scope of moral judgement.

Entropy In Nationalities and Cultures.

The reduction in differences between nations is taken for progress by majority opinion because it is supposed to mean that there will therefore be fewer causes for conflict between them. Here again, there is a general failure to understand these changes in a more than superficial way, even at an academic level, which is shown by the fact that they are always supposed to be happening by human choice for the realization of political agendas. In this way, the stage is set for the whole process to advance without opposition to its conclusion in the name of progress.

On the other hand, the reduction of real distinctions on the personal level gives rise to a general loss of distinction between the different nations and races. This promotes their social mingling, which in turn reduces their differences still further. As with the former examples, there are many who see this change solely as a result of progress, and who ignore the fact that this is connected with a lessening of the abilities of the different peoples to assimilate their own traditions sufficiently to regenerate the ideas around which their cultures were formed. The propagation of the national genius weakens in a manner comparable to the weakening of masculine and feminine identities. The material interests of the different nations remain broadly similar in any case, and the satisfaction of both material and cultural needs requires more international cooperation in proportion as nations and cultures lose what once made them more like self-sufficient little worlds in themselves.

More rapid communications obviously make it easier to diffuse new ideas, but this brings the penalty that they also inhibit the development of new cultures. The plentiful exchange of ideas promotes a dependence on the whole system rather than true creativity, which depends on a deep searching of the resources of individuals and localities in relative isolation. This in turn is directly linked to the qualitative principle of identity which is under pressure. The absence of the qualitative principle results in a void which has to be filled by one means or another, and this, rather than open-mindedness, may account for the welcome which nearly all nations extend to imports of foreign culture. The distinctions between nations may in many cases become much reduced by the use of a common technology and by a common popular culture, but this does not mean that they can be reduced to nothing, although international organizations are liable to treat them as if that were in fact the case. Such treatment, however, rather than making them cease to exist, is calculated to provoke the kind of violent reaction which arises when identity is cornered. Related to this is the phenomenon of interracial conflict, because these distinctions are linked to a number of basic attributes of the different races which do not alter, even when other and more important distinctions have been lost. Such invariants make a dangerous mixture with all the other adopted attributes which are in flux. Where invariants persist intentionally, tokens of national identity are clung to with a greater fanaticism in proportion as individual identity fails to develop, and those caught up in this situation are undeterred by the dangers it causes, because the greatest fear of all is that of the ontological void in the unrealized self. This evil affirms the seeming paradox that peaceful conditions are not produced by the reduction of differences.

HARMONY FROM DIFFERENCES

René Guénon drew attention to the fact that the equalizing process which comes with the 'reign of quantity' results in a uniformity which is in no way the same as unity, and therefore makes conflict inevitable. There is a naively obvious sense in which it is true that differences may cause conflict, on the grounds that at least two different beings are necessary for there to be conflict at all. Friction must have two surfaces. But at a deeper level things are quite the reverse of this, as can be seen from the effects of differences in relation to one another. Suppose the differences between two beings to be increased without limit. Insofar as this happens, they must be taken out of relation to one another, so that they would lose even the physical possibility of conflict. Conversely, if their similarities were increased without limit, their points of common need and interest would also increase without limit, providing the materials for conflict. The fact that there must be at least two beings before conflict is possible does not in any way counteract the condition that, given this initial difference, only similarities between them could make conflict actually operable. The intentional suppression of differences between beings is in any case deluded because the deepest difference of all, namely, that they are so many separate substances, must remain as long as they exist at all. The belief that equalization is realistic is a result of a materialistic philosophy which can only see qualities and attributes as though they were so many accidents somehow associated with their owners which can be manipulated at will, and not manifestations of a central causal principle in the self. Once the latter principle is allowed for, it can be seen that no alteration of externals could remove their central cause.

For the above reasons, it is easy to predict that the more equality there is, whether between nations, social classes, men and women, and age-groups, the more confusion, competition and conflict there will be between them. Only when the differences between individuals and groups are accepted and developed to the full, so that each has its own sphere of action and self-expression which impinges no more than minimally on those of others can there be a truly harmonious world. Far from this diversity meaning mutual exclusivism, it would rather increase the possibilities for human life and so eliminate the privations from which defensive forms of behavior arise. Exclusive behavior is in any case another result of too much similarity, which requires artificial distinctions to counteract it. Genuine diversity unreflectingly creates its boundaries by the fruition of its creative energies, not by the intentional building of barriers for self-protection.

The development of the distinctive natures of individuals takes place primarily in their conscious 'inner space,' rather than in the external world, and this is why materialistic philosophies which cast doubt on the reality of the inner self inevitably work for the spread of uniformity. The consequent inability of individuals and of whole cultures to develop the state of a 'little world' means a denial of something essential in human nature, a denial which creates powerful inner stresses. This evil is nearly always blamed on the other persons and cultures which have also been reduced to the same condition, and the loss of inner diversity tends to impoverish the public world on which the extraverted mind is centered. This connection has been described in Martin Heidegger's observations on the early twentieth century as follows:

> All things sank to the same level, resembling a blind mirror that no longer reflects, that casts nothing back. The prevailing dimension became that of extension and number. Intelligence no longer meant a wealth of talent, lavishly spent, but only what could be learned by everyone, the practice of a routine, always associated with a certain amount of sweat and a certain amount of show. In America and Russia this development grew into the boundless etcetera of indifference and always-the-sameness—so much so that *the quantity took on a quality of its own* [author's italics]. Since then the domination in those countries of a cross section of the indifferent mass has become something more than a dreary accident. It has become an active onslaught that destroys all rank and every world-creating impulse of the spirit and calls it a lie.[2]

This concentration of energies on the material world requires that the higher faculties be reinterpreted as means to material ends, as nothing apart from the material world is supposed to be able to constitute an end in itself:

---

2. *An Introduction to Metaphysics*, chap. 1.

The spirit falsified into intelligence falls to the level of a tool in the service of others, a tool the manipulation of which can be taught and learned.[3]

As the sphere of consciousness always contracts with the passage of time, except where counter-measures are taken, faculties that would serve for the perfection of consciousness are increasingly diverted to short-term practicalities. The natural expansion of consciousness which takes place between infancy and early adulthood tends on average to go less far in successive generations. This does not appear primarily in a decline in measurable intelligence, but in a lessening in the range of different realities to which the mind can relate. Those which remain in the mind's compass become increasingly centered on the demands of self-preservation, therefore, because every reduction of awareness makes survival more precarious. A practical materialism can result from nothing more than a failure of consciousness to achieve its full development. The uniformity which results from this is a material travesty of the unity which Providence has made conditional on the full self-realization which is in fact as much a part of human destiny as the growth of the body. The option of reacting against the suppression of consciousness and reversing the tendency is usually ignored because, as Heidegger further observes, a spiritual decline stifles the very consciousness that any such decline is in fact taking place.

POLITICAL AND ECONOMIC INDISTINCTION

There are a number of realities related to economics which have progressively merged with it, notably politics. The most important practical effect of this is monetary inflation, since this results from the manipulation of economics for political purposes. The confusion of politics with economics and the draining away of monetary value have become attributes of nearly all modern nations, as the powers of the state spread ever more widely. The aims pursued by different political parties differ only in matters of detail, since they

3. Ibid.

are all committed to constantly increasing earnings, industrial production, and national expenditure; the disputes are only about
means, not ends. These things are believed to be subject to human
choice, but in reality they have a momentum which shows them to
be borne along by the cosmic process, not by a human or social one.
Evidence which shows that the indefinite continuance of these aims
is not desirable, especially if it is made to happen by government
decree and not by natural conditions, is never enough to discredit
them. The belief that governments can in effect command prosper-
ity is a fallacy the real price of which is inflation, because governments can only make good their economic claims in the eyes of
those who vote for them by spending their resources on an increasing scale, whether national income justifies it or not. The gap
between income and politically-desirable expenditure has to be
filled by printing the extra money needed. Thus all numerical
quantities rise, while the things they represent are either static or
decreasing.

This is a precise and important example of rising entropy, because a nation's money is a quantitative symbol of its total available
energy. The devaluation of money by inflation reflects the dissipation of national human energy resources, where the division of
money into ever higher numbers of units parallels the way in which
physical energy breaks down into ever smaller and less useful quantities, subject to the Entropy Law. Besides inflation, increasing
taxation is also a result of the conflation of politics with economics,
and at the same time serves to consolidate this conflation. Its tendency to disable or dissolve the individual wherever possible is
so fully in keeping with the general cosmic process that rising taxation is an index of the universal quantitative principle. Its role in the
reduction of distinctions between individuals and social classes is
only too clear, but its ill-effects are by no means evenly distributed.
The most large-scale financial interests are as a rule the ones best
able to thrive in spite of it, and this strengthens the bias toward
quantity and the concentration of energies in the most de-individu-
alizing directions. The benefit of this appears obviously in the enormous abundance created by mass production, but it is an abundance which comes at the price of a standardization in the things

produced, a standardization which may easily communicate itself to those who use them.

The merging of the major functions of civilization can be seen in the central group comprising politics, economics, and industry, therefore, while industry in turn takes in technology and pure science. The avenues open to scientific research are directed to fields which serve technology, which in turn serves industry, besides which, pure science is now conducted almost wholly in and by means of high technology products; how much the natural sciences really have to do with nature is now growing questionable. This erosion of distinctions in the scientific realm affects the distinction, once so clear, between what naturally happens, and what human activity can cause to happen. (Heisenberg's Uncertainty Principle highlights an area where these two things coincide completely.) In this respect there is a significant parallel between modern science and modern literature: just as science-technology is eroding the difference between nature and what man can do with nature, modern literature specializes in the conflation of fact and fiction in so-called 'faction'. Under such cultural conditions, confusions between right and wrong, and between what is natural and unnatural follow almost as a matter of course.

The movement toward uniformity and loss of distinctions also has its effect on architecture, if only because of its connections with industry and science. More than any of the other arts, architecture creates the visible form of a civilization in its cities, and this form is at present naturally one where quantity predominates, as can be seen throughout the world, where modern buildings are designed to give the maximum cubic capacity for the minimum cost. This is a set of conditions which dictates one basic form, namely the cuboid, and this is the form which is stamped on the appearance of modern cities. The reason why the cuboid and cube are a pure expression of spatial quantity lies in the fact that they are not differentiated with regard to the dimensions of space, but match these dimensions exactly with their edges and surfaces. Because of this, their volumes are precisely expressible as products of the three integers representing their lengths, breadths, and heights. All other regular solids have a qualitative distinction which appears in the fact that their volumes are products of irrational numbers such as *pi*, or the square roots of two, three, or five. The qualitative element is represented mathematically by the irrational number.

As much could be said in regard to the gridiron street plans of modern cities. The standard features of quantification, abstraction and equalization are all present, and such appearances are not confined to modern times, but have been found in some ancient civilizations which assumed them in their later phases. In the spread of modern architecture, the confounding of politics, economics, art and science could be said to emerge in visible and tangible forms. The gravity of such changes can be seen from the fact that creation, as in the Book of Genesis, depends on divisive processes; no intelligent combinations can be made except between things that have first been made distinct. For this reason, entropic changes in civilization are in effect a process of 'de-creation'.

CONFLATION OF KNOWER AND KNOWN

The various subjects of conflation considered so far are all concrete and open to simple observation, but the essential reality is so pervasive that it enters into much more subtle realms as well. Modernity has a self-imposed commitment to producing a new kind of human being, radically different from those that have existed before, and there can be no new human being unless there is an equally new way of thinking and a new idea of truth. A radical break with traditional thought is required for this purpose, which nearly always involves the rejection of what I have called the Platonic-Augustinian Paradigm, or just the Paradigm for short. The principal kinds of modernistic thought seek to eliminate the Paradigm by one means or another, because it dictates a fundamental difference between the knower and the known; it thus divides the real into different levels of being.

The situation of the Paradigm in relation to the universe can be made clear by means of an analysis of being into four ultimate levels by E. F. Schumacher,[4] which starts with the level of mineral or inorganic entities. The next level is that of vegetative life, which results from the addition of the vital element to materials drawn from the

4. See E. F. Schumacher, *A Guide for the Perplexed*.

first level. The third level is that of animal life, which results from the addition of consciousness to the combination of matter and vegetative life. The fourth level is the specifically human level, in which another and more internal consciousness is added, one which comprises an interior perception of all the perceptive acts in the 'animal' level of being in relation to the outside world. This fourth level is that of self-awareness, which is spectator, judge, and, ideally, director of the external functions of the person. With this fourth level of being, there is a more radical break with the first three than there is between the latter, since the first three levels of being are all in the world in ways that are open to outside observation, whereas the fourth is not. The interior perceptions of self-awareness are capable of far more than monitoring acts of consciousness in the realm of sense; they extend over objects of all possible degrees of universality and abstractness. In addition to perceiving oneself in acts of sensory perception, self-awareness opens into universal, timeless, and Divine realities.

This is the level of being to which the Paradigm belongs, with its system of ideas or universals common to all minds, and its semantic linkage of words to realities in the ideal realm, and this is the conception which modern thought seeks to eliminate. The alternative to it is the project of making all human activities realizable within what Schumacher called the third level of being, that of immediate sense-consciousness without self-awareness. This is regarded as an act of unification which must make the world more intelligible by being known wholly on one level, without the dualities of matter and spirit, soul and body. This objective of modern thought appears in the systems deriving from the writings of Darwin, Marx, Freud, Wittgenstein, Derrida, and also in Skinner's Behaviorism. The exact ways in which they set out to abolish the Paradigm and the fourth level of being vary considerably, but a general distinction can be made between the scientific approach of those who follow Darwin, Marx, Freud, and Behaviorism, and the nonscientific approach of Wittgenstein and Derrida. For the present purpose, these systems will be treated as phenomena rather than philosophies, because of the common historical purpose running through them all.

A certain amount has already been said in chapter 8 about the way in which Darwinistic thinking eliminates paradigms of any kind, and with them any rational basis for accepting it as a complete account of human origins. However, I include it in the group I call 'scientific' because all the activities involved in scientifically substantiating it proceed exactly as if the Paradigm were an unchallengeable reality. Deductions from facts and observations are presented as truths because they are logical, and the reports of the scientific fieldwork needed for it are offered and accepted as though they belonged in the realm of universal ideas. It is only with the final outcome of all these applications of the Paradigm—that everything in our being results from events in the biosphere—that Darwinism can be seen to negate the means by which it is constructed. Nevertheless, the conclusion that everything results from biological changes satisfies an irrational modern passion for simplification and reduction.

Where Marxism is concerned, truth is supposed to result from the working out of the laws which govern history. (The assumption that universal history is governed by all-embracing laws is just as central to Marxism as it is to the traditional cyclic cosmology, as if to show that this is too powerful an idea for even a materialistic world to exclude.) According to Marxism, all the religion and philosophy in past times consisted in so many provisional stages on the way to the full truth at the end of history (secular man's *Parousia*), and these were in every case the effects of the economic conditions which prevailed in their own times. History will one day find its consummation in the final victory of the revolutionary proletariat, which will be the fullness of truth incarnate, so to speak, though Marxists would avoid such expressions. This system is created by an analysis of innumerable historical facts from its own point of view, and its methods conform to the Paradigm as fully as do those of Darwinism. But as with Darwinism, its final outcome is a state in which truth is merged with a state of existence, besides which, all the truths which have been believed down the ages were, so it is said, really states of mind brought about by economic conditions. The Paradigm is employed constantly to establish this conclusion in regard to non-Marxist thought, but here again the conclusion excludes its own basis.

By its own principles, Marxism arose at a certain time in history when it must have been a by-product of the nineteenth-century capitalist economy of Europe, and so might be expected to cease to be relevant when that economy became replaced by a different one, with different essential industries and distribution of income. Either Marxism is magically immune from its own premise that ideas are produced by economics, or it leaves no reason why it should be accepted as truth at the present time.

The Freudian method of merging thought and knowledge with sensory phenomena leads to essentially the same result. It claims to be able to explain all thought processes and all apparently reasoned convictions by their being prompted by the imperfectly repressed appetites of early infancy. As ever, the Paradigm is employed in the construction of this theory, and where it seeks to explain morbid mentation there is no reason to doubt it. But where it is made into a comprehensive theory of human thought it too must, if everything is to result from submerged passional urges, finally exclude the Paradigm without which it could not be sustained or even communicated. Analogous remarks apply to Behaviorism. It may be that a central contradiction is a necessary ingredient in the new thought, and that inconsistency is only a flaw from the point of view of the traditional intellectuality it is meant to supplant. However this may be, modern man can in fact have no wish to abjure reason to this extent, because the only alternative means of securing agreement seems to be violence, whether overt or threatened; to advocate any such thing is to propose to be governed by violence oneself.

The relation, or disrelation, to the Paradigm is markedly different in the thought inspired by Wittgenstein and Derrida. Truth for Wittgenstein results from the relations of words to other words according to the rules of language. If the language rules are applied correctly, our statement will be true. This approach evidently dispenses with the Paradigm from the start. What is really needed is a correct use of syntactical relations, and, given that, there is no need for concern about the ideal objects the words are supposed to denote. However, this form of thought has been set forth for the same purpose as any other, that of converting other thinkers to it, and it is at this final stage that the Paradigm becomes an issue again. If Wittgensteinian thought is both communicable and able to alter the mental behavior of others, words must be able to engage with realities, and even if this does not necessarily involve ideal realities, they cannot consist wholly of linguistic conventions. Without this final intervention by the Paradigm (with its affiliation of words to natural objects), this form of thought would simply circulate in a sealed world of its own like the events which unfold in a novel. Just as reading a novel creates no rational grounds for imitating its characters, so this kind of philosophy cannot reasonably motivate anyone to emulate it, on its own premises, at least. A truth which by definition results solely from relations between words cannot interact with non-verbal things such as the choices of verbal behavior made by persons. In practice, however, the Paradigm is unofficially allowed in the interests of this philosophy, but not for any others, of course.

A similar conclusion applies to the thought initiated by Derrida which, though not bound by the use of language rules, is still faced with the need to communicate itself as objective ideas which engage with things, if it is to have any consistent effect in the world. Otherwise, this too would have only the self-enclosed interest of an abstract novel. The fact that other thinkers are influenced by it, and in more or less the same way, shows that much more is involved than what could be possible on the basis of Derrida's thought alone. This is just another example of the *genre* which dethrones intellect while the intellect's principles mysteriously revive on its behalf whenever it is a question of social acceptance.

THE SPIRITUAL DIMENSION OF DISTINCTIONS

Heidegger's idea of modernism as an 'onslaught of the demonic' is relevant for the schools of modern thought examined above, because it is only from the interior level of self-awareness that any 'world-creating movements of the spirit' can come. To deny the reality of self-awareness and its level of being is to deny the most essential of human possibilities and to dethrone the intellect with what purports to be intelligence. This is not to say that the work of individuals alone could effect so much, however, because the thought emanating from Darwin, Marx, Freud, Wittgenstein, and Derrida, for all its professed radicalism, merely follows the general downward drift of human consciousness, and rationalizes the limitations which come with that drift. As a result, the development of the personality on Schumacher's 'fourth level' of self-awareness becomes weaker and rarer on average, and spiritual maturity is harder to reach. In all the above philosophical movements, what used to be recognized as a quite ordinary spiritual immaturity (i.e., something essentially negative), is reinterpreted by the new thought as something positive, and those who suffer from it are re-evaluated into torch-bearers of a new wisdom, even of a new dispensation, without their having had to do anything.

Where the same conditions affect religion, the reduction of distinctions has effects which are both similar and more confusing, because in this realm it is possible for a superior meaning to mingle with the more general negative one. The world religions themselves are only subject to equalization to the extent that a global culture equalizes their members, but internally the effect is more marked, as in Christianity, where well-meaning efforts are made to lower the barriers between the different churches. While the same entropic forces are acting here as elsewhere, the question of merging is complicated by the fact that today's diverse churches were at one time all one from quite an early date. The reductive process at its best is therefore working to restore something which had been lost for long ages. But while reunification is obviously desirable in principle, there is no doubt that it is being approached by negative means. An indifference to and an incomprehension of doctrinal issues may make reconciliation humanly easier, but the resulting union would be lacking in content.

Besides, the levelling process has also reduced the differences between believers and unbelievers in a number of important ways, particularly where the natural and the supernatural are concerned. Christians are increasingly drawn into the humanist mindset in which the natural person is not seen as fallen or in need of supernatural grace. This coincides with a major change in the way human nature is understood. The sovereignty of the will and intellect over all the other parts of the personality, always basic to Christian values, is replaced by the relativist view that all parts of the personality are of equal value, so that no one of them should have any powers over the others. In practical morality, Christians as much as humanists now see the ideal of doing good as consisting in the alleviation of suffering at all costs, rather than as conversion and moral enlightenment. Thus barriers between belief and unbelief give way as fast as do barriers between different forms of religious belief. The subject of personal salvation is seldom discussed under these conditions, since it depends on there being a distinction between those with the faith and those without, and because the idea that some are saved must suggest that others may not be. This shows how loss of distinctions has a profoundly static and paralyzing effect in all but the most superficial things.

When things are 'all one' they are at maximum entropy or matter chaos, and at the opposite extreme from the condition of their creation. It is highly significant that the account of the first three days of creation in the Book of Genesis takes the form of a series of acts of division: firstly between the heavens and the earth; then between light and darkness; then between the waters above the firmament and the waters beneath it; then between the sea and the dry land; and living creatures are divided into male and female. Life, growth, and dynamism follow from binary division, therefore, and their opposites follow from its effacement. The fact that the entropic process happens by necessity does not exclude free will's function in regard to its consequences, because mind is not subject to natural forces. Nevertheless, the understanding of this distinction between mental and physical laws is no better able to survive than any of the other distinctions, under actual conditions.

11

'THE ETERNITY OF THE WORLD'

THE AGE OF THE WORLD IN TRADITION

The title of this chapter is a quotation of the rather imprecise expression used in ancient times for debates about the world's age, whether one was arguing that it was endless or that it was finite. The relevance of this subject to cyclic time lies in the fact that the longer the time-span over which the world exists, the more scope and the more necessity there will be for universal change to proceed through cycles. The only other alternatives would be either that historical change be constantly reversible, which would subvert causality, or that it should continue without constraint, in which case it must go beyond the limits within which human life is possible or viable, if continued for more than a few centuries. Even the few thousand years for which civilization is known to have existed is too long a period for historical change to have continued without constant cyclic deviations.

Whether the world is eternal, or whether it is infinitely extended into past and future, or whether it is simply of indefinite duration because it defies all human means of computation, are three distinct issues which the ancients failed to separate. If the world were eternal, it would have an absolute being which would be exempt from addition or subtraction, and it would therefore be effectively self-subsistent as though it were another God. Alternatively, it could be a mass of contingent being, that is, deriving from causes outside itself, which nevertheless exists through an infinite series of time intervals. The third possibility, that the world's duration is not infinite, but transcends human measures, differs from the last in the same way as a relative infinite series differs from an absolute one. All three of these possibilities form a contrast to the idea that the whole cosmic order exists for only an assignable finite time.

The latter idea, that this world is only of a relatively short finite duration and that there was no other world before or after it, is usually identified with the teachings of the Judeo-Christian tradition, which differed from the other ancient traditions in this and in other respects. The fact that Christianity is rooted in the Jewish religion, which taught that the world was created and, apparently, that only a limited number of generations had passed since its creation, must surely have turned Christian beliefs in the same direction, so the argument goes. I shall try to show presently that this conclusion is mistaken. In reality, the belief in the finitude of time and the world is definitely not owing to Judaism, so that it will be found necessary to drop the prefix 'Judeo' from the name of the tradition in connection with ideas about time. The reasons why Christianity adopted this view of time will be considered in general terms later, and in detail in chapter 12.

Cosmic Time In Judaism

Jewish ideas about the world in relation to God do not differ markedly from those of Greek tradition, as might be expected from the fact that Pythagoras acquired his knowledge from the Semitic religions of the Near East. According to Angelo Rappoport,

God and the world are, according to Jewish myth, two inseparable conceptions, standing to each other in the relation of cause and effect.

This is closely linked in the same passage to the manner of creation, where its origin is clearly outside time:

From absolute nothingness All-Father, the Creator, first produced a fine and subtle matter, which had no consistence whatever, but possessed the potential power to receive the imprint of form. This was the first matter, or what the Greeks called *hyle*.[1]

1. Angelo Rappoport, *Ancient Israel*, chap. 1, p5.

Such ideas imply that there must always be a creation of some kind, in order that God's power may be manifest, and because the basis of creation is before all time. What God specifically creates out of nothing is the first matter, which is necessary for the formation of all the elements and all the beings formed from them. Such an account of the creation *ex nihilo* would explain why the Bible does not contain explicit references to God creating the world, or things in it, from nothing. The Book of Job, chapters 38 and 39 for example, while full of examples of God's actions in creation, does not mention creation out of nothing. All acts of creation from the already existing presuppose the first matter or *hyle*, and given this substance, nothing else would need to be created from nothing. In accordance with the cause and effect relation between God and the world, it is held that:

> The present world, however, is neither the first nor the only world in existence. Before the world was created, there existed already many others. The Eternal created many worlds and destroyed them until He produced the present cosmos. Nine hundred and seventy-four generations had existed before the creation of this world, but they were swept away because they were wicked and did not please the Lord of the Universe.
> Thus many worlds preceded the creation of the present one. . . .
> Apart from our cosmos, there are numerous other cosmic systems. God, teach the Rabbis, has many cosmic worlds, and, carried upon the wings of the Cherubim, He manifests His presence in all of them.[2]

While teaching the idea of successive creations and the existence of other universes at the same time as this one, the question as to whether the number of other creations is finite or not is left open. There is a suggestion that this number is finite, whereas proportionality between cause and effect would imply that God's infinity would be reflected in a kind of infinity in creation, but in any case cosmic time is said to extend far beyond the bounds of the present universe. There is, however, no doubt as to which text is responsible

2. Ibid., pp9–10.

for the belief that only the present world is created, and that it is of finite duration. Non-Rabbinical interpreters have long derived this idea from Genesis 1:1: 'In the beginning God created the heavens and the earth.'

To many minds, even up to the present day, this text seems necessarily to imply a beginning of a finite world in time. Because of the modern rejection of metaphysics, modern scholarship usually takes the text in this sense,[3] but the fact remains that this can only be justified if the words 'In the beginning' translate not merely a possible meaning of the original, but its principal meaning as well. In this instance, a long-established practice of translating the first words in a way which does not involve a metaphysical conception dictates that it be rendered 'In the beginning,' even though this is not its primary meaning. The Hebrew word in question is *Bereshith*,[4] which is translated into Greek as εν αρχη (*en arche*) and into Latin as *in principio*. These Hebrew, Greek, and Latin words all agree in admitting a timeless meaning, whereas if a temporal beginning had been the principal idea, the Greek could have rendered it more precisely as πρωτιστα (*protista*)[5] and the Latin could have used the words *inceptium* or *initium*. The timeless meaning, however, would require it to be rendered in the sense of 'in the principle', that is, in the metaphysical power by which things are given their forms. According to Fabre d' Olivet, by the word principle 'they [the Jews] conceived a sort of absolute power, by means of which every relative being is constituted as such.'[6]

This, he says, they represented by a point at the center of a circle. The function of this conception is reflected in the way in which a Form causes instantiations of itself in matter. The same author points out that the emphasis given to the temporal idea of 'beginning' introduces the idea of temporal succession into the different acts of creation in the first chapter of Genesis, where it is misleading.

---

3. See Richard Sorabji, *Time, Creation and the Continuum*, chap. 13

4. As in Gen. 1:1, *Bereshith bara Elohim aeth-ha-shamaim w'aeth-ha-aretz*

5. As in Hesiod's Η τοι μεν πρωτιστα Χαοσ γενετ, 'Verily at the first, Chaos came to be' (*Theogony* 116).

6. Fabre d' Olivet, *The Hebraic Tongue Restored*, pt. 2, p 25.

Nevertheless, nearly all translations have ignored this because of their failure to translate *Bereshith* as 'in principle' or 'at first in principle,' and many misconceptions have resulted:

> In fact, if the word *Bereshith* signified simply, in the beginning, in the beginning of time, as it was said, why did not the heavens and the earth, created at that epoch, already exist at that time; why should there be need of successive development; why should they have rested an eternity in darkness; why should the light have been made after the heavens and before the sun.[7]

Such seeming paradoxes as heavens without light, or the creation of night and day before the sun and moon, which determine them, or the creation of light before the luminaries, are all resolved by the operative word meaning 'in the principle' rather than 'in the beginning'. This meaning, according to the same author, also comprises 'not yet in action, but in power,' and this agrees with the way in which Saint Augustine interpreted it. The idea that the world was created at a moment of time through a certain chronological sequence is thus not dictated by the opening words of Genesis, even if it is allowed. Clearly, this is an issue which cannot be settled by means of an English Bible, even in modern translations. But if the Days of creation are not literally a chronological sequence, they certainly suggest it, and this may well mean that they are a paradigm or Formal cause of cosmogonic sequences.

It can be seen that the Jewish philosopher Philo of Alexandria was true to his own tradition in this regard, even while combining it as far as possible with Platonic thought. Where he speaks of the beginning and end of the world, he does so in a way consistent with what has been argued above. He states that there are only two reasons why God would destroy the world, these being either to create another world or to give up creation as such. The latter alternative is said to be impossible because God's work is that of bringing order out of disorder, not that of reducing order to disorder. The alternative of creating another world is logical, but confused by the question as to whether this was in a relative or an absolute sense. While referring to

7. I.e., the Heavens named in verse 1. Ibid., pt. 2, p29.

the Stoic teaching concerning the final conflagration of the world, he denies that this event could mean a final end of the world, by using the argument that God cannot be conceived to be idle:

> Moreover, if all things are as they say consumed in the conflagration, what will God be doing during that time? Will He do nothing at all? That surely is the natural inference. For at present He surveys each thing, guardian of all as though He were indeed their father, guiding in very truth the chariot and steering the barque of the universe, the defender of the sun and moon and stars whether fixed or wandering and also the air and the other parts of the world, co-operating in all that is needful for the preservation of the whole and the faultless management of it which right reason demands. But if all things are annihilated inactivity and dire unemployment will render His life unworthy of the name, and what could be more monstrous than this? I shrink from saying, for the very thought is a blasphemy, that quiescence will entail as a consequence the death of God, for if you annihilate the perpetual motion of the soul you will annihilate the soul itself also and, according to our opponents, God is the soul of the world.[8]

This argument does not depend on God's being literally the soul of the world, but on an extension of the way in which Platonism understands the soul. It is thought to be of the very essence of the soul that it be a fount of self-generated activity, and consequently upon this, it may be argued that if this is true for the soul, how much more it must be true of God who is its creator and exemplar. While this argument is applied to the question of God's making an absolute end of the world, it applies to an absolute beginning as well. By such arguments, Philo is thinking in a manner which accords with both Judaism and Platonism, but lest it should appear that his thought is more indebted to Platonism, such doubts can be settled by one of the greatest authorities of Judaism, the twelfth-century philosopher Moses Maimonides. In Maimonides' writings the eternity of the universe is denied, while its perpetuity and its

8. Philo, *The Eternity of the World*, XVI, 83.

indestructibility are affirmed. Biblical teachings as to the end of the world are to be taken figuratively, he says, while speaking for Jewish tradition. He also denies that belief in the destruction of the world should follow from belief in its creation, and explains his conception of its perpetuity:

> The following are the words that refer to the indestructibility of the Universe: 'And the earth remaineth for ever.' And those who do not agree with me as regards the above distinction [between the indestructibility and the Eternity of the Universe], are compelled to explain the term le-'olam [lit., 'for ever'], to mean 'the time fixed for the existence of the earth.' Similarly they explain the words of God, 'Yet all the days of the earth' [Gen. 8:22] to signify the days fixed for its existence. But I wonder how they would explain the words of David: 'He laid the foundations of the earth, that it should not be moved for ever' [Ps. 104:5]. If they maintain here also that the term le-'olam va-'ed (lit., 'for ever') does not imply perpetuity, they must come to the conclusion that God exists only for a fixed period, since the same term is employed in describing the perpetuity of God, 'The Lord will reign [le'olam] for ever' [Exod. 15:18, or Ps. 10:16].[9]

According to the meaning of the Hebrew words, then, the perpetuity of God is mirrored by that of the world, and this cannot be denied of the one without denying it of the other. Maimonides also shows that the Psalms speak of the incorruptibility of the heavens, of the laws that govern them, and of the celestial beings, while also asserting that they are created. The term 'for ever' is used frequently in connection with many aspects of creation. The teaching that the works of God are perfect, and admit neither increase nor decrease, and must stand for ever, will also be found in the Platonic tradition in the following chapter. There was no question that either Philo or Maimonides could have been misled by translations of the first verse of Genesis into thinking it stated the beginning of a chronological sequence, because of their familiarity with the Hebrew, and the Old Testament as a whole reads consistently with the timeless

9. Maimonides, *The Guide for the Perplexed*, pt. 2, chap. 28.

conception of the creation. I have dwelt on Jewish tradition so as to make it clear that later developments in the Judeo-Christian tradition took place only on Christian initiatives for various reasons, of which some will be examined in a later chapter. Up to a point the changes made to the doctrine arose only from a need to define the cosmological setting which would answer to the salvation of the soul, but this became exaggerated by a human desire to escape from a wisdom of non-Christian origin.

CHRISTIAN ADAPTATIONS OF TRADITION

Before considering the development of these ideas in Christian thought, a few points must be made clear. Firstly, the argument will, for the present chapter, rely only on quotations from ancient sources rather than on philosophical reasoning, and is not meant to be taken as conclusive. Secondly, part of the purpose of this procedure is to show that Christian belief is not tied necessarily to finitist beliefs about creation, and that it has always been compatible with a world-view quite different from the one depicted by modern scholarship. While scholarship has achieved many new insights into the meanings of biblical texts, its spiritual value is limited by the fact that these advances have been made mostly in a direction dictated by the humanist mindset of modern man. An intelligence distorted by an excess of the reasoning faculty and an atrophy of the intellectual faculty cannot outweigh the wisdom of early tradition, which will be allowed to speak for itself, therefore.

The early Christians lived in a world which was generally believed to have existed for endless ages, and while this idea was not acceptable to Christians as it stood, one can see from Origen's writings that the necessary modifications to it did not have to be too drastic, since the Bible is open to both finite and non-finite views of creation. Origen makes it clear that Christian belief, as much as Jewish, requires that this present world-order should have a beginning in time. Because it is said to be of temporal origin, this world is held to be corruptible, and with the passage of time human weakness and corruption increase to the extent that they can have no human remedy, and only Christ's Incarnation was capable of restoring man to his true nature. Moreover, there was no difficulty in answering the idleness argument concerning what God must have been doing before the world was, if it had a beginning in time, according to the way in which Origen understood the matter:

> God did not begin to work for the first time when he made this visible world, but just as after the dissolution of this world there will be another one, so also we believe that there were others before this one existed. Both of these beliefs will be confirmed by the authority of divine scripture. For Isaiah teaches that there will be another world after this, when he says 'There shall be a new heaven and a new earth, which I will cause to endure in my sight, saith the Lord.' And that there were other worlds before this one Ecclesiastes shows when he says, 'What is it that hath been? Even that which shall be. And what is it that shall be created? That very thing that is to be created. . . .'
>
> By these testimonies each proposition is proved at the same time, namely, that there were ages in the past and that there will be others hereafter.[10]

The biblical teaching that there will be a new heaven and a new earth occurs not only in Isa. 66:22 as quoted by Origen, but also in 2 Pet. 3:13, and in Rev. 21:1, and this is what one would expect if it is true that this world is one of a series of different creations, even though traditional interpretations also treat this as a prophecy of the Redemption. In Origen's treatment of the question, a just balance is achieved between the perspective of this present world and that of the ultimate range of creation. He succeeds at the same time in excluding endless recurrence from the successive worlds by means of a comparison between the lifetime of a world and the outpouring of a bushel of grain, showing a sense of the laws of probability. The idea is that if even two successive worlds should be the same, it would be as though one could pour out a bushel of grain, sweep it all up, and pour it out a second time so that every grain fell in the same spot, in contact with the same other grains as before. Origen alleges that these processes of outpouring and regathering could be repeated for

---

10. Origen, *On First Principles*, Bk. III, chap. 5, 3.

endless ages without there ever being an identical repetition of the order in which the grains fell out. Whether such successive worlds are innumerable or not, he does not venture to decide, but since the contents of a world are incalculably more numerous and diverse than those of a bushel of grain, it would be natural to take the series of creations to be perpetual.

This is supported elsewhere in the same work,[11] where Origen quotes the Epistles in connection with the 'consummation of the ages' as in Heb. 9:26. The present age is said to be made for the consummation of other ages, and there will be yet more ages to come, because Saint Paul again says 'that in the ages to come he might show the exceeding richness of his grace in kindness toward us.'[12] There is at any rate a sufficiency of biblical texts supporting the idea that the process of creation as such is so extended as to have no definable limits, even if there were no direct theological arguments for it. From Origen to Saint Augustine the same basic idea of cosmic time is pursued in a way which agrees with the Christian idea of salvation without too large a divergence from the traditional wisdom. Like Origen, Augustine argues primarily for the uniqueness of each world, whether they be few or numerous or innumerable. The cyclic conception which requires universal recurrence is reasonably seen as the very negation of what religion is there to do, since it would require that immortal souls which had attained wisdom would nevertheless be re-immersed in the world of ignorance and sin after only a limited period of release from it. Whatever sacrifices had been made for salvation, even the grace of Christ, the ultimate result would be as though they had never happened at all.

Nevertheless, Augustine knows better than to try to exclude such a possibility by claiming that 'there was a time when there was no time.'[13] This, he says, is like saying that there was a man when men were not, or that there was a world when the world was not. Such absurdities may look verbally similar to statements that there was a time when Rome was not, for example, but the difference between

11. Ibid., Bk. II, chaps. 3, 4, and 5.
12. Eph. 2:7
13. *City of God*, Bk. XII, chap. 15.

them is essential. This unwillingness to restrict the range of created being can be seen to follow from Augustine's idea of the Creator:

> Wherefore, if God always has been Lord, He has always had crea-tures under His dominion—creatures, however, not begotten of Him, but created by Him out of nothing; nor co-eternal with Him, for He was before them though at no time without them, because He preceded them, not only by the lapse of time, but by His abiding eternity.[14]

The importance of this text lies in the way it shows that God's prior-ity over the creation does not mean that it must be limited at its own level. The eternal has a logical and ontological priority over the whole series of created beings, and this priority is so absolute that one could not increase it by affixing arbitrary limitations to the con-tent of the world. Augustine also quotes Saint Paul in regard to the ages of the world and the 'eternal times', saying that the Apostle speaks as though time were eternal, in relation to both past and future equally, since he says 'In hope of eternal life, which God promised before the eternal times, (προ χρωνων αιωνιων) but hath in due times manifested His word.'[15]

This is a literal translation by Augustine from the Greek, and it confirms that there is no objection to the idea of 'eternal times' as long as they do not imply eternal recurrence. In a text relating to the above, Augustine argues that the divine goodness cannot be con-ceived as ever having been idle, because the idea of God's repenting of a time of idleness contradicts the idea of divine perfection. The supposition that the boundless extension of creation in time must mean the exact repetition of everything in the course of its cycles is said to reveal only the limitations of human minds, since they assume God to be as limited as themselves. Repetition of persons and events would exclude the possibility of salvation for reasons already given. Another consequence of God's being eternal and not temporal is spelled out in Bk. XII, chap. 17, where the fact that God has different purposes in relation to different parts of time does not

14. Ibid.
15. Titus 1:2–3.

imply any temporal succession among these purposes, inasmuch as they reside in God. The same eternal and unchangeable will can bring about different things at different times, and can will an unlimited number of different things over an unlimited time. The idea of 'ages of ages' is treated in relation to creation, and however literally it is to be taken, it gives no grounds for supposing that omnipotence could be obliged to repeat the same things. This is also consistent with what Augustine says about the 'heaven of heavens'.[16]

The treatment given by Augustine to this subject shows how Christian thought resolved the fundamental contradiction in nearly all pre-Christian religion, namely, the conflict between the quest for salvation and a doctrine which denied that salvation could ever be finally achieved. (Modern cults which believe in reincarnation are merely revivals of the same confusion.) The above conclusions are arrived at without any need for the dubious ideas about time and creation which were to come later.

Even though ideas about cosmic time were to change in the West, the change was by no means universal. In the centuries after Saint Augustine, ideas in this realm continued in a similar manner in the Eastern Church, as can be seen from the writings of Saint Maximus the Confessor, in the seventh century:

According to Scripture, there are temporal ages in themselves, and temporal ages which encompass the consummation of other ages. This is clear from the text: 'But now once at the consummation of the ages' [Heb. 9:26]. Again there are other ages or aeons, free of a temporal nature, after this temporal age established at the consummation of the ages. This is shown by the text: '... so that in the ages to come He might display the overflowing richness' [Eph. 2:7]. But we also find in Scripture a large number of past, present, and future ages: there are references to 'ages of ages' [Ps. 84:4 LXX], 'age of age' [Ps. 9:5 LXX], 'agelong times' [2 Tim. 1:9], and 'generations joined together by the ages' [Gen. 9:12].[17]

16. See chap. 12, p164.
17. *The Philokalia*, vol. 2, tr. Palmer, Sherrard, and Ware, 1981, Saint Maximos the Confessor, Second Century on Theology, 85.)

Here again, we have more than enough indication that there need be no conflict between Christian beliefs and a universal conception of time and the world, and that for many centuries no such thing was thought of. When it finally did emerge, it was as a result of undue weight being given to metaphysical arguments which were in any case never very well understood.

TRANSITION TO THEORETICAL ARGUMENTS

There is a necessary difference between the points of view of metaphysical thought and religious belief, but there is no need for any conflict between them on the present subject. Where this does arise, it is probably owing to a misunderstanding as to what the created universe really consists of. The modern tendency is usually to make the universe a mere accident in relation to God. However, this position expresses an unconscious assumption that the universe is primarily a material thing, made up of material parts. If this were true, the modern attitude could be easily justified because there is no reason why God should be committed to a realm of mere objects. However, this is a materialistic view of the world, and an absurd one for the religious mind. Everything is changed when the universe is seen for what it really is, a community of spirits among whom the material structure of the world is subordinate to the souls and intellects which are its principal content.

God's relations with spiritual creatures thus form an integral part of the divine subjective life, and so there is no reason to think that these relations should be curtailed by applying limitations to the scale of creation. Moreover, it is a matter of particular importance from the religious point of view that many ensouled beings participate in the divine nature: divinity is by this means not confined wholly to God, but is shared by innumerable spiritual beings throughout time and space. This collectivity is the primary meaning of the word 'Church,' and because it is an essential part of creation there is no reason to think that God would put an end to creation as a whole in any absolute sense. The idea of the world as a material artifact which is both external to and independent of the craftsman as soon as it is made is also completely at variance with the religious idea that all created beings are continually guided, nourished and preserved by God. Only if it were merely a physical artifact could it possibly be justifiable to make it a mere contingency in relation to God.[18]

At this point religious belief is at one with Plotinus' ideas concerning the Intellectual-Principle.[19] This is where he argues that the self-vision of the intellect is inseparable from its vision of the multiple and external, and without the power of vision it could not be said to exist at all. Thus there follows an argument which will appear more fully in the next chapter, that the higher being does in some sense depend on the lower; that the relation of dependence between them cannot be all one-way. What Plotinus says in this text presents interesting parallels with what was quoted from Philo in this chapter. The very idea of the spiritual principle reducing itself to a 'memberless unity' seems to be self-contradictory, since even this act would involve an act of selective attention which implies the existence of other realities. The following chapters will pursue the philosophical arguments which have arisen in relation to this subject, and which form the background and basis for the cyclic conception of time.

18. See A. Seth Pringle-Pattison, *The Idea of God*, Lecture xvi.
19. *Enn.*v, 3, 10.

12

THE ARGUMENTS
OF PROCLUS

CHRISTIAN AND PAGAN IDEAS OF TIME

Given the cyclic idea of time, the world must exist over so great an expanse of time that it could pass through a general sequence of changes over and over again, even though there be no repetition in detail. Such a world-view would conflict with Christian doctrine if it meant that time and temporal events proceeded with a degree of uniformity that excluded any moment of creation and any end of the present world. For this reason, disputes between Christians and the Athenian school of Neoplatonism in the fifth century AD became centered around the question whether the world as we know it is everlasting. As Christian belief was focused on the end of time and the Last Judgement, this was a logical point of attack for its philosophical opponents. Pagan Neoplatonists like Proclus argued that the world was immortal and divine, and so could neither perish nor be engendered.

Because of the partisan nature of this dispute, neither side would concede that this world might end in some way which would allow the continuation of creation in other worlds after it. Similarly, no one on the Christian side (at least after the seventh century) would concede that a succession of different worlds might constitute a 'world' in an extended sense of the word, and which could well be everlasting. The fact that Platonic opponents of Christianity held so firmly to the idea of a uniformly existing world is the more remarkable in view of what Plato says in the *Statesman* dialogue, quoted in chapter 5, where the world is said to alternately decline and to be restored by God. It is clear that by the later part of classical antiquity neither side was trying to be fair, and that their dispute was conducted on a much lower ethical level than either professed to uphold, at least according to modern ideas of honesty. Prejudice was too strong to allow any examination of ideas which could reconcile them, such as the question whether a temporal beginning of this world must mean that this world is in every way unique, or whether it is compatible with comparable worlds before and after it.

What could be called the uniformitarian view of the world was therefore defended by Proclus, who put forward eighteen arguments in support of it.[1] In these arguments it will be seen that cyclic time is never referred to directly, possibly because its implication that the world could change in some profound way was felt to concede too much to the Christian position. Nevertheless, the idea of a world existing without assignable limits in time remains the basis for the cyclic idea. It is not hard to see why the idea of an endless world-order became suspect from a Christian point of view, in view of its association with such anti-eschatological thinking. The consciousness of antiquity was, in the broadest sense of the word, 'spatial', whereas that of Christianity is 'temporal', and this change of perspective was no doubt an effect of the world-cycle's entry into its latter phases, where the passage of time is necessarily more rapid and more invasive.

THE EIGHTEEN ARGUMENTS

The account I am about to give of these arguments is designed to explain as well as reproduce what appears in the text, and to show how they are related to one another. The names applied to them are of my own choosing, for ease of reference and to help fix them in the mind:

1. *THE CONSUBSISTENCE ARGUMENT.* The Creator brings the world into existence in a way which arises from His essential nature, so that the world itself is a manifestation of that nature. For this reason, the creation has a consubsistent relation to its Creator, while

---

1. Translated by Thomas Taylor in *Fragments of the Lost Writings of Proclus*, chap. 6. Taylor saw himself as a continuator of Proclus' polemic.

still being wholly dependent on Him for its being. This is illustrated by an analogy of the relation between the sphere of light around the sun and the sun itself. As Taylor expresses it:

> as the sun, which produces light by its very being, has the light so produced consubsistent with itself, and neither is light prior or posterior to the sun, nor the sun to light.[2]

While this analogy conveys the relations of consubsistence and one-sided dependence, it does not express the personal idea of creation as an act of choice or intention. The preceding argument would be stronger if creation were indeed as automatic as is the production of light by an incandescent body, or of a shadow by an object in light, but this seems to be an impersonal oversimplification. However, allowance should be made for the fact that the Divine intention is in eternity, whereas the only intentions directly known to us are in time. An eternally-formed intention is emphatically not the same kind of thing as a temporal intention robotically repeated *ad infinitum*.

2. *THE ETERNAL PARADIGM ARGUMENT.* The world as a whole, just like any of the things in it, is an instantiation of an eternal Form or paradigm. This paradigm, along with matter, is as it were a proto-creation, by means of which the material creation is brought into being. The paradigmatic nature of the cosmic Form, being the cause of its image in the material world, is essential to it; without the formation of its image it would be unable to be what it is. If the image ceased to be, the paradigmatic nature would cease to be at the same time. In this way, the image can be said to be as necessary for the paradigm as the paradigm is for the image:

> Thus if the paradigm of the world is eternally the paradigm of it, the world *always* is an image of an eternally existing paradigm.[3]

This is perhaps the most typically Platonic of these arguments. The Forms are above all an extension of the idea of creation beyond the things of time and matter.

---

2. *Fragments of the Lost Writings of Proclus*, chap. 6, p35.
3. Ibid., p36.

3. THE CAUSAL REGRESS ARGUMENT. The Creator must either be a creator in actuality or else in capacity or potentiality. But whatever has a property x in potentiality can only have x in actuality (or 'energy') through the action of something else which has x in actuality already. Thus actual knowledge in one person realizes potential knowledge in another. This points to two alternatives, either that the series of beings changing one another from potentiality to actuality extends to infinity, or else that the series begins from a causal agent whose causal power is always in actuality or energy. Given the existence of this cause, it will follow that the effects proceeding from it will, as a whole, always exist in actuality as well.

4. THE ARGUMENT FROM PERFECTION. Whatever is produced by an immobile cause will share the immobility of its cause. Where such a cause happens to have no effect, therefore, it never will have one, and where it does, it will never cease to have one. The idea that God is unmoving and the mover of everything created is affirmed by Aquinas as follows:

> the mover who is part of the self-moving being moves because of the appetite of some appetible object. This object is higher, in the order of motion than the mover desiring it.... There must, therefore, be an absolutely unmoved separate first mover. This is God.[4]

This immobility in the Creator results from the fact that movement means change, and change means a movement to either a greater or a lesser degree of goodness. But as God is perfect, it would be equally impossible to say that He could become either better or worse. If the creation were to cease to exist, therefore, it would mean that the Creator was thereby attaining to a better state or a worse one, the very things which perfection excludes.

5. THE TEMPORAL INSEPARABILITY ARGUMENT. In the *Timaeus*, it is asserted that time and the universe subsist together, so that they could only be created together and be dissolved together. To say that the universe existed when time did not would be the

---

4. *SCG* I, chap. 13, [28].

same as saying that there was a time when time was not. This is contradictory because if time were to begin or end absolutely in this world it would have to do so at a certain time, and so time would not really be escaped. The perpetuity of time itself results from its being the image of eternity. Accordingly, its nature requires it to realize in a serial manner the full reality which eternity has all at once. The oneness of time with the world implies the same perpetuity for the world.

6. *THE BENEVOLENCE OF CREATION ARGUMENT*. The final dissolution of creation, if it were possible, could not be brought about by any being other than God, as only He who creates the bond can know how to unloose it. But, as Taylor quotes from the *Timaeus*: 'it pertains only to an evil nature to dissolve that which is beautifully harmonized and constituted well.'[5]

Such a supposed action by God against the creation would also be an act of the 'violence' which Aquinas excludes from the Divine nature in *SCG* I, chapter 19, because it would conflict with the perfection of immobility. Now either God has not created the world with the greatest harmony and goodness possible for it, or He has. If He has not, He would not be the supreme artificer, which by definition He must be, but if He has, it could not be finally dissolved without a negation of the Divine goodness. Proclus adds here the idea that if the universe is incorruptible it must also be unbegotten, which is simply a dogma which he does not try to substantiate. If it were true that the incorruptible and the unbegotten were logically inseparable, we should not be able to believe that God could create angels or any kind of immortal soul.

7. *THE SOUL OF THE WORLD ARGUMENT*. That the world has a soul is an idea held on the general grounds that the world itself cannot be lifeless and soulless if ensouled living beings are produced from it. Given that there is a World Soul, it will have the essential property common to souls, that of self-motion. Being self-motive, it will be immortal, and from thence will come the perpetuity of the

5. *Fragments of the Lost Writings of Proclus*, chap. 6, p 44.

material creation it animates. Here again, the idea that the soul is both unbegotten and incorruptible is repeated like a mantra, although these two things are not logically inseparable.

8. *THE EXTERNAL CORRUPTION ARGUMENT*. When things are corrupted, it appears that their corruption is brought about by agencies which are external to them, and which have a nature alien to theirs. But there is by definition nothing external to the universe, as it is the 'whole of wholes'. Likewise things generated require something other than themselves to be generated from, whence the universe cannot be generated, at least not in the manner of the generated things contained in it. The need for an external instrument for either corruption or generation is simply asserted without argument, though it is by no means clear that either of these does in fact require external agency. It is certainly debatable whether corruption must always be owing to external agency. Among material things, for example, radioactive elements break down without any external cause, and so also do chemically unstable compounds. In metaphysical terms, the Aristotelian idea of Privation in all things seems to be an inherent property in them, and one which is not caused from without, and always liable to increase.

9. *THE INHERENT CORRUPTION ARGUMENT*. This is an argument which *prima facie* requires the exact opposite of what is required by the last argument. Proclus quotes Plato to the effect that everything is corrupted by its own evil. This is because it cannot be corrupted either by the good which pertains to it or by the things which are only neutral in its make-up. Before it could perish, therefore, the universe would have to contain something actively hostile to its own good, and this is what Proclus denies, declaring that it contains nothing liable to corruption, and denying that the universe could contain 'the unadorned and the unarranged, into which it will be dissolved.'[6]

If this were the case, the universe would clearly be beyond corruption and generation. However, this argument contradicts what

6. Ibid., p51.

Plato says in the *Timaeus* concerning the material chaos upon which the instances of the Forms are imposed. The disorder of matter is never actually overcome, according to Plato, but only held in check by the Forms. On this basis, the world does contain the source of its own corruption, and in a form which is liable to spread in the manner described earlier.

To sustain this argument, one must concentrate attention on the orderly aspect of the world. Insofar as it is ordered, it cannot *of itself* turn into anything else, but order is always contiguous with disorder, and this is why the amount of order in the world cannot in fact remain at a constant level. This order must be understood to include even the perennial pattern of descents into disorder which alternate with reascents of regeneration. As these alternations always proceed according to the same laws, the total system could be said to be incorruptible inasmuch as its liability to corruption is governed and contained in a way which ultimately neutralizes it.

This interpretation of the argument is really no more than an extension of what is implied in the physical fact that even scenes of disorder in the world around us are only perceptible as such because the propagation of light rays and sound waves always takes place by constant laws, and because our organs of perception are working according to their laws. Thus even the greatest incursions of physical disorder depend wholly on an underlying physical order which makes them perceptible and knowable. In a superficial sense, disorder is the opposite of order, but ultimately order has no opposite; there is only order or nothing. Consequently, this argument is only valid on the basis that the world's inherent evil is counteracted by its Creator.

10. *THE COSMIC ORDER ARGUMENT.* Everything in the world is said by this argument to be either located in its proper place, or else it is moved in a circle, while things which are not in their proper places are all endeavoring to get there. These are typically Aristotelian premises, and if they apply to the world definitively, then their conclusion will be certain, but only because these premises mean the same thing as the conclusion.

All change according to this argument must result from things which are not in their proper places, and in the process of reaching those proper places they are not liable to do any violence to any others which are already in their proper places. Only an external cause could remove things to new places which are alien to them, which would be a departure from nature. Such a change could only mean that the proper places for things already existed prior to the operation of such external causes. Thus the world must be everlasting if all its processes are divisible without remainder into the three categories of: abiding in the proper place; moving in a circle; and returning to the proper place. But to say that everything in the world always abides in its proper place or course of motion is just an expanded way of saying that it is everlasting.

11. *THE PERPETUITY OF MATTER ARGUMENT*. Matter exists for the sake of the universe, being 'the receptacle of generation'. More specifically, it exists for the sake of 'generation,' the endless flow of cosmic change. As the Forms do not change in themselves, their changes take place only in and between their instantiations in matter. Matter is produced from nothing, and for the sake of something else. What is formed by means of it will possess matter fortuitously, because the essence of every being is not in itself material.

Matter is created from nothing before all else, and therefore not in relation to anything else created, but in eternity; at its creation there is nothing else but the eternal. For this reason, its existence cannot be determined by any finite length of time, its origin being outside all finite relations. *Qua* matter, it is not in need of anything else in order to be what it is, or to be able to be receptive of Forms. Thus Forms and matter are both equally perpetual, and by implication so also is the instantiation of Forms in matter, by which the world is constituted.

12. *THE ETERNAL ACTIVITY ARGUMENT*. If God creates by means of the action of Forms on matter, it may seem that created things could cease to exist through the annihilation of either Form or of matter, or of both, although this idea is actually excluded by the foregoing arguments. Annihilation might also result from a failure by matter to be receptive of the Formal causes, or by a loss of productive power by the Formal causes, or again by both of these things.

But matter cannot undergo any change in its own nature because any such change would require an internal diversity which matter by definition cannot have. Neither can there be any loss of power either by God or by the Forms. This seems not to exclude the possibility that God might choose to cease to exert this power (figuratively speaking, as though God acted in time). This, however, could only be either trivially true or not true at all. It is true to the extent that God or any free agent can both retain a given power and decline to use it in some limited context, but it is false if this choice of inaction becomes final and definitive. This would amount to an actual loss of the power in question. Such would be the case if the Divine action was temporal. If, however, it is in eternity, the very question of such an internal change or abrogation could not arise.

13. *The Circular Motion Argument.* This argument depends on the Aristotelian dogma that the heavens are immutable because they are spheres of an indestructible matter which turn in circles. The rectilinear and disorderly motion necessary for corruption can exist only on earth, therefore. All generation and corruption come from the actions of things with properties contrary to one another, and no such contrarieties can exist in the celestial realm. This was the argument used by Hakewill (see chapter 6).

14. *The Co-Adaptation of Form and Matter Argument.* Matter and the 'vestiges of Forms', and order are said to have a simultaneous existence. Unlike human fabricators and artists, God creates the matter from which His creation is made. This reiterates what has been argued already, that the world must be everlasting if all the basic components of creation have always existed, and have always existed for one another. This line of argument is clearly not free from circularity; what is made of things that always exist must always exist if they always act in the same way.

15. *The Platonic Authority Argument.* This again is an argument which adds little to the ones above, but which emphasizes the role of the paradigmatic Form of the world, as well as Plato's

expressions for it, these being 'only-begotten', 'eternal', and 'all-perfect'. The latter expression is said to be applicable to the universe. As before, the similarity between the world and its paradigmatic cause must imply perpetuity for the world. The world is conceived as a divinity, and therefore not dependent on God.

16. *THE ORDER AND DISORDER ARGUMENT*. This concerns the Divine will, as it is inferred that the will to create the world implies a further will that all confused and disorderly phenomena should not exist. It thus preserves what is ordered and destroys the inordinate, and this will is not subject to any temporal change, because time is not in God, but exists only as a consequence of the creation. Only through disordered things could the world be corrupted, and their existence and increase is opposed by the Divine will. Disorders are in any case never created as such, but result from deviations in time to which originally ordered things have become subject.

17. *THE GENERATION AND CORRUPTION ARGUMENT*. Here again is an argument which adds little to the previous ones, one in which Plato is cited in a manner more religious than philosophical. What is generated must also be corruptible, and whatever is unbegotten must be incorruptible. The world contains order, and order is a manifestation of the eternal and unbegotten paradigm, whence it too must be incorruptible, and in any case, no benign creator could destroy a world which has been ordered with wisdom.

18. *THE DIVINE UNIFORMITY ARGUMENT*. This is a lengthy argument which reverts to the Argument from Perfection. God will not be able to act differently in different parts of time because His nature, and therefore action, cannot vary. The world is conceived as a created divinity, therefore dialogues such as the *Statesman*, in which the world is described as alternately falling into disorder and being re-ordered by God, must not be understood to mean any such alternation of activity in God himself. Our temporal trends both to order and to disorder result from a single uniform action by God which proceeds from outside time. In support of this, it is asserted

that God's presence in, and absence from, the world must be taken 'in conception only', a subjectivization of the ideas which is clearly selective. The objective nature of uniformity is never questioned.

RELIGIOUS ORTHODOXY AND TIMELESS CREATION

The above arguments are typical of the thinking of the pre-Christian world in antiquity, to which only the Judeo-Christian tradition made any exception. In the absence of revealed teachings which show God to be essentially other than the universe, the idea that the creation should share in the attributes of the Creator is practically irresistible. If God is infinite and eternal, then any creation worthy of Him must have the same properties. Failing this, God must have produced something less than the greatest creation possible, which is not to be supposed inasmuch as God is defined as the being than whom there can be none greater.

At the same time, however, creationist critics of this idea are not free to go to the opposite extreme and deny that the universe reveals anything of the Divine nature. To do that would be to fall into the Manichean doctrine for which this world is effectively a hell which completely conceals God from human awareness. For this reason, it follows that Christian criticism of the Proclan arguments is hampered by the fact that it cannot oppose them very radically, if one is committed to the belief that the world is created by God and is expressive of the highest goodness and wisdom. In these respects, it is clear that one must agree with the pagan view that the world does manifest attributes of the Creator, while still dissenting from it on the grounds that not *all* the Divine attributes are manifested in this way.

Thus there is a problem as to why some of the attributes should be excluded from the world, but not others. Nevertheless, this can be reasonable in principle, if the truth is taken to be a *via media* between an inclusion of all the attributes, which would effectively make the world and God the same thing, and a Manichean exclusion of them, which would make it utterly evil. The pagan side of the issue can acquire a measure of irrational support from the fact that human nature (without the influence of revelation) nearly always tends to make a God of the world in any case, so that God is then perceived as a rather shadowy entity behind it with little or no power over it once it had been created. The history of ideas and religions shows that human intuition naturally tends to a mixture of pantheism and idolatry, and this negative element can easily be allowed to sway the argument.

Some of the above arguments rest on grounds common to the different traditions where they proceed from the idea that God created an intelligible world (νοητος κοσμος) of everlasting Forms and the primary matter of creation, besides the material world known to the senses. The inclusion of the spiritual order of creation in the general category of 'world' or 'universe' has an appreciable effect on the arguments for the world's perpetuity. If creation were solely a thing of stocks and stones, there would be far less reason to expect it to be everlasting. However, the central role of consciousness in the world makes materialistic views of creation unrealistic, and once consciousness is taken into account, we find that consciousness is determined just as much by ideas or intelligible realities as by sensory ones. Consequently, it appears that a full account of the world must include subtle and suprasensible things whose laws are not those of matter.

Besides this, the study of human consciousness shows it to have the attribute of infinity, even if it is an order of infinity in its own kind. This also reacts upon the nature of the world inasmuch as it shows how the world contains infinite constituents as well as finite ones. Intelligible realities and infinite ones are both profoundly unlike the material substances which the senses perceive to be generable and corruptible, and when the latter are seen to be caused by the former, it must seem that the world as a system containing mutable things will as a whole participate in the everlasting nature of the ideal causes which interpose between it and God.

This way of thinking is also supported by the traditional idea that God can never be conceived to be idle. R. Sorabji explains Philo's use of this idea as follows:

God made it (the intelligible world) to serve as a pattern (*para-deigma*) for making perceptible things. There are as many perceptible kinds (*gene*) as there are intelligible. The intelligible world consists of ideas (*ideai*), and we may compare them to the plan in an architect's mind. In the same way, God first thought up the imprints (*tupoi*) and put together an intelligible world which exists in the divine reason (*logos*).[7]

This conception was continued by Origen, who treated the Forms or intelligibles as an earlier creation which was later to be the means for creating the material world, while the intelligibles had existed without temporal origin. Sorabji comments on this idea as follows:

> Not only did God create *material* worlds earlier than the present one, but he also created an earlier (or a timeless) *intelligible* world. Origen offers this twice as a solution to the idleness problem.... From Philo to Augustine there was a continuous tradition of belief in a separate intelligible heaven, and Augustine discusses a 'heaven of heaven', somewhat like that of Origen, in *Confessions* XII.[8]

Augustine deduces the heaven of heavens, the eternal heaven of Christian belief which specifically belongs to God, from the text: 'In the beginning God made the heaven and the earth.' This can mean that God created a heaven *before* the six days of creation in which the earth and the visible heavens were made. At the same time, the original matter which was said to be without form and void was also made before the six days of creation, and therefore it too must be beyond the conditions of corruption and evanescence which reign in the material world. Augustine denies that the heaven of heavens is coeternal with the Trinity (or it would be another God), but asserts that it partakes in God's eternity. It is possible that the heavens could still be consubsistent with God without being consubstantial as well, as the persons of the Trinity are.[9] Not much

---

7. R. Sorabji, *Time, Creation, and the Continuum*, chap.15, p250.
8. Ibid., chap. 15, pp251–252.
9. *Confessions*, Bk. XII, 8 and 9.

more is involved in this idea of the universe as a quasi-divine creature than is involved in Catholic teachings concerning the nature of
the Church, in which the natural and the supernatural are also
combined in this way.

The mode of duration corresponding to the heaven of heavens
would naturally be that of the 'ages of ages' or 'eternal times' referred
to in chapter 10. This may be eternity, or a very high order of duration. The tendency of this thinking shows that the Christian idea of
creation was by no means completely opposed to that of the gentile
tradition, and as a result, the latter had to be distorted by the pagan
faction into a strict uniformitarianism to ensure the existence of a
difference worth contending over. A corresponding extremism arose
later on the Christian side, as will be seen. But in the first place it
was enough for Christian thought to deny the pagan belief that the
world was a god, while still allowing it an intelligible dimension
which comprises far more than appears to common sense or to
materialism.

Transition to a New Cosmology

Historical changes have a way of preparing the ground for contin-
uations of themselves, more as a result of their acquired momentum
than of any practical necessity, as a pendulum must go to an
extreme. This seems to have been the case where the doctrine of creation was concerned. In the sixth century AD, things were taken a
stage further by Philoponus, a Christian philosopher in Alexandria.
He engaged in a dispute against Proclus and the older philosophical
tradition, and found a hitherto unsuspected weakness in their arguments (see next chapter). It appeared that he, unlike previous philosophers, was able to sustain the idea that this world was not only
of finite duration, but was as it were a unique episode between two
eternities in which there was no creation. His ideas were found
acceptable by the authorities of Church and State, and as a result
they came to be widely regarded as defining the truly Christian position for a long time afterward.

That this idea was believed to be more Christian was probably
owing to the fact that the thinking involved was more directly

opposed to that of the older tradition, rather than to the idea's inherent content. Philoponus' work on this subject appeared in 529 AD, and thereafter his arguments had an influence on what theologians taught about the world in relation to God, even down to the time of Saint Bonaventure, seven hundred years later.

These arguments must be considered next, but first of all one should have a general idea of what else was taking place in the sixth century, so that this doctrinal change can be seen in context. A new kind of world was being born, with an idea of reality which must certainly be called different, if not exactly new; for more than a century before this time, some Fathers of the Church had been teaching that the earth was flat, mainly from a desire to dissociate Christians as much as possible from pagans, who were occupied with the sciences that showed it to be round. There was possibly also a belief that if human beings knew too much about their world they would feel too much at home in it. During the sixth century this flat earth also began to become official, with the help of the writings of another Alexandrian, a monk called Cosmas:

> The first comprehensive cosmological system of the early Middle Ages, destined to replace the teachings of pagan astronomers from Pythagoras to Ptolemy, was the famous *Topographica Christiana* by the monk Cosmas.... The first of its twelve books is entitled: 'Against those who, while wishing to profess Christianity, think and imagine like the pagans that the heaven is spherical'. The Holy Tabernacle, described in Exodus, was rectangular and twice as long as it was wide; hence the earth has the same shape, placed lengthwise from East to West at the bottom of the universe.[10]

This flat, rectangular earth was said to slope from North West to South East, and was surrounded by four walls. Such was the idea of the world which became equated with orthodoxy during the next three centuries. Only during the ninth century was it again possible for it to be publicly acknowledged that the earth was round. Even so, there is evidence from maps like the *Mappa Mundi* in Hereford

10. Arthur Koestler, *The Sleepwalkers*, pt. 2, chap. 1.

Cathedral that many in the Church continued to teach that the earth was flat, nearly up to the fourteenth century. In the latter example the earth appears as a flat disc with Jerusalem at the center. The need to create a Christian cosmology even without regard to actual observation, would today be called a category mistake between facts and values, but it had a certain psychological relevance inasmuch as the formation of a different kind of human being is made easier if one can get him to believe in a different idea of the universe. It should also be appreciated that the question of our world's being a unique creation can only be a serious one on the basis of a geocentric cosmology, with creation effectively centered on this planet. Once creation is extended to innumerable stars and planetary systems, all coming into being at different times, the question of an absolute beginning for this whole universe must lose human significance, even if it could be exactly determined. The importance today of an absolute beginning lies rather in the way in which the possibility of such a beginning tests the arguments which are used in support of the perpetuity of the world.

13

The Arguments
of Philoponus

Ancient Beliefs About Creation

The early Medieval cosmology referred to in the last chapter shows how easily the human mind was able to slip back from the sophisticated ideas necessary to penetrate the appearances of nature. But there is never any escape from the alternatives, either that reality is only intelligible if we see through its appearances, or that reality is not intelligible if it is taken to be simply what it appears to be. The latter option is easy, but always a dead-end. The changes which took place in the sixth century were occasioned by the fact that the infinite and the indefinite were not very well understood at that time, which would excuse the reaction against them.

However, the after-effects of this situation have continued to shape some of the cosmological ideas which orthodoxy uses to this day, where the finitude or otherwise of creation is concerned. But in the light of what is known about infinity today, this subject should no longer be a stumbling-block in doctrinal matters. Much of the original problem was owing to the prestige of Aristotle, whose idea of the infinite was so defective that it could scarcely be distinguished from a very large finite quantity. His bias in favor of the finite is the negative side of an appreciation of the finite which is peculiarly Greek. It was the Greek genius which saw beyond the vulgar perception of the finite as just a very small bit of the infinite, and discovered that the finite was an equal counterpart of the infinite as a qualitative principle.

The Christian doctrine of the Incarnation depends on this insight, so that it could hardly have taken root in cultures where these ideas had not been developed. However, in its original context, this understanding of the finite went so far as to exclude the irrational and the unknown, an imbalance which Christianity was to correct. Nevertheless, finitist views still prevailed for a long time in areas where they were not relevant.

THE INFINITY ARGUMENTS

Because the thought of pagan antiquity was not at ease with the idea of infinity, it often failed to distinguish between it and the indefinite. Clear and distinct knowledge was sought, which requires finite objects and not the kind at which the mind staggers. One indication of this attitude can be seen in the Pythagorean table of opposites, where the infinite is placed on the same side as Evil, and the finite on the same side as Good. Philoponus saw how this negative view of the infinite could be exploited in relation to theories about the age of the world. If the world was without any temporal beginning, it could only mean that an infinite length of time must already have passed, and that this must be an actual and no merely potential infinity.

The importance of the latter point derives from Aristotle's treatment of this subject, which was accepted without question by both sides of the issue. For Aristotle, the infinite was to be conceived on a finitist basis, as an ever-extendable finitude, built up by a continual addition of finite increments. If a truly actual infinity were to exist, this process of addition would have to have been completed, but in practice this could never be, if endless addition was all that was involved. Where it is a question of dividing up a line, there is no limit to the number of points on it which can be constructed, so that one can say that the line amounts to a potential infinity. Because the infinitude of points in it is only a potential one, the traversal of the line presents no problem. But where there is an actual infinity the situation is quite otherwise, because an actual infinity could only be traversed through all its successive elements, which would amount to making a full count of them. Such a count was held to be impossible, and therefore it was also held to be impossible to traverse or go through an actual infinity, which was supposed to be unrealizable in itself.

According to Aristotle, the infinite had a rigidly-defined nature which made it impossible to add anything to it. It was by definition the quantity than which there could be none greater; any increase in it would thus be contradictory. For reasons related to this, Aristotle took issue against Anaxagoras who held that the infinite could be made up of lower-order infinities. Such a possibility would mean that the infinite could in some real sense be multiplied, since the absolute infinite would thus be the product of infinity by the number of its infinite component groups. This would be even more opposed to its unique nature than being subject to addition. The Aristotelian idea of infinite quantity made different orders of infinity contradictory, as also additions to it.

At this time, no one was believed to know more about this than Aristotle, and the idea that infinite quantities could be capable of operations analogous to those of finite quantities was still unknown. But the Aristotelian idea of infinity existed alongside the conception of creation discussed above, according to which the world had existed over beginningless time. Now it was Philoponus who first realized that there was a contradiction between these received ideas concerning the infinite and the supposedly infinite age of the world, and his new insight was to enable Christian thought to take the initiative against the domination of Aristotelian and Platonic ideas over the intellectual life of the time.

If there was no time at which the world began, must it not mean that an infinite length of time has passed up to the present time? This, moreover, must be a fully actual infinite, realized by the accumulation of an unlimited number of years. The present era has been reached by the passage of time over an infinite multitude of years, therefore, in which case an actual infinity must have been traversed in finite increments. Yet other apparent impossibilities were involved: although an infinite length of time may have passed up to the present, time is still passing, and so the infinite time-span is continually having new days and years added to it. But according to Aristotle, no such additions to the infinite were possible.

Moreover, an infinite time must mean various multiplications of the infinite as well. In an infinite time there must have been an infinite number of human beings, but then there must have been an infinite number of horses as well, and the total number of humans and horses must be two times infinity. If there had also been an infinite number of dogs, the result would make three times infinity, and so on. Similarly, in an infinite length of time, Saturn must have completed an infinite number of revolutions, but in the time for each one of these, the sun will have completed about thirty revolutions, so that in total the sun will have made thirty times infinity revolutions. At the same time, the moon revolves about twelve times for every one of the sun, so that it must have revolved twelve times infinity in relation to the sun, to say nothing of three hundred and sixty times infinity in relation to Saturn.

Since an actual infinity, its traversal, and its being added to or multiplied were all held to be impossible by general agreement, the only alternative seemed to be the conclusion that the world could only have existed for a finite time. Clearly the Proclan arguments did not meet this kind of attack, and the pagan side of the issue had no satisfactory reply. Simplicius, one of the last philosophers of the Academy, argued that the humans and other creatures which had existed over infinite time had all ceased to exist with the passage of time, so that they could not be said to make up infinite quantities. However, as Sorabji points out, while they as individuals do not at any given time make up an infinite quantity, their time-sum does, and in any case the non-existence of past things is only true in the weak sense of no longer being present to us.

Because no new developments arose in connection with the idea of the infinite, therefore, Philoponus' infinity arguments prevailed, and left the Christian side free to date the beginning of creation by a literal reading of biblical chronology, to a date around 4000 BC, which remained without any serious challenge until well into the nineteenth century, when geologists began to work out the age of the earth. During the intervening period, the arguments of Philoponus continued to be repeated in the context of a geocentric idea of creation by Christian, Muslim, and Jewish theologians right up to the thirteenth century, when they were still being used by Saint

Bonaventure, as this account of his work shows:

> If the world had existed from eternity, it would follow that it is
> possible to add to the infinite . . . but it is impossible to add to
> the infinite . . . if one considers simply the past, then one would
> have to admit an infinite number of lunar revolutions. But there
> are twelve lunar revolutions to one solar revolution. Therefore
> we are faced with two infinite numbers, of which one is twelve
> times the other, and this is an impossibility.[1]

As this quotation indicates, even the same examples as those of
Philoponus were still being used. The idea of the infinite had not
developed, and would not begin to develop until the fourteenth
century, when new advances were made in logic beyond Aristotle.
But even when the Aristotelian conception was known to be wrong
it did not bring about a reassessment of the belief that the world had
a beginning in time, partly because there was a continuing belief
that Christian identity needed to be made secure by heightening its
differences from pagan ideas about the universe. Even after Coper-
nicus, the theological reaction in support of Aristotle had the effect
of preventing the exploration of the theological implications of the
new science.

Corrections to the Idea of Infinity

The belief that there cannot be an actual infinite quantity was
owing to a failure to see that infinity is a reality in its own right,
independent of the finite. There is in any case something contradictory in setting up the idea of the infinite and making it a result of
adding up finite increments. One is not far from saying that infinity
is self-contradictory. However, the infinite is now known to be a
quantitative reality in an order of its own, where it is distinguished
from finite quantity in essential ways, one of which is that the relation of whole and part has a quite different meaning. In finite quantity, the part is in every way less than the whole, while the size of the
whole is determined by the number and sizes of the parts. In infinite
quantity, these relations do not hold, because it can gain or lose

1. Frederick Copleston, *A History of Western Philosophy*, vol. 2, pt. v, chap. 27 (3).

finite parts without alteration, and just as importantly it can have parts which are themselves infinite.

A clear example of an infinite quantity which is made up of infinite parts is the series of natural numbers. It can be divided first into two parts comprising the odd and even numbers, both of which are infinite, despite the fact that they each contain only half the numbers which make up the whole. Similarly, an unlimited number of infinite series can be set up on the basis that each pair of numbers in them differ by the same ratio. There is no limit to the number of infinite series which can thus be drawn from the natural number series, since any series containing any systematic selection from the natural numbers will also be infinite. Innumerable further possibilities result when these common differences and common ratios themselves change according to numerical laws. To these may be added infinite series of fractions with the same possibilities of development. The ancients were familiar with the series of triangular, square and pentagonal numbers, which were clearly infinite while containing fewer numbers than does the natural number series, but nevertheless the conclusion that an infinity can be made up of infinite parts was never generally realized.

The natural number series is thus an infinite collection which is not merely made up of an infinite number of finite members, but also of an infinite number of infinite members, in the form of all the different infinite series. On this basis, the existence of actual infinities and the multiplication of infinities are established beyond question. The objection that it is not possible to add to or subtract from an infinite quantity is similarly groundless as soon as the question is considered outside the bounds of Aristotelian definitions. The length of an infinite series cannot be affected by the addition of finite quantities to it. If it could be so affected, there would have to be a common measure between the finite increment and the infinite series itself, which could only mean that the latter was in fact finite and not infinite at all. Thus the fact that new time units are being added to a supposedly infinite time span does not mean that it was in any way 'less infinite' before the addition, or 'more infinite' after it.

As for the argument that the past cannot be of infinite length because it ends at a determined point, the present moment, this needs no refutation beyond the fact that the natural number series begins from unity (or from zero, if we make allowance for the fact that this beginning is not specific to number as such). Here, an infinity obviously proceeds from a fixed point.

There is even a spurious argument against the immortality of the soul which results from this belief that an infinite series cannot have a terminus. Could the soul be immortal if it begins from a fixed point like that of birth or conception? In fact it can be so, similarly to the way in which the natural number series is infinite while starting from unity or zero.

Such is the mathematical context of Philoponus's argument that an actual infinite quantity cannot be traversed. Despite appearances, this is based intentionally or not on an argument used by Proclus in *Elements of Theology*, Prop. 206. (This no doubt made it so much the more effectual when used against the Neoplatonic position.) Here, Proclus argues that a series with no beginning can have no end, and vice-versa; that there must always be a symmetry in this respect. For this reason he states in the same place that the soul can only reincarnate without end, since there would have to be an end to this beginningless process if the soul were finally to escape it. While this property of having neither beginning nor end is true for some kinds of infinite quantity, Proclus' mistake was to conclude that it must be true for *all* such quantities. The existence of infinite series ending or beginning at one fixed point refutes both this argument of his, and Philoponus' argument that an actual infinite cannot be traversed.

As the present time must needs be an 'end' of an infinite length of past time, it could of course never have been reached if no beginning had always to mean no end. But in view of the number series, starting from or ending with 1, there is no reason to believe this. Thus it was ironic that one of Proclus' very few erroneous arguments should have been considered effective against his philosophy. The idea of infinity involved in this argument is all too dubious for more reasons than those just given. If the word 'traversed' was just a synonym for 'counted', this statement would be nothing more than a repetition of the original assertion that there cannot be an actual infinite. If, however, it should refer to the action of a real agent, one need only ask 'By whom?' to reveal the confusion involved. If the answer was 'By God,' it would be obviously untrue, since omnipotence cannot be so incapable. But if the answer was 'By any *finite* being,' it would be just a statement of the obvious, like declaring that one cannot measure the depth of the ocean with a six-inch ruler.

The idea of traversal springs from a half-instinctive belief that the temporal continuation of the universe somehow depends on whether an imaginary agent can live through it all. To think in this way is to presuppose that there must have been a first day of time, an infinite number of days ago, and that from this Day Zero an eternal wanderer begins his career, having to live through an infinite number of days, that is, an actual infinity, in order to reach the present time. The argument then goes that no such result can be reached by this method, so that the present could only have been reached over a *finite* length of time. Such a finite past time means that there must have been a first day of time or Day Zero, of course, but this was precisely what had to be assumed in order to rule out an infinite traversal. If an infinite length of time were to follow a first day of time, the time series could never conclude now or at any other time without ceasing to be infinite (two fixed points have to mean finitude). Thus the traversal argument is really one of question-begging; to argue from a first day of time is the same as to say that all past time exists between two fixed points (the first day and today), i.e., that it is finite. It should hardly now be necessary to add that the existence of an endless time series cannot really depend on the activities of imaginary time travelers, and that to think otherwise would be a subjectivist delusion like thinking that Mount Everest only began to exist after it was first climbed.

The fact that this argument continued to be quoted like an oracle for centuries is a sign that it pointed to a result which was too desirable to allow room for criticism. The resulting finite view of the universe fulfilled a spiritual need which could not otherwise be met except by means of metaphysical ideas which were not popularly explicable. Unless man is a significant actor on the stage of the universe, spiritual values will seem to have no more than a purely subjective meaning; they can only have a cosmic role if man has one. Accordingly the world must be seen to be finite, if man is not to appear to be nothing in relation to it. A valid alternative to this is that the relation of man to the world should be understood more profoundly in terms of microcosm and macrocosm, an idea not suitable for popularization in the present era.

THE MATURE CREATION PARADOX

If the arguments of Philoponus are compared with those of Proclus, it is easy to see why they are only of historical interest. Their essential content consists of controversial devices relevant only in late antiquity. The Proclan arguments, on the other hand, have most of them a timeless quality. They express a set of universal realities which stand by themselves above the flux of cultural conditions, despite Proclus' uniformitarian bias; and however they may be criticized, most of them are not liable to be shown not to be arguments at all. Nevertheless, a lack of substance in Philoponus' counter-arguments does not mean that one can ignore the position which they were used to support. It could still be true that time as such is of finite length, for reasons which so far have never been determined. If this were the case, a number of important results would follow, not least where our ability to relate to a real past is concerned.

This is because, contrary to common sense, an absolute beginning of time and movement brings with it the possibility that it could have begun at *any* moment, even up till a moment ago. In the face of this paradox, it is not relevant to argue that the world contains written records and artifacts produced in the past, or persons with memories. If time and the world were of recent origin, it would contain all such things from the start, and no deliberate deception need be involved. Even if the time of the beginning was as remote as is usually believed, so that it contained only Adam and Eve, they, being complete human beings in early maturity, would be in that state without having lived through the previous twenty-odd years of development that their mature state would require in the course of nature. The equivalent of this would apply to the earth, sun, moon, and stars which made up the world in which they were created. Insofar as creation has to mean *mature creation*, therefore, it must begin from a state which manifests the outcome of a history which has not happened. If we allow that time and the world began at some moment in time, we cannot assume that we have the right to relegate that moment to some period in remote antiquity which is too far off to concern us.

In practice, no one is willing to sacrifice common sense to this paradox and believe that the world began a moment ago, or even a few centuries ago, even though there is no logical basis for dismissing such an idea. The reasons for this are of more than psychological interest, although on a basic level the rejection of the paradox is no doubt owing only to the shock it gives to customary ideas of reality. But more significantly, the general disbelief results from something most minds feel instinctively about their knowledge of time. This is an intuition that the temporal process is *per se* an endless continuum, in which continuity is an intrinsic property. The intuition is that if we do not know that much about time, we do not know time at all. There is a connection here with the Principle of Plenitude, which concerns not only the self-extension of the totality of being, but of each modality of being, such as time. This does not exclude any number of relative limits which arise from external causes, such as those of world-ages, but it does exclude the idea that time may be limited of itself. If this idea of the temporal continuum embodies a true insight, there need be no doubt that historical events have actually happened, even if not always in the ways supposed.

On the other hand, the idea that time began at a moment in time would mean that we could have no such assurance. There would in fact not be a single historical event which need actually have happened, no matter how much evidence there was for it. Besides the shock to common sense, this is an impossible conclusion from the point of view of the monotheistic religions, which are so largely based on historical revelation, and consequently it is paradoxical in another way that the idea of a temporal beginning of time should be so much associated with orthodox beliefs. The alternatives thus seem to be either that time is, if not infinite, an indefinitely-extensible continuum, or that our knowledge of the past should be theoretically unfounded.

THE QUESTION OF COHERENCE

I have added the phrase 'at a moment in time' in connection with the beginning to emphasize the fact that the very idea of an absolute beginning of time in this world would make time itself begin (and end) just like any series of events in time. There is something deeply incoherent in this, as can be seen when it is understood that time is definable as the condition subject to which all things capable of beginning and ending do in fact begin and end. On this basis, to speak of a beginning or an ending of time in an absolute sense is as much a category mistake as to speak of a 'history of time'. The mistake involved can only appear subtle because of the intangible nature of time, but its crassness is clear enough when one sees how it invites comparison with an idea that a cinema might be wrecked by an explosion which takes place in one of the films shown in it. Such a view of time is of a piece with Cosmas' idea of cosmic space, which was said to be contained within four walls, as if they could be anything but boundaries in an even greater spatial extension.

In case this form of the above argument should seem to concede too much to the conventional distinction between time and its contents, it may also be expressed in a way which shows it does not rely on this distinction. If the world of time were of finite extent, it would have to start at one moment and end at another. But neither starting nor stopping are ever known except as contained in a time-process. Thus 'starting' presupposes a continuous passage of time before, during, and after the event, and so likewise does 'ending'. Therefore if the world-time process itself started and stopped, this could only take place in a higher-order time or 'meta-time'. But the introduction of the latter would clearly defeat the object of reducing time as we know it to a finite quantity. If we were to argue that this higher-order time was also finite, the question of its starting and stopping would similarly require an even higher order of time, and so on in an infinite regress. In this way, a supposedly finite time gives rise to its opposite, so that there is no possibility that time could be overcome on its own level.

If then there were no intermediate reality between eternity and time, the idea of time as such 'beginning' could only be a confusion,

for the reasons given. However, the continuity of being requires that
the interval between eternity and time should be filled by at least
one kind of 'meta-time', one which possesses attributes both of
finite time and of eternity. Such a higher kind of time was known to
the Scholastics as *aevum*, and it is conceived as having a duration
greater than historical time by whole orders of magnitude, so that
cosmic cycles or world-ages would only be successive moments relative to it while, possibly, the whole extent of time on our level of
being would amount to just one cycle of *aevum*. If time and the
world as we know it were to 'begin' and 'end' in *aevum*, therefore,
this would imply finitude for one special kind of time, not for time
as such; endless duration would still be there in a different form.[2]
Time and the world have been treated as being inseparable in the
above discussion, not only from Platonic premises, but because the
idea that there was an 'empty time' before and after the duration of
the cosmos would extend the idea of time into a realm in which it
could have no meaning. The fact that such time before or after this
world was made up of successive moments would be completely
unverifiable. There would be nothing at any one of its moments to
distinguish that moment from any other before or after it, and by
the Identity of Indiscernibles, such moments, being indistinguishable, would thus be all one and the same moment, and therefore
there would be no temporal extension. Some such confused idea
of a 'time before time' enters into the supposition that somehow
time was already passing when God created the world at a certain
moment, and it shows how little substance there is in the idea of an
absolute beginning in this world.

Curiously enough, the doctrine that the world was created *ex
nihilo* provides yet another reason for excluding the idea that time
and the world are of limited extent, in a way which is hardly ever
noticed. If the material world were created out of nothing, not only
would there be nothing before and after it, there would be no other

2. The idea of time as self-extensive by its very nature expresses a property it has
in common with all modalities of being. All of time's limits, like those of cycles or
world-ages, are only imposed on it by other realities, as spatial extension is acciden-
tally limited by some kinds of objects in it.

cosmic reality related to it in any way. In this case, the world is *bounded by nothing*, which is to say unbounded. This argument requires only that the word 'nothing' should mean what it says, and not signify some formless quasi-something which may fill up all the unwanted space and time beyond a supposedly limited world. However, Aquinas claims that this way of thinking serves to make the world eternal in the same way as God:

> The assertion of the world's eternity; the assertion of the eternity of the world's matter, out of which at a certain time the world began to be formed.... For in all these cases, something beside God is claimed to be eternal; and this is incompatible with the Catholic faith.[3]

The assumptions made here are that there is only one way in which a being can be eternal, and that the only alternative to eternity is time of finite length, whereas it has already been shown that we are not confined to these alternatives. Eternity comprises the whole of reality in a *totum simul* which has no need of change for the realization of its possibilities, since they are all realized together once for all. Between this and finite time, the natural intermediary is that of endlessly extended duration, which we have just encountered as *aevum*.

From an orthodox point of view, Aquinas' argument here cannot be acceptable without considerable qualification because the Christian faith also teaches that the saints in heaven participate in the Divine eternity, so that they too must effectively be eternal, even if in a dependent relation; they cannot be supposed to exist only a finite time in the hereafter just because only God is eternal *per se*, an elaboration of the idea of the eternal which Aquinas seems to ignore. Elsewhere, however, he argues implicitly in the opposite sense, where he argues that creation must have the maximum possible diversity if it is to correspond to the power of the Creator:

> Now by the fact that the active power is actualized the effect receives the likeness of the agent. Hence there would not be a perfect likeness of God in the universe if all things were of one

---

3. *SCG*, vol. II, chap. 38, [16].

grade of being. For this reason, then, there is distinction among created things: that, being many, they may receive God's likeness more perfectly than by being one.[4]

Here it is frankly allowed that there should be a correspondence between the power of the Creator and the range of content in creation, and it is therefore all the more strange that no account is taken of the way in which this also applies to the quantitative extent of the creation in time. This must be requisite if 'the passive potentiality of matter' is to be 'completely actualized.'[5]

Aquinas' argument in the above, and the quantitative extension of it I am suggesting, are logically connected by the idea that the realization of all the possible species and grades of beings should naturally require an unlimited expanse of time. Such a conception need involve no more than the idea of indefinite extension, without applying terms like 'eternity' and 'infinity' which cause confusions because they apply primarily to Divine attributes. In conclusion, therefore, the theological reasoning against this idea is not much more effectual than the philosophical, and is more naturally able support than contradict the notion of indefinite extension. While the time in which human experience takes place may be finite in relation to higher orders of being, it can only be perceived as finite on its own level by a confusion of thought.

4. Ibid., chap. 45, [3].
5. Ibid.

14

An Ontology of Time

A Dependent Mode of Being

While it cannot coherently be said that time itself begins at a given time, or that it exists between a starting date and an ending date, it is nevertheless a contingency as a whole, just as much as any of the events which occur in it. Although it is of indefinite length, it is a derivative and dependent reality in relation to the whole of being, by far the greater part of which is non-temporal since the whole of being comprises God, and the angelic and intelligible worlds. The manner of time's non-temporal origin can be understood in the light of the Principle of Plenitude. On this basis, the temporal process as a whole can be shown to come into being in a manner which is no different from the way in which its component phenomena arise.

There is no reason why a subordinate mode of being should not be realized by a non-temporal process. For example, the conclusions and answers reached in logical and mathematical problems follow from their premises in just such a timeless manner, even though these connected statements are traced by thought and verbally expressed in temporal sequences. Thus the conclusion 'Socrates is mortal' follows logically and timelessly from 'all men are mortal' and 'Socrates is a man,' even though these statements may be written down in a temporal sequence. Another example comes from what theology teaches about the Holy Trinity. The Son proceeds from the Father, and the Holy Spirit proceeds from the Father and the Son, and these processions are eternal, even though we have to think of them temporally. The same thing can be seen in another way by means of the series of natural numbers. This is a timeless system of quantitative relationships whose non-temporal succession is translated into a temporal one by our act of counting.

The time process in which we exist comprises a real mode of being, but it is nevertheless a very limited one, which is assigned to the lower levels of the scale of being because the amount of reality it contains in each of its moments cannot be increased without the cessation of what went before. In contrast to this are the archetypal realities in which every mode of being and reality has its greatest amplitude. Subsequent to these are kinds of being which are real by participation, but which have progressively greater degrees of privation, in the Aristotelian sense of the word. This is the principle by which temporal things derive from states of being which are superior to change and corruption, while all the instantiations which are comprised in the temporal condition are much attenuated in the process, just as every greater possibility implies a lesser one as well.

That this applies to the contents of time appears in three different ways in which temporal existence differs from eternal being. Firstly, even the longest temporal durations are insignificant compared with the eternal; secondly, only a tiny amount of even this very limited share of being is ever realizable in any one moment of time; thirdly, temporal existence is contingent, that is to say, it always depends on its relations to many other temporal existences which are contemporary with it. (For example, each living creature is physically dependent on the existence of innumerable others, both like and unlike itself.) These properties of temporal existence are also part of the difference between a Form and its instantiations, say between the Form of an axe and the material axes which manifest it; while a Form and its being are inseparable, its instantiations are under no necessity to exist. From this point of view, the passage of being from eternity to time is of the same nature as the descent of the causal power of the Forms into their material instantiations. These relations in the macrocosm are of course reflected in the microcosm inasmuch as the realm of Forms is present in each individual mind. Consequently, this ontological movement has its reverberations in the subconscious mind, where it may well have inspired Coleridge's lines:

Where Alph, the sacred river, ran
Through caverns measureless to man
Down to a sunless sea.[1]

The 'sunless sea' would therefore be the material world in which the
Forms reach their final level of instantiation. The more usual interpretation, that this is an allusion to the rivers of Paradise, is also a
symbol which could convey the same idea, since Paradise manifested, in a relative sense at least, the fount of the realities which
make up this world.

The relation between Forms and their instances is of one nature
with the reduction of being into time, but this does not explain the
Principle of Plenitude. On the contrary, it follows from Plenitude
that Forms automatically cause their instantiations in matter, since
Plenitude conveys the general principle of the Form-matter relation
in its ontologically 'downward' sense. This way of accounting for
time in terms of its solidarity with instantiation is in conformity
with what has already been argued against the idea of 'empty time',
because the formation of the time-series and that of its contents are
of one and the same nature on this basis. Moreover, the necessity for
change and movement in the realm of time is also explained by the
effect of Plenitude as it operates in its 'downward' or cosmogonic
sense. Given the progressive reduction of being and reality implicit
in this process, there is a corresponding reduction in the potentialities of the instantiated beings, which can only be counterbalanced
by the quantitative principle of continually increasing their number,
and ensuring that they replace one another as rapidly as possible. As
this cosmogonic descent tends to its extremity, therefore, the rate at
which temporal change takes place should rise to a maximum, as a
greater number of small quantities must compensate for a smaller
number of large quantities. However, one must carefully observe a
distinction here, between the timeless cosmogonic descent implied
by Plenitude which produces the whole time-series and material
instantiation, and the changes which reflect this descent in minia-
ture in the various cycles of time. The 'temporality of time' thus

1. *Kubla Khan.*

increases between the beginning and the end of a world-cycle, as the quantitative reality increases.

THE THREE LEVELS OF BEING

Without looking further into the dynamics of time for the present, I shall enlarge on the idea of time's issuance from eternity. As the origin, eternity has the peculiarity that, being exempt from change, it is more open to definition. Starting from this conception, time may be conceived from the suppression of some of the eternal attributes, which Plotinus speaks of as follows:

> We know it as a life changelessly motionless and ever holding the Universal content in actual presence; not this now and now the other, but always all; not existing now in one mode and now in another, but a consummation without part or interval. All its content is in immediate concentration as at one point; nothing in it ever knows development . . . for ever in a Now. . . .[2]

The cosmic reality which we know only as divided, discontinuous and often without coherence is, at its origin, an integrated and undivided whole to which nothing can be added. All that derives from the absolute reality emerges increasingly fragmented, even though it may still manifest the same total content in a disarticulated manner. The unchanging nature of the eternal is not the same as its being simply static, which would in any case be a temporally-conditioned property. It rather combines immutability with the dynamism of change without any of the corruption, loss, or conflict which change involves in the material world.

But since Plenitude entails that all possible levels of being should be realized, time could not follow directly from eternity if it were possible for there to be another mode of being which possessed properties peculiar to both, and which would mediate between them. The difference between eternal and temporal being is sufficiently extreme to make a third mode of being necessary. It is conceived as being like time in that it develops through moments which

2. *Enn.* III, 7, 3.

succeed one another in a series, while on the other hand it is like eternity inasmuch as the duration of everything in it is endless. Such is the endless temporal existence called *aevum*, which seems to have been originally conceived by Plotinus, even though he does not distinguish it very clearly from finite time:

> Existence for the [generated] All must similarly consist in a goal to be attained; for this reason it keeps hastening toward its future dreading to rest, seeking to draw Being to itself by a perpetual variety of production and action by its circling in a sort of ambition after Essential Existence.[3]

Temporality, whether finite or non-finite, appears as a state of deprivation of all but a minimum of real being, and the need to fill the vacuum allows no rest from the drive to ever more prolongations of itself, as if this could remedy the deficiency of temporal being. This is what Plotinus expresses in the same passage about the dynamics of time, as being a process which 'seeks perpetuity by way of futurity', although the 'futurity', when it arrives is necessarily of the same nature as the present time, whether it be in time as we know it or in the higher form of time. The latter is a whole of temporal wholes which is an archetype in relation to the finite and fragmented change of this world. The reduction of being from eternity through *aevum* to finite time can be compared with the process of representing a complex three dimensional object like a house in two dimensions by means of a set of elevations covering all its aspects. Such a transition from a higher-dimensional state to a lower one requires a certain increase in quantity so that the lower medium can in some sort match the higher on its own level.

That this ontological movement requires three, not two, universal categories of being is argued by Proclus in a way which depends directly on Plenitude:

> For if all process is through likeness [prop. 29], and the first term of any series is immediately succeeded by terms which are like it rather than unlike, the wholly unlike having a lower station

---

3. *Enn.* III, 7, 4. (The All is both spiritual and material.)

[prop. 28] and if it is impossible to attach directly to the eternals things which come-to-be in a part of time [since the latter are doubly distinguished from the former, both as things in process from things which are and as dated from perpetual existences], so that there must be an intermediate order which resembles the eternals in one respect but differs from them in the other. . . . It remains that the mean is that which perpetually comes-to-be: which in virtue of its coming-to-be is attached to the inferior order, while in its perpetuity it imitates the eternal nature.[4]

These three orders thus comprise the concentrated simultaneity of the eternal, the endless succession of *aevum*, and the lower temporal level which contains only finite durations. The latter comprises many different orders of duration, ranging from that of *aevum* itself down to forms of duration so short as to tend to non-existence. This descending series of possibilities, implicit in the idea of Plenitude, is essentially the same by nature when it proceeds from *aevum* to finite time, as when it proceeds from eternity to *aevum*. This continuous scale of durations is a property of time which will be looked at more closely in the next chapter.

TIME, SOUL, AND COSMIC PROCESS

The acceleration of finite time, or the shortening of the duration in which its phenomena develop, is never directly observable, and so it may well appear that we should have the right to ignore it. The rotation of the earth on its axis, and the cycle of the year always bear the same ratios to the length of a human lifetime, for example, regardless of the absolute duration comprised in them. Cosmic processes, and the constructive mental activities of mankind share in the same overall pattern of change, at least wherever mental activity is devoted to the production of changes in the outside world.

The possibility of evil is also implicit both in the production of finite time itself, and in the acceleration of change in it, because the instantiation of eternal Forms in the material world means that they

4. *Elements of Theology*, prop. 55

acquire the possibility of forming combinations quite unlike their mutual relations *qua* Forms. Instantiation thus involves a process of disarticulation which allows the material world a range of possibilities wider in many respects than those of the archetypal world, albeit at the price of negative potentialities for conflict. Thus destructive conflicts can result from the juxtaposition of cultural forms and human types which would not be nearly related in the realm of their archetypal causes.

In the human microcosm there are correspondences between the intellect and the realm of Forms and between the soul and the physical world. There is also the difference that the conformity of the intellect to the Forms is intrinsic to it, whereas the soul's conformity to them is only conditional, which is why the soul, unlike the intellect, is in need of salvation. Soul and cosmos are both subject to time; just as the soul grasps intelligible realities in a serial manner, so in the macrocosm the archetypal reality is realized in a series of moments, the sum total of which will be in some sense equivalent to the original archetype. What Plotinus says of the soul in this connection applies *mutatis mutandis* to both the human soul and the world-soul. In either case, it is said to contain 'an unquiet faculty' whose passion is to recreate what it originally knew in the Authentic Realm. This is what gives rise to the endless series of different acts which aims to recreate that realm on a lower level of being, as where a centuries-long history of a nation would be much more adequate to its archetypal cause than its attributes over a few years.

This view of time and the world differs from that of subjectivism, however, inasmuch as the temporal world is not created as such by the conscious movements of either the individual soul or the world soul. The soul could be said to recreate the world by its representation, while this representation is based on the self-subsistent realities of both matter and the Forms. In addition to the representing power, the creative function of the soul appears in the dynamism and forward momentum which passes into nature from it. This dynamism can be qualified by innumerable different dispositions of the soul, depending on the combination of faculties which predominates. For this reason, a majority of minds or souls which have a broadly similar disposition can impart to their world a quality which goes far deeper than the material works they undertake.

Insofar as we are subject to this psychic force, it is very difficult to see truth and falsehood apart from what they are taken to be by the prevailing ethos.

At times when only the sense faculties are operative in the majority, metaphysical truths will be made to seem more obscure than they are in themselves. The dominant properties in the collective consciousness give rise to different forms of the world, partly as a legitimate realization of new possibilities, and partly as a smothering of higher values by lower. The qualification of time by its mode of representation in individual minds has also a bearing on the fact that miracles are recorded much more in some periods in history than in others, not because divine intervention is more present at some times but because of the receptivity of the general state of mind. This receptivity is linked to the value which is placed on time and temporal development. While the soul and its world are both subject to time, there is a margin of choice within which the soul can choose how far its energies are absorbed in things of process and how far they can be committed to a reality which transcends time. This is not a mere choice of options; it is a creative act which decides the nature and value of a world. There is no reason in principle why any given individual should not thus recover, even in this life, a conscious participation in the eternal source of the material world, as numerous mystics have been known to do.

The choices made by the individual can thus be such as to either accelerate or to slow down the passage of time, even though the effect owing to that person will not be noticeable unless a similar choice is made by a large number of others. The modern preference for temporal movement is the opposite of that of the mystic, and it contains a denial of any final and enduring state to which the time process could tend, because the domination of short-term purpose excludes the ultimate purpose which can make life meaningful. Since the soul is under no inherent necessity to convert itself to the flux of time and matter, it belongs by nature to the world of the spirit, even though it does not yet exist in eternity. This means, as Inge has pointed out,[5] that the spiritual world cannot be equated with eternity. While it includes eternity, it also includes other modes

5. *The Philosophy of Plotinus*, vol. 1, (vi–viii), 'Time'.

of being which are characterized by an authentic relation to the eternal. The fact that ensouled corporeal beings are not *per se* spirit does not prevent them from the completest participation in the essence and the power of the spirit.

This idea of the dynamics of cosmic change gives a much lower status to the role of the material universe than does scientific thought. The Forms, and material existence, constitute a reality shared in by all beings, but in addition to them there is the sum total of all the world-representations formed from them in conscious beings or monads. This is why the creative activities of minds are components of the real world with as much or more right as are the cosmic bodies. While this conclusion about the real world was reached most clearly by Leibniz, it is also implicitly the cosmology of the Neoplatonists. Much of the opposition it meets with is owing to the fact that it is not open to the reductions and simplifications so much desired by modern thought.

TIME, CREATION, AND THE FORMS

The creation of the material world has been spoken of so far as the working-out of an ontological movement which appears to have nothing to do with the idea of a world being created by a personal choice by God. But the fact that the realization of Plenitude is in no way compatible with a personal choice made by a finite mind operating in time does not give us the right to presume without further ado that it is not compatible with a choice made outside time by an infinite mind. All the contingencies which characterize human choice are owing to its being exercised in time, and this cannot be a model for acts of choice by God.

We must also avoid setting up an absolute distinction between the original act of creation and the propagation of universal existence from moment to moment, which could be called a constant re-creation. Being is by its very nature extensible in time in a way which has no dependence on logic, that is, the existence of a given object in the future is not deducible from its existence now. As God has created it with this property, it is reasonable to conceive the creation of the material world as distributed along the time dimension in an infinite series of separate acts as well as to conceive it as a timeless ontological movement. Neither of these accounts can be taken as complete or exclusive, therefore. They closely parallel the distinction made in the above between the soul's causal power over nature and the efficient causality the world at a given time has in regard to its being in a later moment. There is in fact more than a hint of a 'creation out of nothing' in the prolongation of all states of existence through time in the life of the cosmos as it is known in subjective representation. There is room for doubt here as to whether the ontological self-propagation takes place by a constant direct divine intervention, or whether this propagation is an inherent property created originally as an attribute of temporal being.

It is a fact supportive of the idea of creation out of nothing that the forward projection of existence from moment to moment reveals something of this level of creation. The continuation of existence does not result from logical relations, but is rather a contingent reality which shares in the continuous being of soul and intellect. Every moment of the material world which is future in relation to the present is in a sense a 'nothing' which is turned into a real existence by some power external to it. This conversion of future into present is only a relative 'creation out of nothing,' of course, because the future can be shown to be more than nothing because we can think constructively about it, and make plans in relation to it. Nevertheless, it could reasonably be taken for a natural image of an eternal act of production.

Such ideas about time and creation contrast with Plotinian ideas, according to which the emergence of a world and its contents comes as an almost automatic result of the relation between the eternal archetypes and the receptivity of matter. It is yet to be seen whether one can reconcile these perspectives of an almost motiveless creation or emanation on the one hand, and on the other hand one by which everything is intentionally brought into existence by the Creator for a specific purpose inclusive of the good of the beings created.

The word 'creation' as used in the Bible does not, by itself shed any light on the question, as its derivation is from the Latin *creare*, which seems to be impervious to analysis. The operative part of this word is simply the syllable *re*, meaning 'thing,' while the ending *-are* serves only to make this noun into a verb. The word 'creation' therefore conveys nothing more than the conferring of thinghood upon a thing, or an act of 'enthingment'. This difficulty is not solved by means of the Hebrew for *creare*, since it also has a construction which parallels that of the Latin word. The use of the word 'created' in Genesis would therefore seem to be a barrier against theoretical explanation. Whether it is primarily an act of intelligent choice which realizes itself in particular individuals, or whether it is an inevitable ontological descent, the idea of creation is as unanalyzable as that of Being.

There is no reason why these two approaches to creation should not be reconciled, however, because individual and universal realities need not exclude one another. There is a great difference in perspective between the theory of electromagnetic energy and the construction of radio transmitters and receivers but their mutual integration is complete. As man's mind bridges the divide between the laws of energy and the structures which employ them, an analogous synthesis may well reside in the act of creation. The nothing which precedes creation is first of all a nothing on the cosmic plane, prior to the creation of matter, and of the Forms. The latter contain no will or purpose of their own as a collectivity, so that in themselves they have no co-ordinating and marshalling power which could ensure that their manifestation in matter will result in a cosmos and not a chaos.

God's relation to the Forms can be understood as being like that between Plato's Form of the Good and the Forms, that is, as a higher instance of the way in which a Form relates to all its instantiations in time and matter, in the sense of being their cause and pattern. But in addition to this, however, God has the power of determining which Forms shall be instantiated at a given time, and which shall not, and in which combinations.

There is an Aristotelian criticism of this view of creation by Saint Albert the Great which can also yield a conclusion supportive of it for those who are not committed to Aristotle on principle. Albert discounts the idea that the Formal causes of particular things should be essentially separate from them, on the grounds that 'the proximate principles of particular things are particular, and the proximate principles of corruptible things are corruptible.' He adds that 'by universals which pre-exist and have beforehand the being of things, no thing is known; and thus they are useless to the knowledge of things.'[6]

This argument is either a statement of the obvious like saying that dogs are always produced by dogs, and cats by cats, or it is very dubious inasmuch as the Forms do not have to be understood as proximate principles, since it will be seen later how they can subsist with other and more physical causes. Platonists were not using the idea of self-subsistent Forms because they were unable to understand physical or efficient causality and needed a substitute for it. (Aristotle himself teaches the simultaneous working of Formal, Final, Material, and Efficient causes.)

The text just quoted proceeds to another objection to the idea of the Forms as subsistent realities which brings us back to what has just been said about God's relation to the Forms. It is, moreover, an objection which looks strangely unmindful of the role of the Creator, and shows how the materialistic tendency of Aristotle's thought makes it unhelpful for discussions of this kind:

> Moreover, if they [the Forms] were separated, [i.e., subsistent realities] what would make them touch matter and cause a natural being in it? For the *etymagium*[7] which he [Plato] speaks of, does not touch wax for the purpose of sealing *except when someone moves it* [author's italics]. But what there is to move separated Forms of this sort is impossible to say, although some wish to suppose some such thing.[8]

This objection has some matters of substance which deserve a fuller statement. Given that the Forms transcend their instantiations, they give us no means of deducing where or when these manifestations shall arise. Likewise, they give us no clue as to just how many such

---

6. Saint Albert the Great, treatise II, chap. 5 (*Selections from the Medieval Philosophers*, Scribners).

7. Latin for εκ μαγειον or 'out-imaging'.

8. Saint Albert, ibid.

creatures would come into being, and neither do they reveal what combinations they would form with other entities like themselves. Finally, the question of purpose seems to have no place. The point seemingly ignored by Saint Albert is that the agency answering to the above conditions is that of God, and moreover in respect of a function specifically divine, even though the manner of the action involved is according to Plenitude. This objection against self-subsistent Forms, that they cannot by any volition of their own create a world or any part of one, is a rather strange one to be raised from a Christian point of view, and not only because it regards merely the natural level. If, conversely, it were possible to attribute such autonomous action to the Forms, there would in effect be as many creators as Forms, and this would be rejected at once as polytheism. For this reason Albert's Aristotelian criticism of Formal causes requires that we should ignore their relation to God, without adequate reason.

The combination of the theistic conception of creation with the instancing of Forms as its *modus operandi* is recognized by a number of those who have studied the traditional cosmologies. For example, Titus Burckhardt[9] speaks of the 'vertical genesis of species' into material existence, at a time when the material medium is still receptive to such large-scale changes. He conceives the Forms as causing a certain 'condensation' of themselves at ever-lower levels, so that they have prior instantiations in a more subtle matter than the matter of this world. These subtle kinds of creation play the part of Formal causes in relation to the creatures in this world in a strictly relative sense, and are in effect what Saint Albert thought of as their 'proximate causes', with which they are equally individual. But since causes of this kind result from the instantiation of subsistent Forms in a superior kind of matter, there is no question of conflict between these two kinds of explanation, except where Aristotelian thought would restrict all thinking to just one of them.

The resulting descent of these mediated Forms into this world would, according to Burckhardt, be quite sudden, and therefore

9. See Titus Burckhardt, 'Cosmology and Modern Science' (in *The Sword of Gnosis*, Jacob Needleman, Ed.).

without any previous evolutionary development. Each life-form would be complete from the start, and would be as it were a coagulation of a more subtle kind of being. However, it will be possible to see a pattern of evolution in the order in which these ontological descents take place, only with the difference that the sequence is owing to a power acting on matter and not to the generation of one species by another. In a related context, Proclus argues that the Form of Man is instantiated in three realms before this one,[10] where the constitutive matter consists of the philosophical elements fire, air and water respectively, men being formed from each of these four elements in a kind of hierarchy. Man in this world is the fourth instantiation in order, that of the earth element. Such a descent of a Form through increasingly gross kinds of matter is matched in each one of them by the way in which the matter becomes increasingly opaque in the course of a cosmic cycle. This conception closely follows the Plenitude idea of each type of being filling all the levels of existence possible for it. In Proclus' account a similar cosmogonic progression is applied to most other Forms, including the Horse Itself and the Lion Itself.

UNIFICATION UNDER ONE CONCEPT

Not only is the 'Platonic creationism' consistent with the theistic idea of creation, it is also a means of correcting materialistic tendencies that can enter into the latter. Saint Gregory of Nyssa even took this metaphysical approach to the extent of eliminating the role of matter in it, on the grounds that all things could be explained by God's gathering groups of Forms together in appropriate bundles by the action of His will alone. For example, a conjunction of hardness, coldness, heaviness, whiteness, and extension would account for marble without need for a material substance. If things were so made directly from ideas from the Divine mind, one could indeed speak of a creation out of nothing, as there would be nothing where there was supposed to be the prime matter or *hyle*. However, this use

10. Proclus, *Commentary on Plato's Parmenides*, Bk. III, 812 (G.R. Morrow and J.M. Dillon translation).

of the Forms in creation is too similar to the manner in which the Divine Word is generated from the Father, so that this theory is only spiritual in a way which would confuse God with created beings.

Without taking this conception to the lengths to which Gregory took it, however, it sheds light on the question as to whether the immediate object of creation consists in individual beings and physical objects. If the idea of omnipotence acting in eternity is taken by itself, there is no logical reason why the Creator should not be directly concerned with making individuals, right down to individual atoms. However, God's action in creation must be conceived as commensurate with Divine intelligence and that would not normally include things that could be delegated to subordinate beings. The precise nature of the ingress and egress of the Forms in relation to the material world will no doubt always be obscure to those who live in this world, quite apart from the manner in which the material world is under Divine direction, but that is not an objection to arguments which imply that this ingress and egress does in fact happen. Neither does this obscurity detract from the complementarism which has been inferred between the theistic creation doctrine and the Platonic account of its means. Besides this conception of the working-out of creation, the account given here makes it possible to say what time really is, provided the metaphysics involved is accepted as reflecting the constitution of the real, and not merely as a way of discussing its appearances. No other type of philosophy leads so directly to the resolution of this ancient problem, and it does so in a way which does not require that one should first solve the paradoxes to which time gives rise. Nevertheless, such problems must be confronted, as the technical aspect of time becomes more relevant where it is necessary to explain the changes that take place in the course of a cycle. Problems of this kind are the subject of the next chapter, which will prepare the ground for a numerical treatment of the subject.

15

TEMPORAL CURVATURE & CONTRACTION

A MODERN ANALYSIS OF TIME

The account of the whole time series as the issue of a reductive sequence which divides being and reality into ever-smaller quantities implies that all kinds of entities must displace and replace one another the more frequently in proportion to the degree to which reality is reduced to smaller quantities. But beyond the aspect of displacement of one thing by another, or of the displacement of one state of a given being by another state, this is still too general to help us understand the mechanism by which time is concretely experienced. This is a matter of analysis which has received much attention in modern philosophy. When numbers and calculations have to be applied to time, the detailed dynamics of the temporal flux are of special importance. The cyclic form of time is, among other things, the condition upon which time can be quantifiable, as in the case of the cycles of hours, days and months. Time's observable workings and its cyclic principle can be connected by a theory of time which was put forward by J. M. E. McTaggart.[1]

This takes the form of an analysis of time into two distinct series which run in parallel, these being referred to as the *A* series and the *B* series. The *A* series answers to the common sense perception for which temporal events function in the three compartments of past, present, and future. McTaggart draws attention to the contradiction which appears in this conception owing to the fact that membership

1. *The Nature of Existence*, chap. 33.

of any one of these three categories is always exclusive of the other two, that is, things in the past or in the future can never be present, and vice-versa, while at the same time every member of these three categories constantly transforms itself into a member of the other two. Thus everything in the past was once future, and then present; everything present was future and will be past; and everything future will be present and then past. This aspect of time was made the basis of arguments to prove that it is unreal, though without that implying the unreality of the temporal world, since it was believed that time could be sufficiently abstracted from its contents for this purpose. This contrasts with the Platonic cosmology which does not allow such a separation, and so assigns time and temporal things to an inferior degree of reality without having to make them unreal. Such a conception avoids the complication that the temporality declared unreal still goes on existing, and has to be given some kind of connection with the real if it is to be explained.

Everything in the A series, and not merely the present, is however in constant flux, because the passage of time means that everything in the past is moving ever more deeply in to the past, while everything in the future is moving ever nearer the present. The contents of past and present are thus in constant change by virtue of their changing relationships to the present, and the A series cannot, of itself, determine what is to occupy a place in past, present or future. In other words, it depends on a standpoint *outside itself* whence a given event is seen to fall into one of the three categories. This contrasts with the B series which is essentially static by nature. It comprises all the events and contents of time in a series where every member is fixed in the relations of being 'earlier than' one thing and 'later than' another one. Thus Queen Victoria is always later than George IV and always earlier than Edward VII, while Gothic architecture is always later than Romanesque and earlier than the Classical revival.

However, the relations 'earlier than' and 'later than' clearly derive from the temporal relations of the A series, whence its derivative position, despite its fixity or immunity from change. Every part of the B series must occupy a position in the A series, ranging through future, present and past, so that the time we experience consists in the movement of these two series in relation to one another. In this way, the content of the *B* series would be manifest in the present of the *A* series like a train passing a window. But which one is still, and which one moves? Common sense would see the *B* series as still, and the *A* series moving over it from past through the present into the future, though it could be the opposite way round, with the B series moving the other way, from the future through the present and into the past. McTaggart observes this ambiguity, but does not draw the consequences from it which it is capable of yielding.

A and *B* Series and Cyclic Order

The first and most general point to emerge from the above relative motion is that time, to give the experience of change, must form a combination of static and dynamic elements. A time series which consisted of pure dynamism could not supply any kind of experience because every element in it would have become something else before it could be known. On the other hand, a purely static time would not be temporal at all. Only a mingling of the changing with the unchanging can constitute time, and this is consistent with the idea of time as a lower degree of reality and not an unreality. The static and the dynamic elements may be related by a 'forward' or a 'backward' movement between past and future, but this is by no means an exclusive choice. If both were equally real it would have important consequences for the nature of time. A two-way flow through the present would in fact break down the distinction between past and future which can appear all but invincible.

To begin again from the common sense position, the immediate past issues in the present, through which the future is brought into being. From this point of view, one can see the future being formed from what is past. However, it remains equally true that everything in the past was once in the future, and this means that the contents of the past which we see to be the generator of the future have all come to it out of that very future, by virtue of an equal and opposite flow toward the past. On this basis, the present time is the scene of two equal and opposite flows which build up the future out of the past and build up the past out of the future. The present could thus be compared to a window through which one observes two columns of troops marching past each other in opposite directions. The relevance of this to cyclic time could not be more direct. Given this relation between past and future, the recurrence of the past in some form or other is inevitable inasmuch as there is a preponderance of persons, objects, and events which have to exist in a similar way in both past and future, owing to the constant interchange between them. Such is the basis of the repetitive aspect of time which is known to Buddhists as the 'wheel of *Samsara*'.

If every transition from past to future and vice-versa involved only a new combination of pre-existing elements which belonged to past and future equally, the balance would be tilted too far in the direction of pure repetition despite the possibilities of new proportions and combinations. Natural processes are not the only ones involved in this, since there is always the question of new content entering the temporal flow from outside its own course, both by creation and human ingenuity. However, it is possible that the above conception of temporal flow could still give rise to identical recurrences if the A and B series were both of finite length and returned upon themselves. To return to the above comparison, if the two columns of troops were both arranged in circles, one inside the other, the individuals seen through the window to be passing one another will inevitably recur, and so similarly with time, if its extent was finite in this manner. Given that time is a two-way flow, therefore, it must be of indefinite length if the possibility of identical recurrence is to be ruled out.

An absolute beginning of time would imply that time could start from a point at which the past contained nothing, which must be impossible if the essence of its flow is twofold. If such a beginning were to be made to occur, the contents of a past time would have to be specially created for it, in accordance with what has been said before about mature creation. This, however, seems to mean only that there cannot be an absolute beginning of time at its own level. If a general pattern of repetition is just as inevitable as the continuation of change, a starting-point for it, if there was one, would have to be arbitrary. The comparison with two counter-moving circles is still relevant in this connection, but the question is, how to combine it with the other image of two indefinite series passing one another? One way of doing this is to substitute for the circles two spirals of similar radius, traveling as it were around the walls of cylinders, one closely inside the other, like two springs. As these rotate on their common axis in contrary directions, nearly in contact, one can observe a crossing-over point between them which travels over each turn of the spirals. The completion of each turn provides the element of repetition, while the endless length of the spirals causes continual new variations.

CYCLIC FORM AND COSMIC CHANGE

This conception of past and future adds to what has been argued earlier for the cyclic order, where it is the basis of calculation in any field, whether it be that of sunspots, ice ages, the courses of the fixed stars, or human activities in the rise and fall of stock markets and levels of trade in different goods. There is no need to make an exception of the time-scale of universal history in this regard. The truth of cyclic time can be tested by calculation of the lengths of universal eras, and even by the matching of some historical periods with periods defined by cyclic laws. Such calculations can enable us to estimate our own position in the universal era from its beginning to the present and from the present to its end. For this purpose we shall have to look further at the mathematical aspect of this subject, and explore it by means of the analogy between spatial and temporal structures.

The comparison already made between spatial and temporal cycles is still too limited inasmuch as the successive turns of the spirals are conceived as being of constant radius. While the theory is not dependent on its geometrical expressions, the latter are of value because spatial relations are more open to the imagination, and without them, many things said about cycles of time may seem not to be part of a coherent system.

The development of a world cycle undoubtedly involves a greater range of changes than can be accounted for by the periodic repetitions implied by the two spirals with cylindrical symmetry. One reason why a more complicated spiral model is required lies in the property of finite time already referred to, namely, that the finite degrees of being it allows to its contents vary widely. A progressive general reduction of these degrees of being in the course of a cycle, giving rise to more rapid change and greater instability in all things, could best be represented by continual increase in the radius of the curve. Thus each successive turn of the crossing-point of the two spirals would encompass a larger circuit, and therefore a greater number of successive existents. Being of larger radius, its curvature would decrease at the same time and this would represent a decline in the qualitative differences between its successive states. (This is assuming that the two spirals rotate on their axes at a constant rate.) In this case, the two spirals would no longer trace paths around the walls of cylinders, but rather about the walls of cones, one inside the other. With the radius constantly changing in this way, the two spirals will pass one another slowly where their radii are small, and more rapidly the larger they get. When the spirals have wound outward to a maximum, as if at the base of a cone, they will start to contract again down to a minimum answering to the apex of the next cone, and then outward to the base of the next one, and so on.

Successive moments of time are separated from one another in two ways, one of which is a qualitative change which makes each one unique in some respect, and the other lies in the way in which each present moment lies outside past and future. These two aspects of time are represented by two properties of the spiral. Each point on the spirals is like a position on a curving path which is fenced on either side so that there is no view before or behind. At the same time, the radius of curvature changes as a point travels along it, and this corresponds to the change in the prevailing quality of the successive parts of time. If time really was the rectilinear process it is usually taken to be, there would be no barriers to obscure one's knowledge of the past. There would be an intercommunication between different times which would contradict the essential nature of time, which is to distribute being and reality only in very small and isolated quantities; this would be to confuse it with eternity.

As the change in the radius of curvature of the spiral answers to a steady change in the qualitative composition of time, it follows that as each moment affords a representation of all other times from its own point of view, the quality of that moment will be imposed on all other times for the experience which resides in that moment. From the present period, all other periods assume the aspect which is imparted to them by the temporal quality of this present time, as though seen through a colored glass. Each age has its human point of view, but this point of view is founded on cosmic conditions. By this means, man's perception of his past is controlled in a manner more fundamental than that achieved by fashion and prejudice. In this respect, each part of time could be said to contain all others (within the lifetime of a civilization, at least) in a way which is comparable to the way in which each consciousness contains a representation of the world from its own point of view.

In the early stages of a cycle, the rate at which time elapses is at a minimum, reflecting its proximity to the next-higher reality, *aevum*. This is represented in the 'clock spring' spiral by the relatively short lengths of the curve which are traversed in one revolution when one starts near its center. Relevant to this early stage are the superhuman ages attributed to the early Patriarchs in the Book of Genesis, and the shortening of human life during the *Kali-Yuga* referred to in the *Bhagavata Purana*. It is probably in connection with the latter text that Guénon states in *The Reign of Quantity* that human life is now shorter than it has ever been in this world-cycle, this being not in relation to the other natural cycles, but in relation to absolute duration. This contradicts the modern perception that human life is now longer than ever, because this greater length of life, which is measured in time units such as years, is purely relative to the duration of other phenomena. From the principle that the cyclic process involves an ontological contraction, the amount of duration comprised in a year, or in one revolution of the earth about the sun, will grow progressively less, though in a way which is not directly detectable, since all other phenomena are affected similarly.

The property of the spiral mode of change implies that the passage of time must accelerate in proportion as the end of the cycle is approached. However, this cannot cause perceptible accelerations in the natural order, for all its impact on human life. This amounts to a much more universal relativity of time than that which results from the velocity of the observer, according to the Theory of Relativity.

But the idea of universal contraction may seem to give rise to the scientific objection that, if duration really was contracting in this way, the earth and the other planets would be having to travel ever faster in their orbits around the sun, in order to cover the same distance in less time. This, if it happened, would cause their orbits to lose their approximately circular shape, and become ever more elliptical until they became like the orbits of comets. This, however, would be a mistaken inference because it rests on the assumption that the planets would be traveling faster *subject to a time-flow which was the same for all times.* No such thing is envisaged, of course, because that would contradict the basic hypothesis that the rate of time-flow is not constant.

Nevertheless, the contraction of duration is a major human issue, even though it cannot be studied by physical methods. While everyone is subject to it, the choice remains of either counteracting it or of forming part of it. Such a possibility depends on a radical division between the human state and the natural order, already referred to in connection with the microcosm. This idea excludes the common sense belief that the real world is solely a physical system in which persons are as so many passive components, along with plants, animals and physical objects.

While mankind has a world in common, each person's perceived world is a unique personal reconstruction of that world, characterized by their scale of values and priorities. Thus the real world includes innumerable inner worlds. We need some understanding of this idea in order to understand the traditional idea of time. Because each person's world is represented by an outgoing act of an inner state of being, there are two directions in which consciousness can be deployed by preference. The will holds the balance between two realms, those of physical process and of the unchanging, i.e., God and metaphysical reality. It is free to devote the best part of its energies to the one or the other. On the one hand, this means that one can identify the self either with the represented realities or with a reality which is present at first-hand, that is, without mediation.

On the other hand, the self may become identified with the external, that is, with the products of its world-representation, in which case its mode of being becomes almost wholly temporal. The latter choice means that the self becomes part of the flux of phenomena, not in a neutral way, but as a motor principle which adds its force to the temporal condition. Temporality is humanly generated. Such is the basis of the draining away of the self-aware level of mind, the only one which is specifically human.

While this self-aware or intellective consciousness needs time to develop, like anything else, it depends on the content of duration in a way that the external faculties do not. For example, a loss of duration in the time in which one can walk a given distance takes nothing from the nature of the action, because, like all physical action, it is made up of a series of discrete elements which can be more or less compressed or expanded without essential loss.[2] Our physical and practical activities, being based on the natural order, can for this reason be accelerated in the same manner as nature as a whole. However, the truth-seeking activities of the mind are not capable of any such acceleration. This is because the grasp of truth depends on a causality which is of the mental, not the physical order. Any intrusion of the latter would invalidate it. In Scholastic terms, the soul's independent being in relation to the body and nature means that it has an *operatio absoluta* which is exercised temporally, but not subject to natural forces. Thus the contraction of duration allows ever less scope for the maturation of the intellect, while there is no detriment to the natural life. In this way, the passage of time increasingly empties human life of spiritual content.

The modern prolongation of human life in comparison with the lives of other creatures or in relation to the cycles of nature need not

---

2. This can be proved by means of geometry, where radii are drawn across two concentric circles which represent space, where any points A_1, A_2, A_n, on the larger circle can be chosen and joined to the center C. These radii cut the smaller circle at points B_1, B_2, B_n. No matter how many such points on the larger circle are joined to the center in this way, we never find one for which there is no corresponding point 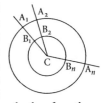 on the smaller circle. However much larger the outer circle is made, therefore, there will be no point on it for which there is no corresponding point on the inner circle. Even if the inner circle is reduced until it approaches the central point C, this equality remains, showing that the center contains *in potentia* all the points on the circles around it; and that spatial figures (and by implication bodies) are expansions of the same origin.

mean very much, therefore. While the addition of years must make some difference, this will be more than offset by the reduction in the absolute duration they contain. An increase in the relative chronological length of human life is a compensating factor which helps to prevent its absolute reduction from being a human disaster. The great ages attributed by the traditions to our remote ancestors would thus be firstly a symbol of the superior temporal duration in which they lived, while at the same time this would also reflect the greatness of their being in the supernatural order.

CONTRACTION AND INTERNAL INFINITY

The ancient chronologies ascribe shorter periods of years to the latter parts of the world-cycle, such as where the *Kali-Yuga* amounts to only one-tenth of the complete cycle. This outward and visible reduction corresponds to an inner reduction in the 'time value' or duration in these years, in which case the Iron Age or *Kali-Yuga* would be the shortest age both extensively and intensively. The multiplication of time-units without corresponding temporal content suggests a natural phenomenon resembling inflation in the sphere of economics. If the content of time-units became vanishingly small at the end of the cycle, the effect could be to make the end theoretically unattainable, since an infinite number of them might be required actually to reach the limit.

This property of diminishing time can be illustrated by means of a mathematical model in which a certain enclosed space allows objects inside it to have their full size only at its center. As they move toward its periphery their dimensions contract according to a mathematical function of their distance from it, so that the units of length would reduce to zero if the boundary was actually reached. However, the boundary never can be reached in this system, because the successive steps taken toward it diminish until they become infinitesimal before it is reached, and therefore an infinite number of them would in fact be needed. An observer in such a world would be convinced he was in a realm of infinite space, although it would be obviously finite to any observer outside it. The properties of worlds where space is relative can also be applied to the time of a cosmic cycle, showing how an apparent temporal infinity could result from a law of contraction if it went to an extreme degree. Such a pattern of development would make each cycle more completely a world in itself than if it were merely a measured segment of uniform time. Its finite nature would be balanced by an internal infinity by which it is symbolically the total cosmos.

The variation in the amount of duration contained in the cycle's measures of time has its effect on our attempts to rediscover and reconstruct the past, and to establish dates in remote ages. Inevitably the time-measures used to fix such dates will be those of the present era, with the result that very large numbers will often be involved, where periods of the geological and cosmological order are involved. There is in effect a 'chronological hyper-inflation' in modern attempts to explore the origins of the present world. Besides the telescoping of time's measures, another aspect of the cycle is that of a continual and accelerating removal away from the cyclic origin where there was the greatest fullness of being. This change is represented by the ever-lengthening radius at which a point traversing a spiral is removed from the center. This change is felt in an increasing loss of continuity between past and present and a loss of participation in the truth of the original state, even as a race memory. The increase in the radius of curvature in the outer part of the spiral (undergoing a reduction in curvature), represents the loss of qualitative distinction between the different parts of the world as well as between its successive states. In the limit, where its outer curve approximates to a straight line, it would reconnect with its eternal origin, from a state which was the polar opposite of the beginning of the cycle.

The irreversibility of time is represented in the same model by the way in which each new increment along the curve is at a slightly longer radius than the last. The curvature or constant change in direction which separates the points on the spiral illustrates the way in which moments are separated from one another which would not be possible if the points were arranged in a straight line. The different degrees of expansion of the spiral also reflect the manifestation of the spatial world itself, starting from a center in which all its realities are present and concentrated in a point. Creation has an aspect of ejection and dispersion and progressive dilution, which runs its course till it ultimately rejoins its supernatural cause.

The inherent relativity of time, as it appears in the cyclic concept, is both natural and traditional, since the modern rectilinear view of time was only created to provide the simplest conditions for calculations which were applied to the solution of technical problems. In earlier civilizations, which depended on the motion of the sun for their practical measures of time, it appeared obvious that time did not pass uniformly. The varying lengths of shadows cast by sundials and obelisks showed the constantly-varying speeds at which the tips of the shadows moved, these being most rapid in the early morning and late afternoon, and slowest around midday. Thus the hours around midday were taken to be the longest, and for similar reasons it was thought that all the hours were proportionately shorter in winter, when the sun's course was lower and shadows were therefore longer and so faster-moving. Even when water clocks were invented, the Egyptians ensured that they worked at varying speeds, or to varying measures, to match the times of the day and of the seasons as reckoned by the sun.

IF TIME CEASED TO PASS

The study of temporal being by means of metaphysics and mathematics is objective inasmuch as these disciplines derive from a reality which is not in time at all. Their independence of natural conditions makes them true manifestations of the non-temporal principle in human consciousness which has already been indicated as the means whereby we can discriminate between the past, present, and future contents of the temporal *A* series. Does this mean we could also become conscious of a cessation of time, in a way which was not the same as a cessation of existence? The fact that the intellect is superior to time implies that our own true being may be independent even of this. At the end of a world-cycle there must be a cessation of time, if only as a transition to the next time series. Whether it be the end of a world or the end of an individual life, the question remains: does our being depend on the continuation of time? Past, present, and future have each a meaning only in relation to the other two; take away one, and the other two have either no meaning or a very different one. Consequently, if there were a 'last moment' there would no longer be a future, or in other words, the future would cease to be future, and for the same reason *the past would cease to be past* at the same moment. The last present moment would merge with what had been the past, which would then form a supra-temporal present in which everything dispersed by the passage of time would be reintegrated. It is only because of the forward impetus of time that past times are lost to us, and if this condition ceases, either because of the ending of a particular time series or because of the mystical attainment of a state of being outside it, the conclusion will be a fullness of being.

16

THE STRUCTURE
OF CYCLES

NUMERICAL CLUES FROM ANTIQUITY

The mathematical model used in the last chapter to illustrate cyclic properties is applicable only to the arguments to show that time as a whole is cyclic, in a way which remains confined to generalities. But this conception must be pursued into particulars if it is to connect with what is known about history. For this purpose it will be necessary to examine the structure of actual time-cycles as they have been understood in the past, though without any attempt to attach historical dates to them at this stage. Direct connections with history, although important, are often unsatisfactory because history always shows a greater complexity than can be accounted for in theory. Nevertheless, this still does not mean that the broad outline of history cannot be grasped theoretically, as I shall try to show later.

The most important quantity to be ascertained is the length of the cycle which contains the era of recorded history, a quantity which has frequently been given in chronologies, but nearly always by means of symbolical numbers. A study of such chronological periods shows them to be made up of shorter cycles, and these in turn are made up of yet shorter ones. This property alone makes it very difficult to determine whether the beginning of a given cycle really coincides with the origin of the human race, or whether that origin only goes back to the beginning of one of the lesser cycles of which it is composed. The subordinate cycle recapitulates within its own compass many of the features of the greater cycle, providing more grounds for confusion. To illustrate this, it may be useful to examine the symbolic quantity of 432,000 years, which has an important place in chronology because of the way in which it recurs in widely differing cultures apparently unconnected in time or place, and because of its astronomical connections.

A UNIVERSAL NUMBER

The writings of the Babylonian historian Berossos contain an account of ten kings who reigned in succession from 'the descent of kingship from the courts of heaven,' to the great Flood, a period corresponding to the biblical period from Adam to Noah, the age of the Patriarchs. He gives the length of each reign, which in each case is a period far in excess of any human lifetime measured in years, and their grand total comes to exactly 432,000 years. The figures seem to have a symbolic meaning, as also is the case with other ancient texts from Sumeria which give total periods of 241,200 and 456,000 years for these same antediluvian kings. These numbers are related to 432,000, moreover, inasmuch as all three are multiples of 1,200, the factors being 360, 201, and 380 respectively. (A period of 12,000 years also divides exactly into two of the above three numbers, and this period was reckoned to be a 'divine year' in some traditions, including that of India.) There is no apparent relation between these numbers and those given in the Book of Genesis for the same period, but I shall examine the meaning of this divergence in the next chapter.

When we turn to another tradition as different as possible from those of the Near East, that of the Icelandic *Eddas*, there appears an apocalyptic verse which is translated as follows:

Five hundred doors and forty there are,
I ween, in Valhall's walls;
Eight hundred fighters through each door fare,
When to war with the Wolf they go.[1]

---

1. Joseph Campbell, *The Masks of God, Oriental Mythology*, chap. 3.

The 'war with the Wolf' is another expression for the last battle, the *Ragnarök*, when the powers of darkness overwhelm the gods. The number of combatants who are said to emerge here is thus 540 x 800 = 432,000. Appearing as it does in connection with the end of a world, this number will have a relation to its total duration, and such a recurrence is too much for coincidence. This number also appears in ancient tradition in higher multiples, including 4,320,000, and this number has a particular astronomical significance.

It has hardly been noticed that this number could have been found from an astronomy which required only naked-eye observation of the planets and records of them extending over one or two centuries. The planetary bodies, including the moon, have each at least one cyclic period after which they return to the same place in the zodiac on the same date as at the beginning of the cycle. For the moon, this is 19 years, the period of the Metonic Cycle. For Mercury and Mars, by a strange coincidence, it is 79 years in either case; while for Venus it is 8 years. For Jupiter it is taken to be 12 years, though this is less exact, being rounded up from 11.86 years, and for Saturn it is 30 years, this being rounded up from 29.45 years, and so also less exact.

Now with these quantities it is possible to define a universal era by means of the time it takes for all six of these bodies to return to the same positions in the sky they had at the beginning of the era. One way of calculating this period would be simply to multiply all these numbers together, without attempting to take out common factors. The resulting figure would be exactly divisible by each separate planetary cycle and therefore common to all six bodies. Thus the time for the moon, Mercury, and Mars to return to their same relative positions would be 19 x 79 = 1,501 years, which for the present purpose will be rounded to 1,500 years. Likewise, the time for the moon, Mercury, Mars, and Venus to return to the same places would be 1500 x 8 = 12,000 years. For these four bodies and Jupiter so to return, it would be 12,000 x 12 = 144,000 years; and for these five together with Saturn, it will be 144,000 x 30 = 4,320,000 years.

Thus with slightly idealized and unsimplified factors, this fundamental cosmological quantity of 432,000 has a direct relation to the phenomena of the Solar System. It constitutes a measurement for what the ancients called the 'mundane apocatastasis', some estimates for which went into many millions of years. It can be seen that the separate factors of 12 and 30 for Jupiter and Saturn did not have to be included if the shortest period of recurrence was all that was required, since 12,000 (the period for the moon, Mercury, Mars, and Venus) is exactly divisible by either 12 or 30. This gives an additional reason for the importance of the 12,000-year period in ancient chronology, while underlining the symbolical nature of the 432,000 years. This is by no means the only astronomical explanation of it, as will be shown later.

Returning to the subject of apocalyptic images which contain numbers relevant to the cosmic periods, these appear in the New Testament in its account of the New Jerusalem, of which each side measures 12,000 furlongs, the height being also 12,000 furlongs.[2] The area of each of the sides would thus be 144 million square furlongs, and its volume would be 12^3 or 1,728 million cubic furlongs (1,728 is also equal to 4 x 432). Elsewhere in the same text a similar number system arises where it is stated that 'there were sealed an hundred and forty and four thousand of all the tribes of Israel,'[3] that is, 12,000 from each of the twelve tribes. (The sacred significance of twelve in Jewish tradition is exoterically owing to there being twelve tribes of Israel.) There are twelve gates in the walls of the New Jerusalem, one for each of the twelve tribes, each numbering 12,000, again expressing the number 144,000. The connection between this number and the number in the *Edda* is a factor of three, as 144,000 x 3 = 432,000, and a second factor of three makes another of its astronomical connections, as will be shown.

To explain the significance of numbers made up of products of 12 and 1,000, it should be realized that 1,000 symbolizes totality since it is the cube of 10, and therefore a product of length, breadth, and height, and therefore in a sense the whole of space and the whole of creation. Twelve, on the other hand, symbolizes fullness in a more qualitative manner, being a product of three and four, where these numbers stand for the Forms and the material cosmos respectively.

---

2. Rev. 21:16.
3. Ibid., 7:4–8.

This aspect of twelve is acknowledged in innumerable groupings of twelve in both the Bible and in folklore.

If the factor of three is applied once more to this number system, i.e., 432,000 x 3 = 1,296,000, the result is 100 times 12,960, which is a very close approximation to a period in years which is of importance in astronomy as the semi-period of the precession of the equinoxes. This period is the time taken for the sun's positions at the Spring and Autumn equinoxes to retreat halfway round the zodiac, and so change places. Thus, if the sun was at 0 degrees Aries at the spring equinox (as it was about two thousand years ago), and at 0 degrees Virgo at the autumn equinox, it would take nearly 12,960 years for these positions to move until the sun was at 0 degrees. Virgo at the spring equinox and at 0 degrees Aries at the autumn equinox. This relative shift between the sun's circuit and the fixed stars is very slow, therefore, about one degree in seventy-two years.

However, this is the cosmic movement whose length is related to those of 432,000 and 144,000 years by simple factors. It also reappears in the so-called 'Nuptial Number' in Plato's *Republic*, where it defines a cosmic period in accordance with which human affairs such as marriages should be arranged.[4] In this discussion of number, the favorable times, which are presumably proportioned down to the measures of human lifetimes, are said to be governed by the product of 3, 4, and 5, raised to the fourth power. These three numbers are those of the first Pythagorean triangle, and their product is sixty: 3 x 4 x 5 = 60; 60^2 = 3,600, and the square of this, $(3,600)^2$ = 12,960,000. Two ways of reaching this result are given, one of which involves squares, i.e., 36^2 x 100^2, and the other involves a product of unequal quantities, i.e., 27 x 48 x 100^2, from a different arrangement of the 3, 4, and 5.

A very similar connection between the precessional period and the 432,000-year period is to be found from the sexagesimal arithmetic of Babylonian astronomy, in which the longest period, the Great *Saros*, was equal to 60 x 60 x 60 = 216,000 years, and where two of these periods add up to 432,000 years. It is remarkable that the ancient chronologies should be linked so closely to a cosmic cycle which is supposed not to have been measured accurately until

4. *Rep.* VIII, 546.

modern times, as Joseph Campbell has pointed out.[5] Either there were sources of scientific knowledge in antiquity which are now unknown, or the arithmetic based on powers of sixty has given rise to an extraordinary coincidence.

THE PERIOD FOR THE *KALI-YUGA*

Another source for this universal quantity is to be found in the chronology of ancient India, which gives a period of 4,320,000 years as that of a world-cycle, usually called a *Manvantara* or 'era of *Manu*,' who was India's original lawgiver. (Guénon argues that he may also be the lawgiver of the Romans, since the Roman *Numa* is simply Manu with the syllables transposed. The name *Minos* in Greek tradition seems to be of the same origin.)

This universal era is said to be divided into four lesser cycles or *Yugas*, corresponding to the ages of Gold, Silver, Bronze, and Iron, as described in chapters 5 and 7. However, the Indian chronology assigns symbolic periods of time to each of the four *Yugas*, which are listed in order as follows:

Krita-Yuga	1,728,000 years =	4 x 432,000 years
Tretā-Yuga	1,296,000 years =	3 x 432,000 years
Dvāpara-Yuga	864,000 years =	2 x 432,000 years
Kali-Yuga	432,000 years =	1 x 432,000 years
	4,320,000 years	

The shortest of the four, the *Kali-Yuga*, is thus one-tenth the length of the total cycle. The order of these cycles, it should be noted, follows that of the Pythagorean *Tetraktys* in reverse: $4 + 3 + 2 + 1 = 10$. This numerical symbol shows how the first four numbers are in a sense the equivalent of all numbers, as they produce the decad.

If these numbers are taken literally, the present era of Manu would extend far beyond the longest time assignable to recorded history, and this has resulted in this subject's confinement to the realms of myth. But this attitude results from the loss of means of

5. Joseph Campbell, *The Masks of God, Oriental Mythology*, chap. 3, III 'Mythic Time'.

estimating the historical length of the present world, since the problem is precisely that of discovering what practical time values are contained in the symbolic periods. We are at least given an exact date for the beginning of the *Kali-Yuga*, i.e., February 16, 3102 BC, and it is obvious from the perspective of the present time that this cycle must have only just begun if the above numbers had to be taken literally; there would still be some 427,000 years more before its end. One reason for not taking such numbers literally is that mathematicians in antiquity preferred the use of very large numbers to the introduction of decimal points or fractions. By making the unit quantities small enough, exactness could be obtained with whole numbers.

Concerning the date, 3102 BC, it is a date which lies at the furthest limit of historical knowledge. Even the *Pyramid Texts* are dated only a little earlier than this time. The latter are an exception to the lack of intellectual contact with civilizations dating from before the present 'iron age'. The general lack of evidence for still earlier civilizations is consistent with the discontinuities between cycles which are implied by the theory, although it is dangerous to support any theory on a mere absence of evidence. In fact this is not necessary because there are always at least vestiges of the long-lost ages. Both human remains and artifacts of an antiquity extending over many millions of years have been found, and however isolated and scattered they are, it should be clearly understood that just one such item of geological antiquity would be enough to explode the entire edifice of evolutionary theories as to man's so-called 'primitive origins'. One human bone or metal artifact dating from the Carboniferous era is all it would take, and in reality there are more than one. J. Davidson gives an account of a number of such finds which have been collected and described by geologists.[6]

The barriers between world-ages are thus by no means absolute, even though they rule out any spiritual or cultural transmission

---

6. John Davidson, *Natural Creation or Natural Selection?*, chaps. 9 and 10. According to this author, 'A human skull, completely mineralized to iron and manganese oxides and hydrates was found in a 100 million year old coal bed near Freiberg [East Germany] and described in detail by Karsten, in 1842.' Fossilized shoe prints of a similar period have also been described.

from one to another. They are formidable enough, even where they divide only secondary cycles like the *Tretā-Yuga* and the *Dvāpara-Yuga*, and this suggests the possibility that there may be more such barriers even during such cycles as these. This would be the case if they were made up of yet smaller cycles, for example if the *Kali-Yuga* itself went through four cycles of its own. That this should be so would follow from what was argued earlier in chapter 3. The shortest cycles of time in ordinary experience, like those of day and night, would truthfully reveal the nature of temporal change as it extends to even the longest periods. There would in this case be no reason why there should not be a continuous range of cycles from the longest, like the *Manvantara*, down to the shortest, like a year or a day. This would mean that the longest cycle would be made up of a very large number of cycles, and the effect of this would be a superficial disorder similar to that of a large number of musical instruments playing together. The note played by each instrument will make a regular pulsation, but the sum of all these regularities will be highly irregular, if a profile of the sound waves is constructed. Similarly to this, the superimposition of numerous time-cycles will account for much of the apparent disorder of history.

FURTHER NUMERICAL RELATIONSHIPS

The numbers given for the four *Yugas* give a hint of this possibility of further subdivision in the number of zeros they contain. By the repeated division by ten which they allow, we can reduce the four *Yugas* to further sets of lower sub-cycles. Thus if the *Krita-Yuga* or Golden Age is also divided in the same ratios of 4 : 3 : 2 : 1, the last and shortest of them will likewise be one-tenth of the whole:

Golden age of golden age: 691,200 years = 4 x 172,800
Silver age of golden age: 518,400 years = 3 x 172,800
Bronze age of golden age: 345,600 years = 2 x 172,800
Iron age of golden age: 172,800 years = 1 x 172,800
                          1,728,000 years (total for *Krita-Yuga*)

Similarly, further divisions of the cycle by 100 and then by 1,000 will yield yet smaller cycles, still with the same ratios as those of the first ones. This is how it could be said that the *Krita-Yuga* or Golden Age has its own golden age, and then its own silver, bronze, and iron ages. Likewise the three other *Yugas* will have their own golden, silver, bronze, and iron ages, and in this way all the permutations will be worked out until the final limit is reached with the iron age of the Iron Age. Such a process of recapitulation inherent in time would be a natural cause of confusions between remote periods and later ones in which they re-emerge on a different scale. There may also be confusions between critical events which may be the same in form while differing widely in their range of effects, as with various major inundations which have been taken for the biblical Flood. Such confusions could not be resolved until the durations of the cycles divided by such events were ascertained.

The cyclic recapitulation as described so far can be expressed much more economically by means of numbers. Taking the *Manvantara* as the primary cycle, one may represent the secondary cycles, i.e. the Golden, Silver, Bronze and Iron Ages by 4, 3, 2, 1. The same numbers will then also be used to denote the next subordinate cycles with the same qualities, which we may call the tertiary cycles. Thus the Silver Age of the Golden Age would be denoted by $4 + 3$, and the Iron Age of the Bronze Age would be denoted by $2 + 1$. The numbers 4 to 1 will be added in turn to the numbers 4 down to 1. By this means, sixteen tertiary cycles can be expressed as follows:

Golden Age	$4 + 4$,	$4 + 3$,	$4 + 2$,	$4 + 1$
Silver Age	$3 + 4$,	$3 + 3$,	$3 + 2$,	$3 + 1$
Bronze Age	$2 + 4$,	$2 + 3$,	$2 + 2$,	$2 + 1$
Iron Age	$1 + 4$,	$1 + 3$,	$1 + 2$,	$1 + 1$

Each cycle is represented here as a composite of secondary and tertiary cycles by a sum of two numbers which stand for the respective qualities of the parts in question and fix their place in the whole order. The highest sum, 8, is found only in the first, and the lowest, 2, only in the last, whereas all the others are repeated once, twice, or three times, as the following summary shows:

Golden Age	Silver Age	Bronze Age	Iron Age
8, 7, 6, 5	7, 6, 5, 4	6, 5, 4, 3	5, 4, 3, 2

This sequence with its partial reversals shows a vital aspect of the cyclic rise-and-fall pattern, which can be summed up in a law that *the first and highest state of a lower sub-cycle always comprises a return to a higher state than that of the lower parts of the next-higher sub-cycle before it.* It is essentially owing to this naturally self-reversing property of time that belief in progress finds confirmatory evidence, as every advance into a lower range of possibilities will be compensated by the realization of values in it which went unrealized before. Such changes deflect attention from what has been lost in order to make these new relative goods possible, so that lost values fall into oblivion while things gained have immediate evidence. Different ages can thus vindicate their own value in relation to others thanks to the re-ascending movement of time, though this is always deceptive by absolute standards because the reascending movements are always incomplete, while the descending movement goes further each time.

In the above numerical illustration, the end of the Golden Age is followed by the Silver Age which begins with a tertiary cycle (its own golden age), equivalent to the *second* tertiary cycle of the previous cycle, and it is represented by 7 in either case. The highest and lowest members of the whole set, represented by 8 and 2 respectively, are both unique in the set, whereas the one represented by 5 occurs in all four secondary cycles, showing among other things an equivalence between the lowest part of the highest of the four secondary cycles and the highest part of the lowest secondary cycle. The numbers 6, 4, and 3 are repeated in a similar way, but less frequently. From these facts, there follows another cyclic law to the effect that *when history enters an age which is in a category of its own in relation to the past, it must be the last part of the total cycle.*

The total numbers which denote the tertiary cycles, 8, 7, 6, 5, can be seen to follow another numerical rise-and-fall pattern which has already been observed in connection with degrees of complexity in chapter 3, as the intermediate order of possibilities has the greatest frequency in either case. Again there is a symmetry of extremes and a maximum development at the center. The example worked out above concerns only the tertiary degree of complexity, but there is no reason why it should not be pursued next into quaternary cycles in the same ratios as before, as follows:

4 + 4 + 4,	4 + 4 + 3,	4 + 4 + 2,	4 + 4 + 1,
4 + 3 + 4,	4 + 3 + 3,	4 + 3 + 2,	4 + 3 + 1,
4 + 2 + 4,	4 + 2 + 3,	4 + 2 + 2,	4 + 2 + 1,
4 + 1 + 4,	4 + 1 + 3,	4 + 1 + 2,	4 + 1 + 1,
3 + 4 + 4,	3 + 4 + 3,	3 + 4 + 2,	3 + 4 + 1,
3 + 3 + 4,	3 + 3 + 3,	3 + 3 + 2,	3 + 3 + 1,
...	...	...	...
1 + 1 + 4,	1 + 1 + 3,	1 + 1 + 2,	1 + 1 + 1.

On this basis, each member of the previous sixteen-term se-quence acquires a set of four changes of its own, giving a new set totalling 64 members. A further set, developed in the same way would therefore have four times as many members again, that is, 256. In the above example, the first and last numbers total 12 and 3, and are unique in their set in the same way as 8 and 2 were in the previous one. The first four three-number totals in this set are 12, 11, 10, 9, and the last four are 6, 5, 4, 3. This system again shows an increasing frequency for numbers the closer they are to the average between 12 and 3, similarly to the pattern for the set which ranged from 8 to 2. This method of cyclic division can be pursued as far as required, or until the smallest sub-cycles come down to a length approaching, say, a year.

All that can be done at this stage is to find how the cyclic order can be divided, without attempting to link its divisions to historical dates. However, one application to history is possible, in view of the fact that no other period has had so little continuity with past centuries as the present one. This historically singular character of the past hundred years means it can reasonably be identified with either of the final and unique terms 2 and 3 in the above examples. Here is a possible clue as to the length of the *Kali-Yuga* and consequently of the *Manvantara*, since the essential changes that gave rise to the modern world date from no more than four hundred years ago at most. If a length of three, four, or five centuries could be assigned to the last tertiary cycle or 'iron age of the iron age,' the lengths of all the other cycles could be calculated, as they are all related by proportion. However, that would only be the solution for one system of cycles, which would not rule out other kinds of cycle acting at the same time.

17

CYCLIC PERIODS
IN HISTORY

CONNECTION OF THEORY AND FACT

       The conclusions that have been reached about cyclic processes have the consequence that these processes inform all the eras of history and their changes, regulating them from within as the rules of harmony and counterpoint inform the audible properties of music. This analogy can help clarify the problems inherent in the application of a theory of time to history. Just as it can be argued that one can have music without musical theory, so it could be argued that knowledge of history will not be improved upon by relating it to a system of periodic functions which is not part of it. In either case it can be answered that the theoretical structure must be there, whether or not it is ignored, and that it can in any case only be ignored in a quite external manner. The limitation in this analogy is that music is an activity under human choice and direction, whereas history is an indefinite extent of activities which determine human choice as much as they are determined by it.

An analogy free from this limitation is provided by the realm of biology, which reveals the same kind of duality between the abstract and the concrete. From one point of view, it can be seen that this realm consists of species, genera, classes, orders, and phyla, while from another point of view it could be argued that it really consists only of individual living creatures; that the classifications are wholly products of human mentation. Like history, the realm of living organisms is something which simply exists and is not the expression of any conscious human purpose. There is an empirical sense in which it can be said that in the one case the true reality consists solely of individual historical events and periods, and in the other case it consists solely of individual animals. But if the conceptual counterpart is denied in either of these cases, the result is an inability to understand the relationships among the individual entities and the reasons for the differences and similarities between them. The confinement of knowledge to individuals and particulars is in any case futile in the long run because even knowledge of the particular is only possible because of an underlying knowledge of a universal. Even to know something solely as 'an individual' is dependent on the universal category of Individuality, and for this reason there is something artificial about attempts to make concrete realities independent of ideal ones.

The question of finding connections between the legendary and metaphysical realms and the facts of history is not in principle any different from the discovery of species and genera in nature. In the latter case, this discovery is a possibility by virtue of the inclusion of individual things in universals, however unnecessary it may seem for those whose interest in nature is either that of practical utility or aesthetic delight. If the historical application of the cyclic concept achieves nothing else, it should lead to a deeper understanding of the pitfalls involved in all attempts to work out a date for 'the end of the world'. Doubts regarding the validity of these efforts, as well as the above difficulties in relating the abstract and the concrete, create resistance to theories of history, but this also comes from a fear that such theories would mean a denial of free will. In reality, the study of world-cycles presupposes a free will which is able to adjust to them and counteract their ill-effects. No one can be morally good or bad solely because of the age they live in.

MYTHICAL HISTORY AND THE BIBLE.

A preliminary step in the connection of theory and history can be made in a realm where cyclic laws remain almost unsuspected, namely, that of biblical history. One of the most surprising results of numerological research has been the discovery of the universal cyclic number in the Bible despite a complete lack of *prima facie* evidence for it. It has been shown to enter into the measure for the period of the Patriarchs from Adam to Noah, thanks to the discoveries made by the Assyriologist, Julius Oppert,[1] with the result that there is no unbridgeable gulf between the chronology of the Book of Genesis and that of the ancient cyclic systems. It has already been mentioned how the writings of Berossos give a total period for the antediluvian kings as 432,000 years, this being the biblical period from the Fall to the Flood. From the figures given in Genesis, the period in question evidently totals 1,656 years, this being the total of the ages of each of the Patriarchs at the birth of the sons who succeeded them (not their total lifetimes). According to the Talmud, the Patriarchs were rulers of all mankind, so that the distinction between 'patriarch' and 'king' is only conventional in this context. The names and figures given by Berossos[2] can best be appreciated in conjunction with those given in Genesis chapter 5, as follows:

Berossos		The Bible	
King	Years	Patriarch	Years
Aloros	36,000	Adam	130
Alaparos	10,800	Seth	105
Amelon	46,800	Enoch	90
Ammenon	43,200	Kenan	70
Megaloros	64,800	Mahalel	65
Daonos	36,000	Jared	162
Euedoraches	64,800	Enoch	65
Amempsinos	36,000	Methuselah	187
Opartes	28,800	Lamech	182
Xisuthros	64,800	Noah (until Flood)	600
	432,000		1,656

These two totals, like the numbers they are respectively made up from, would seem to be as unrelated as any figures could be, but Oppert began by showing that they have a common factor of 72: 432,000 = 72 x 6,000 and 1,656 = 72 x 23.

---

1. See Joseph Campbell, *The Masks of God, Oriental Mythology*, chap. 3, III, 'Mythic Time'.
   2. Ibid.

These factors of 6,000 and 23 are then treated as though the Babylonian figure were expressed in days and the biblical figure in years. Both periods are then converted to periods of weeks by dividing the larger figure (6,000) by the number of days in the Babylonian week and by multiplying the smaller figure (23) by the number of whole days in a year. Both periods are then enumerated in the same kind of unit. For the Babylonian period, this means division by five, since the week in question was one of five days, i.e., $6,000 \div 5 = 1,200$ weeks of this kind.

The biblical factor of 23, taken as a period in years and multiplied by 365 gives: $23 \times 365 = 8,395$ days. As this period is between twenty and twenty-four years, there will be five leap-year days to be added. This brings the figure up to 8,400 days precisely, and it derives from figures belonging to Jewish tradition for which the week contained seven days, no doubt as a reflection of the seven days of creation. Thus the period of 8,400 would have to be divided by seven for the same purpose as before: $8,400 \div 7 = 1,200$ (seven-day) weeks, just as there were 1,200 Babylonian weeks.

The original removal of the factor 72 was only to obtain a simpler basis for the demonstration, and it can now be restored to both periods, so as to show that they are both periods of cosmic weeks, i.e., $72 \times 1,200 = 86,400$ cosmic weeks. (N.B., This is also 200×432). If this period is now taken as a period of natural Babylonian five-day weeks, it gives a period in days as follows: $86,400 \times 5 = 432,000$ days. Thus two different traditions, one of which is supposed to have no use for cyclic concepts, can both be seen to reckon sacred history in quantities which depend on numbers beginning with 432 and 864. The implications of this conclusion go beyond pure chronology, since it unites biblical tradition which includes the idea of free will with a cosmic conception which is widely believed to exclude it. This is an indication that the common sense conflict between free will, and a position tied to cosmic rhythms that underlie outward events, will need to be considered more closely.

THE PLATONIC YEAR OR GREAT YEAR

For the present purpose, this recurrence of the number 432 in the Bible underlies the need to find an identifiable historical period to which it could correspond. If such a historical period could be ascertained, the one known date in this system, 3102 BC, would enable us to calculate the other cycles that form part of the system, including the beginning of the *Manvantara*, and the relevance of that for the present era. In the previous chapter, the relation between the 432 number and the precessional period of the equinoxes and the 'nuptial number' in Plato's *Republic.* (1,296 = 3 x 432) was considered. The period of 12,960 years is also said to be the period of a Great or Platonic Year. It is the length of periods referred to in Plato's *Timaeus*[3] as the 'long intervals' at the ends of which the world is devastated alternately by catastrophic changes in the natural order: at the end of the last such period the world was said to be devastated by flood, and it would be devastated by fire at the end of the next.

The importance of this cycle lies in the fact that its length in years is both scientifically determined as the precessional period, and has a numerical value which places it among the symbolic numbers of cyclic arithmetic. It is therefore an essential means of building a bridge between the realms of symbolism and historical fact. In the same text quoted above, it is claimed that the destruction of Atlantis was part of the latest of these devastations, which was by flood. If a realistic date for this event could be established, we should then be able to estimate the time of the next one, and the position of the present century in the course of this 12,960-year period. Plato continues the same account by quoting an Egyptian sage who claimed that the sacred records kept by the institutions of his country spanned a period of eight thousand years. The dialogue refers to the time of Solon, so that the cataclysm must have taken place at least 9000 BC:

The age of our institutions is given in our sacred records as eight thousand years, and the citizens whose laws and finest achievements I will now briefly describe to you therefore lived nine thousand years ago.[4]

3. *Timaeus* 22d.
4. Ibid., 23e.

This means nine thousand years before Plato's time of course, (about 350 BC), in which case it would seem that the Atlantis cataclysm must have happened somewhere between eleven and twelve thousand years ago, possibly a period approaching that of the Platonic Year in length. There is still a margin of uncertainty here, owing to the length of time which must have elapsed before the resumption of the civilization recorded eight thousand years earlier in Egypt. Modern estimates for the date of the disappearance of Atlantis range from 8000 to 11000 BC, which is consistent with a gap of one or two thousand years between this event and the beginning of the eight thousand year history which Solon was told about in the dialogue. It also indicates that the present time is relatively close to the next devastation, the one with which cycles of this kind end and by which they are divided from the succeeding one, since it would thus be between twelve and thirteen thousand years from the last one. This is a period of six 'Platonic months' of 2,160 years each (as 6 x 2,160 = 12,960), this being the time taken for the sun's position at the spring equinox to traverse thirty degrees of a sign of the zodiac. It can easily be seen that the Great *Saros*, or 216,000 years, is one hundred 'Platonic Months', i.e., 60 x 60 x 60.

THE LENGTH OF THE *KALI-YUGA*

Although one cannot be quite sure that the end of the present Platonic Year will coincide with the end of the *Kali-Yuga*, it is at least a precisely-known period by which the four *Yugas* can be measured. Their apparent total period, 4,320,000 years, can be taken to represent a whole number of Great Years or Platonic Years in view of the simple relation between their length and the multiples of 432. Given the starting date for the *Kali-Yuga*, it would be possible to fix the length of this cycle if that of the *Manvantara* was known. The simplest assumption is that the latter, the sum of all four *Yugas*, comes to just one Platonic Year. In this case, the length of the *Kali-Yuga* would have to be only 1,296 years, since it is one-tenth of the whole. But this would mean that it had already ended, as 3102 BC–1,296 = 1806 BC. The impossibility of such a result appears from the fact that historical records go back to 1800 BC and beyond, whereas the end of the *Kali-Yuga* is by definition a cosmic revolution too great to allow any such continuity.

Similarly, if the total period were taken to be two Platonic Years, the length of the *Kali-Yuga* would then be 2 x 1,296 = 2,592 years, whence its end would have been at 3102 BC−2,592 = 510 BC; if, once more, its supposed length were three Platonic Years, it would have ended at 786 AD, as 3 x 1,296 = 3,888, and 3888 AD−3,102 = 786 AD. These answers are useless for the same reasons as before, but a new range of possibilities opens up if the main period is taken to be four or more Platonic Years in length. If the required number were four, the *Kali-Yuga* would be of 4 x 1,296 = 5,184 years, so that its end would be at 5184 AD−3,102 = 2082 AD, which is the first date in the sequence to lie in the future, and therefore the first to be a possibility. Bearing in mind that the first three results of this calculation are impossible by definition, we may now tabulate a number of them so as to draw attention to those which are possible:

	Possible Length of the Four *Yugas*			Date for End of *Kali-Yuga*
1	Platonic Year:	3,102 − (1 x 1,296)	=	1806 BC
2	Platonic Years:	3,102 − (2 x 1,296)	=	510 BC
3	Platonic Years:	(3 x 1,296) − 3,102	=	786 AD
4	Platonic Years:	(4 x 1,296) − 3,102	=	2082 AD
5	Platonic Years:	(5 x 1,296) − 3,102	=	3378 AD
6	Platonic Years:	(6 x 1,296) − 3,102	=	4674 AD

As this table is extended, the end of the *Kali-Yuga* recedes by an additional 1,296 years for every additional Platonic Year assigned to the whole period, so there is no arithmetical limit to the number of possible answers. However, the answer closest to the present time, 2082 AD, deserves special attention, and not only because the final crisis of the present age is said to be in the 21st century, according to many estimates of material resources. A theoretical reason for considering the date nearest the present time arises from the property of cycles according to which the first and last subordinate or secondary cycles always have a unique character within the whole system.

This property can be applied in reverse, so that it could be said that if a period has no historical parallel, it must be the last cyclic subdivision of which the whole is capable. This conclusion is not affected in substance by the question as to whether such a concluding cycle be one-tenth or one-hundredth of the full universal era. If it were the hundredth, it would have the same ratio to the *Kali-Yuga* as the latter has to the total cycle, in which case it could be called the 'iron age of the iron age'.

Since the historically unprecedented character of the modern world results from the rise of modern science, we may reasonably take 1600 AD as a not-too-arbitrary date for the beginning of the final era. (It was in the first decade of the seventeenth century that Galileo made his discoveries.) In this case, 1600 AD would by definition be the date at which nine-tenths of the *Kali-Yuga* must have passed, since this last part of the *Kali-Yuga* similarly bears a proportion of one-tenth to the whole of it. The period in question would thus extend from 3102 BC to 1600 AD, that is, 4,702 years. As this is nine-tenths of the period we wish to determine, we need only divide it by nine to obtain the tenth part to be added, i.e., $4,702 \div 9 = 522$ years to the nearest whole year. When this period is added to 1600, the total will be equal to the date at which the cycle should end: 1600 AD + 522 = 2122 AD. There is an arbitrary element in this date which stems from the choice of 1600 for simplicity's sake. For all that, it falls only about forty years beyond the date 2082 AD and this difference would in any case be very small in comparison with the intervals of 1,296 years. This method is independent of the previous one, so that its approximate date of 2122 AD is close enough to confirm the date of 2082 AD. The latter date can therefore be provisionally accepted, as it is based on criteria which are perfectly exact in their relations, regardless of whether they are valid as a whole.

According to the assumption that the whole universal era is equal to four Platonic Years in length, the total period is one of $4 \times 12,960 = 51,840$ years, of which one-tenth or 5,184 years, forms the *Kali-Yuga* ending in 2082 AD, as 5184 AD $-3,102 = 2082$ AD. If a late date is chosen for the onset of the modern age, say, the beginning of the Industrial Revolution around 1770, a date for the end of the *Kali-Yuga* or Iron Age can be worked out by the same reasoning as before. As the last age, or 'iron age of the iron age' is by definition one-tenth of the Iron Age, and therefore one-hundredth of the whole, nine-tenths of the *Kali-Yuga* would have passed by 1770 AD, and its length up to this date would have been 3,102 + 1,770 = 4,872 years. Dividing by nine as before, the tenth part is given by 4,872 ÷ 9 = 541 years. In this case, the *Kali-Yuga* would end at 1770 AD + 541 = 2311 AD. This date is over two hundred years beyond 2082, but even this difference is quite small compared with the additional 1,296 years there would be if the total cycle was of five Platonic Years and not four. Despite the lack of a clear starting date, the modern age certainly began between the latter part of the sixteenth century and the middle of the seventeenth, in which case the end of the cycle should be within one or two centuries from the present time.

THE MAYAN CHRONOLOGY

There is at least one other ancient chronology which contains a precise date for the beginning of the present universal era, namely, that of the Mayas. Their 'long count' dates the present world from what was apparently a recreation of the world dated at 12th August 3113 BC in terms of our calendar. It is significant that this date lies only eleven years before that of 3102 BC given by Aryabhata. This system uses a conventional year of 360 days, the *tun*. Four hundred of these make up an important cycle, the *baktun*, which comprises 144,000 days, as 400 x 360 = 144,000.

The present world-cycle is defined by this system as a period of thirteen *baktuns* or 1,872,000 days, as 13 x 400 x 360 = 1,872,000. If this period is divided by 360, i.e., 1,872,000 ÷ 360 = 5,200, this answer is 5,200 *tuns* or 360-day years. To convert this period to our years, the period in days must be divided by 365.242 instead of 360, i.e., 1,872,000 ÷ 365.242 = 5,125 years to the nearest year. From this period it is easy to show that the end of the cycle must be in 2012 AD, as 5125 AD − 3,113 = 2012 AD.

This date lies in the same century as 2082, but there is a difference of seventy years between them. A difference of this order is quite small in relation to the world-cycle, but it is large enough in relation to a human lifetime for it to be a serious issue for those who live anywhere near the dates in question. Most investigators seem to be content to conclude the matter here, although it is still possible to reach a different result. From the above arithmetic, it can be seen that if we substitute a correct figure for the year in place of the 360-day *tun*, the full period in days results as follows: 13 x 400 x 365.242 = 1,899,258.4 days. If this period is now converted to years, the result is 1,899,258.4 ÷ 365.242 = 5,200 years. This answer is of course exactly 5,200 because the calculation eliminates the 365.242-day period just as completely as it eliminates the one of 360 days, leaving only 13 x 400 = 5,200 in either case. This shows that the number 5,200 could refer to years just as well as to *tun*s. The Mayas knew as well as we do that the year contains 365.24 days, so it is possible that their system allowed all periods in *tun*s to be numerically identical with periods in years. The round number 360 could then have been simply an arithmetical symbol for the year, and its exact length would not be an issue in calculations of this kind. It is obvious to anyone, let alone the Mayas, that a figure like 360 days could only yield exact dates in the trivial sense of points along a series of numbers, but never in relation to the solar year, unless some compensating factor is involved. At any rate, it is hardly conceivable that the Mayas did not wish to evaluate their world-cycle in years, and unless there are original Mayan calculations converting periods in *tun*s to years by substituting 365.242, we have the right to take the 5,200 as meaning solar years.

In this case, the cycle would now end at: 5200 AD – 3,113 = 2087 AD. This date is within five years of 2082 AD, the one calculated for the four *Yugas*, and these two dates are roughly as close as the corresponding dates for the beginning, 3102 and 3113 BC. These two results are mutually supportive, the more so as the Mayas in the Yucatan Peninsula and the inhabitants of ancient India are about as geographically and culturally unrelated as any two cultures are likely to be.

To Find Intermediate Dates

Since the lengths of all the cycles deriving from the *Kali-Yuga* are fixed by the proportions 4 : 3 : 2 : 1, there will be no difficulty in finding the dates at which their component parts begin and end, now that we have a figure for the overall period. This can be done on the basis of a total length of the four Platonic Years proposed earlier, but before using this quantity, at least one alternative to it should be considered. It appears that Guénon held that the full period of the universal era was not four, but five Platonic Years, totalling 64,800 years: 5 x 12,960 = 64,800.

As a tenth of the above, the *Kali-Yuga* would be of 6,480 years.[5] Thus if the date 3102 BC is used, this cycle would not end until 6480 AD −3,102 = 3378 AD, i.e., there would be another 1,296 years. However, it does not appear that Guénon was dating any cycle from 3102 BC, so that his date for the end of the cycle should be held inconclusive, especially as a date so far in the future conflicts with his known belief that the end of the *Kali-Yuga* was historically quite close. There is of course the possibility of maintaining the end-date at some time in the 21st century, say 2080 AD, and reckoning backward to a different beginning, which would have to be at about 6480 BC −2,080 = 4400 BC It would still be necessary to find some special significance for the latter date, either in the ancient chronologies or on the borders of prehistory, which seems not to be possible.

The choice between four and five Platonic Years is also affected by the fact that the unit in question, 12,960 years, is just half the time taken for the sun's equinoctial position to traverse the whole ecliptic. Consequently a universal era of four such periods would bring the sun back to the original position at its end, whereas an odd number of them, such as five, would leave one half of this solar cycle uncompleted.

From the figures which have now been reckoned, the date for the beginning of the Golden Age or *Krita-Yuga* can be placed at 51840 BC −2,082 = 49758 BC, albeit with the reservation that time spans of this length will be subject to the contractive distortions which were outlined in chapter 15. The division of this period into four Platonic Years is further supported by the complement they make to the four unequal divisions of the *Yugas*. This would be in keeping with the 'cosmic' character of the number four which corresponds to the

5. See Gaston Georgel, *Les Quatre Âges de l'Humanité*, chap. 3.

emergence of the physical creation after the last of the transcendental realities. Consequently there are the four cardinal points, the four seasons, the four states of matter (or philosophical elements), the four solar stations of the year, the four natural levels of being (mineral, vegetable, animal, and human or rational), the four branches of the animal kingdom, the four forms of physical energy, the four elements of organic matter, and the four worlds of the Kabbalah (*Atziluth*, *Briah*, *Yetzirah*, and *Assiah*), of which this world is the fourth. The centrality of the number four in this system can further be seen where the defining numbers of the four *Yugas* are all simple multiples of 4 and 108: 4 x 108 = 432; 2 x 4 x 108 = 864; 3 x 4 x 108 = 1,296; 4 x 4 x 108 = 1,728.

Any further confirmation for the dates for the beginning and ending of the cycle can only come from the relevance, or otherwise, of the historical applications the system gives rise to. The first set of dates to be deduced is that of the four secondary cycles, these being four-tenths, three-tenths, two tenths, and one-tenth of the 51,840-year period respectively:

Krita-Yuga (Golden Age)	49758 BC	—	29022 BC
Tretā-Yuga (Silver Age)	29022 BC	—	13470 BC
Dvāpara-Yuga (Bronze Age)	13470 BC	—	3102 BC
Kali-Yuga (Iron Age)	3102 BC	—	2082 AD

These four periods are roughly of 20,000, 15,000, 10,000, and 5,000 years, and have boundary dates which are obviously far too remote for historical relevance, but within the *Kali-Yuga* itself we can now repeat the same analysis in the ratios of 4 : 3 : 2 : 1 as before, using the names of the symbolic metals for convenience's sake:

Gold-of-Iron	3102 BC	—	1026 BC	2,076 years
Silver-of-Iron	1026 BC	—	528 AD	1,554 years
Bronze-of-Iron	528 AD	—	1564 AD	1,036 years
Iron-of-Iron	1564 AD	—	2082 AD	518 years
				5,184 years

This latest set of four comes third in order of size from the 4 x 12,960 years with which we started, and the periods comprised therein are roughly 2,000, 1,500, 1,000, and 500 years in length. Between them they cover almost the whole of recorded history. When it comes to showing how they correspond to some of the most fundamental divisions of history, the most difficult correspondence to make is with the first, or golden age of the iron age. This is the period of the earliest recorded antiquity, which saw the building of the pyramids at Giza and Dashour, and the megalithic monuments of north western Europe. The next date in order, 1026 BC, has a historical relevance inasmuch as it is about as early as Greco-Latin civilization can be traced. It comes within about a century of the Trojan War, which was about as far back as classical civilization was accustomed to trace its own history. By 500 AD the barbarian invasions had triumphed, so that the period roughly from 1000 BC to 500 AD gives therefore realistic limits for classical antiquity, while it corresponds to what I have called the silver age of the iron age.

The calculated date of 528 AD has some symbolical historical interest on its own account because it was only one year after this that Justinian caused the Academy to be closed down after it had existed for over nine hundred years. This termination of one of the major institutions of the ancient world gives an effective 'official' date for the end of that civilization. By 529 AD a process of transition which began over a century before reached completion, and the next tertiary cycle had begun, corresponding to the 'bronze age of the iron age' which has a duration of just over a thousand years according to the figures shown above. In fact the Middle Ages do occupy a period of about one thousand years, for which the boundary dates of 500 AD and 1500 AD are clearly appropriate. In most of Europe the sixth century was a time of obscurity besides being the time of most rapid transition to the new age, while the sixteenth century saw the most rapid and decisive changes from Medieval to modern civilization. While it is true that the sixteenth century contains a number of dates which could be taken as historical turning-points, it is not inappropriate that the calculated date, 1564 AD, is also that of the Council of Trent, which established the new post-Medieval Christendom, divided between the Catholic and Protestant faiths. It also has some symbolic significance from the fact that it saw the births of both Galileo and Shakespeare.

According to the same system of dates, the minor cycle containing the twentieth century should extend for some 520 years up to 2082, and we must now have entered the final century of this period. Thus the latter part of the twenty-first century should see the end of the whole 'era of *Manu*' or, in Mayan terms, thirteen *baktuns*. Although this final half-millennium is short in relation to the other cycles, its importance for us makes it worth analyzing numerically into its own secondary cycles in the same ratios as before. In theory no cycle is too short to reproduce within itself the greater order of which it forms part, only the shorter they are the less the impact of the historical changes which mark its divisions. Even so, the dates calculated on this basis have enough relevance to the major transitions of the past four centuries for there to be more than coincidence involved:

'Golden age'	1564 – 1770	206 years
'Silver age'	1770 – 1926	156 years
'Bronze age'	1926 – 2030	104 years
'Iron age'	2030 – 2082	52 years

The first internal date here, 1770, is appropriate for the onset of the Industrial Revolution, and however localized it was at the time, its later impact on the rest of the world makes it a significant point in the historical process.

The second date, 1926, is at least near the beginning of the new era following the First World War, the aftermath of which saw the end of Europe's thousand-year order of its imperial monarchies. (In early Christianity, prayers for the Emperor were justified on the grounds that the end of the Empire was believed to herald the reign of the Antichrist, and tradition maintained this view.) This new order was completed by the political East-West polarization owing to Russian communism which prevailed for over seventy years. The date at which this period ends, 2030, is a realistic date for the completion of the transition from one Platonic month to another, that is, from the Piscean to the Aquarian ages. This would give a date of 130 BC (i.e., 2,160–2,030 = 130), for the beginning of the Piscean Age, though these dates cannot be precise because the 30-degree

arcs assigned to each sign of the zodiac cannot be positioned definitively, owing to the shapes of the constellations.

What may be said of the final half-century which then follows is
dependent on the assumption that the end of the *Kali-Yuga* would
also be the time of the Second Coming. In that case, the last half-
century should culminate with the Antichrist and a bringing to
completion of the anti-spiritual order which has imposed itself to an
increasing degree for two centuries now. If the same cyclic proportions are applicable to this present period from 1926-2030, it should
be noted that two important internal dates that result are 1968 and
the notorious 1999. The indication is that these are both times at
which change is at its most rapid and decisive. One can in any case
see an effect of the cyclic principle in the twentieth century when at
certain times events seem to be racing forward to an apocalyptic
conclusion, and at others the pace subsides and a relative stability
prevails once more, without this being attributable to any visible
agency.

The only way in which such unseen forces are ever manifest
directly in the general consciousness is in the form of an expectancy
both strong and vague at once. Eventually, the pace of change rises
toward a new climax, under pressure from a confused popular
expectation of some event which is never really defined. This moti-
vation, repressed most of the time, is a catalyst for change which
works unrecognized for what it really is, an inverted and secularized
form of the Messianic hope. This disposition is inbuilt into human
nature, and it will still attach itself to something or other, even when
the religion it belongs to is not believed in. The modern appetite for
change at any price can readily be explained as a materialized form
of the striving toward the infinity of God which was a catalyst in the
older civilization. The separation of this essentially spiritual drive
from its native 'vertical' dimension and its relegation to the 'hori-
zontal' one of natural life is thus part of the means whereby our
experience of time is made to elapse the more rapidly, in conformity
with the contraction of duration which increases markedly at the
end of temporal cycles.

Apart from cyclic theory, there are material reasons for thinking
that at most the present world cannot continue for more than

another century. Natural resources are being consumed on an unprecedented scale which has no prospect of decreasing as long as world population remains anywhere near its present level. The modern technology and industry which consumes these resources has penetrated to every part of the world, with the effect of making the whole human race into a single collective entity. This means that the world has lost an essential means of survival and renewal, namely, a large and uninvolved section of the human race, unaffected by the onrush of the same civilization. At the same time, there is no prospect of history taking a different direction because all cultural changes which may arise and form the conditions for an alternative value system are smothered or absorbed by the existing system before they can establish a sustainable identity and produce consequences of their own. This means that no change is likely to be made to the pattern of overpopulation and exhaustion of natural resources, whether as mineral deposits, topsoil, or forests.

Such destructive forces, together with those of global pollution, are all comprehended under the conception of rising entropy, which has been outlined in earlier chapters. Contrary to appearances, entropy rises nearly as much in the finished products of industry as in the destruction and waste involved in their production. In itself, this is wholly inevitable, but its evil comes from the vast scale on which it is conducted. Even when new, industrial products are part of the dispersal of materials into smaller and ever-less recoverable quantities, and when their useful life is over, this dispersal is aggravated by their lack of re-usability, except of course when subjected to processes which disperse yet more ordered matter and available energy. Nevertheless, these things can be seen to form part of an over-riding order. The theoretical explanation of these things matches observation, and the temporal divisions deduced in the foregoing match the main transitions of recorded history.

An Alternative Time-Scale

Reverting to the period of 51,840 years calculated for the total cycle, another reason for this, with its consequent period of 5,184 years for the Iron Age or *Kali-Yuga*, can be found from the date for the mid-point of this era: 5,184 ÷ 2 = 2,592 years, whence the mid-point is at 3102 BC – 2592 = 510 BC. From the mid-point of a cycle it is natural to find a new beginning, and the longer the cycle the more marked this kind of change is liable to be. Binary division is also manifest because the division in the ratios 4 : 3 : 2 : 1 dictates a significantly greater complexity in the second half compared with the first, and this will in itself give the appearance of a new beginning. In this instance, 510 BC, or the early part of the sixth century BC, is a specially significant time because it is from this time onward that a true historical continuity emerges. In the actual year 510 BC, Rome became a republic, marking the end of the half-legendary era of the kings. Around this time, the Jews were returning from their Babylonian exile, and their history under the successive empires which ruled the Near East was beginning. Athens also entered a new era, and soon afterward defeated the Persian invasion. This was the time when Pythagoras was publicly teaching the spiritual wisdom he had gathered, so as both to spiritually regenerate the ancient Mediterranean world and to prepare the way for Christianity. In Asia, Confucius and the Buddha were living and creating the spiritual traditions descended from them. From all these sources in the later sixth century BC continuous lines of historical development can be traced, and for this reason one can date the effective beginning of history from this period.

It is also significant that if the period 510 BC to 2082 AD is divided in the ratios 4 : 3 : 2 : 1 as before, the divisions it gives coincide with those already worked out at 528 AD (as on p 233), while the subsequent ones have historically relevant relations with them. They would, however, end the Medieval period over two centuries earlier, in the early fourteenth century, which would correspond to the decisive interior changes in Medieval civilization which set in train the events culminating in the Renaissance.

18

THE TIME
OF THE END

IMITATION, COUNTERFEIT, AND CONFUSION

According to orthodox teachings, the lower culmination of the world age sees the realization of the horrifying possibility known as the reign of the Antichrist. To the modern mind, with little belief in God and none at all in either the devil or objective evil, this subject raises peculiar difficulties when taken for a real possibility and not as a subject for sensational fiction. What meaning could there be in a counterfeit Christ? A counterfeit so effective that hardly anyone could unmask it? Strange as it may appear, such a being is an integral part of the traditional cosmological conception, and results logically from it, besides which this climactic evil also results physically from the collective will of man and belongs necessarily with the sovereignty of human free will.

To understand this, one must look closely at the exact nature of imitation, and of counterfeit, which is imitation intended to deceive, as with forgery, so as to see that it has a cosmological role, and is not merely a human activity. In the modern world, tangible examples of imitation are everywhere, since the modern way of life depends largely upon them. The ability to create imitations in realms where it was never possible before is pushed further and further, and in this regard the biological technique of cloning is just one of the more dramatic developments in this field. The production of imitations defines about nine-tenths of the programme of applied science. These include the replacement of natural fibres by synthetic ones, along with the spread of ever more advanced petrochemical products so that there are now very few things that cannot be made of them. The transmission of sound and visual images also comes under the heading of imitation, as also do the methods of mass-production in industry. In the realm of computer technology, the scope of imitation expands practically to infinity, since computer programs are designed to imitate every conceivable natural process down to its minutest details. A certain kind of power is achieved by this, since the imitations of reality so produced are a richer and more concentrated source of experience for most people than is the real world they are based on. Above all, computers imitate intelligence, without anyone being able to see what ill effects should arise from engaging with reflections of the real world and not the world itself. That such things answer to a universal need is only too obvious, and it is evidence of an equally universal starvation of reality.

It can be seen that when imitations are made, the thing imitated plays a part in relation to its imitations which bears an analogy to the relation of a Form to its instantiations. Even though nothing more is involved than relations between physical entities, this imitative relation is in some sort a reflection of the primordial Form-instantiation relation. The material world comprises everything which is contained in the realm of Forms, albeit in an inferior and very fragmented form, and this totality could not be complete unless the original cosmogonic relation is included. Such is the universal generative act. But if this relation has a necessary place in creation, it must still be explained why it should rise to such prominence at a time in history like the present. The answer to this has already been indicated in what was said concerning rising entropy and the universal reduction and dilution of all individual qualities and identities. There is an intrinsic three-fold relationship involved here, namely rising entropy, weakening of individual identities and qualities, and counterfeit qualities and identities. The connection between the first two of these three is direct enough, and from thence it can be seen that this creates a void which has to be filled somehow. This void is the increasing extent to which instantiated beings fall short in relation to their archetypes, that is, the increasing inadequacy with which they instance their Forms, even by the standards of material existence. A solution to this imbalance is achieved by making qualities and identities into a kind of convertible currency (both in human life and in industrial products), regardless of how appropriate they may be for the subjects on whom or on which they are imposed. The result is a world where hardly anything ever is what it appears to be. Aside from moral considerations, this condition results necessarily from the descending cosmic process which has been explained earlier. This means that there is nothing, from the most material to the most subtle, that can be held exempt from imitation and counterfeit under the conditions that prevail in the 'last times'. The positive side of this is that it gives maximum scope to investigations that extend knowledge, but it is at the price of loosening the connection between consciousness and its ontological roots. Those who are affected most by the dilution of identity and the confusions resulting from attempts to supply it from outside itself will also be at a disadvantage when it comes to testing the genuineness of new spiritual phenomena or supposed revelations. Hardly anyone is wholly immune from this evil, and for this reason very few will be able by their natural faculties to see through the ultimate act of counterfeit.

THE ROLE OF EVOLUTIONIST BELIEFS

Another question which this subject naturally raises is how the human race as a whole could ever get itself under a direct domination of evil without first losing its mental faculties. No matter what cosmic pressures may be acting to this end, natural forces should not be able to outmatch awareness. Something must therefore prepare the way by neutralizing innumerable adverse reactions which the approach to this final state should arouse. Ideas with living force in today's world are few, but a clear example among them is the revaluation of events made under the influence of evolutionist thought. Regardless of its scientific relevance, evolution has acquired the status of a lay dogma which teaches that everything that comes into being in the animate world does so by replacing something else of an inferior nature. Whatever is latest to appear is therefore accepted as the best of its kind so far, so that it could be said that intrinsic merit has been replaced by historicity.

The evolutionist creed is a logical fruition of the historicist mentality which places everything in a linear progression where all interest is centered on the part of the linear process which has not yet been lived through, regardless of its qualities or lack of them. The domination of this outlook makes society like an organism without an immune system, as mere historical opportuneness ensures an entry and a validation for just about anything. This historicist mentality and its works is governed above all by the Principle of Plenitude, and exemplifies it, even though progress and evolution are the only criteria which are consciously believed in. The role of the latter is quite independent of the scientific or philosophical validity of evolution, because this theory derives from a belief in progress which was adopted long before Darwin's time. In the popular mind evolution is valid because there is always progress, and there must be progress because nature always evolves, while the circularity of this thinking is ignored.

The direction of a civilization by evolutionist and progressist beliefs makes the emergence of the Antichrist all but inevitable, because for this outlook, there can be no such being as an Antichrist. For minds conditioned by the linear progressist conception, such a being could not be less than genuine, that is, the Son of God. Such is the ultimate nemesis of the linear-historical mystique. Since the great evil of the last times is foretold in the Bible, it is worth considering whether a possible reference to the evolutionist doctrine is also contained there. Concerning mankind in the last times there is the passage which states that satanic activity will bring a 'wicked deception' upon many of mankind, along with deceptive signs and wonders because, as the Epistle states:

> They refused to love the truth and so be saved. Therefore God sends upon them a strong delusion, to make them believe what is false, so that all may be condemned who did not believe the truth.[1]

This shows at very least that neutrality or plain indifference in regard to truth cannot be a viable option, for the working of the

---

1. 2 Thess. 2:10–12 (Catholic R.S.V.).

cosmic process compels everyone to embrace either truth or false-hood. The sending of the 'strong delusion' is in any case a providen-tial response to man's self-determination by his own free will. All tendencies, whether positive or negative, create a metaphysical attraction to experiences cognate with them, and make them in a way self-verifying.

The great delusion in the above passage forms part of a text which is concerned with the coming of the Antichrist, and the importance attributed to the delusion in this connection implies that it must be a false doctrine which spreads everywhere, and which darkens the understanding so that those so affected would not be able to see through the 'power' and the 'pretended signs and wonders' referred to in the same text. It is true that the modern world is full of dubi-ous doctrines which have spread in proportion as traditional doc-trine has lost influence, but the fact remains that only one of them could be said to have attained universal acceptance, and that is the pseudo-mysticism of evolution. If this could not be identified with the 'strong delusion' there would be no comparable belief to put in its place. The essence of the delusion referred to in the above text is a 'faith' which is calculated to break down resistance to the invasion of falsehood under the guise of novelty, and there is no equality among the possible contenders for this role. One notable victory for the 'delusion' is the way in which it has taken away nearly all belief in the objective reality of evil or of sin. In proportion as more is known about the natural causes of behavior, the distinction between cau-sality and justification grows lost in confusion. The mere fact that the sources of moral and religious teachings belong to the past is taken to mean that these things must be 'dated' and obsolete; when values are lost, therefore, this is taken to mean that they are of no further use or relevance. Such attitudes engage with a near-instinc-tive belief that the truth of a religious faith or of an ideology depends on the amount of worldly success it enjoys. The influence of democracy is such that the will of the majority is taken for the source of truth and value, and for this state of mind the intellectual conviction that things can only be either true or false or right or wrong in themselves appears almost as a kind of malevolence. No other result could be expected from an ideology which allows no limit to the extent to which values are made subject to the will, not the intellect.

THE REAL OPPOSITE OF ORDER

The situation described so far would not seem to have any prospect beyond steadily mounting disorder, ending with a social chaos so complete as to put an end to history. Such a perspective is also that given by Plato in his *Statesman* myth, where the world is rescued and restored by God every time it descends to the verge of dissolution. While this is based on undoubted realities as far as the natural order is concerned, it still does not give the full picture. Among natural forces it is indeed true that disorder is the only opposite to order, as high-entropy states are the counterpart of the low-entropy states from whence they originate. But things are very different where the subject under discussion is order created by human, not cosmic, means. There are many forms of order which, being both human and divine in origin, are created for the specific purpose of guiding minds and wills in accordance with the will of God. Such is the meaning of traditional civilizations, and order of this kind implies the possibility of an inverse kind of order which would have the opposite effect. It would certainly still be order from a short-term human point of view, while by absolute standards it would be the extremity of disorder inasmuch as it set human life at variance with the law of God. This idea has been expressed by Joseph Pieper in connection with the possibility of a final world government:

> the End will not be chaos in the sense that the opposition and conflict between numbers of historical powers will cause a progressive dissolution of historical ties and structures, and finally putrefaction. On the contrary, the End will be characterized by one single governmental structure equipped with prodigious power, which, however, fails to establish any *genuine* order. At the

end of history there will be a pseudo-order maintained in being by the exercise of power.[2]

While the time of the End will not be simply a time of chaos, however, the way toward it will certainly be prepared by the other things referred to, the dissolution of historical ties and structures. Destruction and confusion will be caused by the Antichrist so as to create a popular demand for a restoration of order at any price. The malefic nature of this new order will be skillfully concealed and will form a powerful illusion:

> The description 'pseudo-order' is also valid in the sense that the 'illusion' is successful; it is an element in the prophecy of the End that the 'desert of order' of the Antichrist will be regarded as a true and authentic order.... Perhaps the pseudo-order of the Dominion of Antichrist, after a 'period of chaos' on a vast scale, such as, in Toynbee's view, always precedes the establishment of a universal State, will be greeted as a deliverance (which would exactly confirm the character of the Antichrist as a pseudo-Christ).[3]

This points to a kind of world state of which the totalitarian dictatorships of the twentieth century were so many adumbrations. The popular tendency to identify the State with God is at the present time far advanced in the modern world, as people have recourse to government for deliverance from evils which in the past were accepted as willed by God. They act as though human beings had the power to elect an immunity or preservation from evils which result from the abuse of their own free will. This *ad hoc* attribution of ultimate power to the State is widely desired because it is seen as an empowerment of those who vote for it. Consequently, the State increasingly performs functions which are material parodies of the actions of God as provider, sustainer, avenger, enlightener, and protector. Although this power is false because it means a transfer of a power which should be inward and spiritual to a system of more or

---

2. Joseph Pieper, *The End of Time*, chap. 3 pp119–120.
3. Ibid., p120.

less fragile practical relations in the outside world, it is hard to oppose, because the desire for a God-substitute is so strong and so widespread. (A substitute which is even felt to be preferable to God, as it does not require the responsibilities that God requires.) In proportion as belief in God declines, belief in the power of the State increases, and with it, the range of powers over individual lives which the State can assume. If this tendency went to completion it would be bound to result in a formal claim to divinity by the head, or figurehead, of the ultimate government.

Another aspect of the ultimate anti-order of the age can be seen by means of the law of the three phases referred to in chapter 3. This law expresses an aspect of symmetry between the first and last states which occur in a progression, or between the highest and the lowest. Thus the inverted anti-order of the latter days will be as a lower reflection of the true world-order which existed in primordial times before the 'confusion of tongues'. (According to the Talmud, Adam, Seth, Enoch, and their descendents before the Flood were rulers of all mankind.) The transition from the higher order to the lower one will be made by way of all degrees and forms of disorder which increase in number between the two unities. The realization of this final anti-order is a necessary condition for the end of the world cycle. A state of civilization which simply lapsed into manifest chaos would reduce to the tribal or even zoological level which could in principle go on for ever. Its very lack of form would make it too ineffectual to give rise to the kind of disruption implied by the End.

This disruption results not merely from a failure to manifest the archetypal realities, but from the realization of a world which positively denies or perverts them. Only a certain kind of order could do this. Neither God nor the archetypes need bring about the End by direct action, since the essential opposition to them by human wills generates the necessary negative force. An anti-order implies a rising tension between the outside world and the universal order which it nevertheless depends on. An inversion of relations in regard to God and the higher values must first take place in the collective consciousness, so that they are no longer seen as realities independent of mankind to which human wills must be subject, but rather as mere projections of human ideals and desiderata. At the same time, democracy fosters a confused conviction that there could be nothing that is not subject to the will and choice of society. This anti-order is appearing in the creation of societies where moral and spiritual norms can increasingly be violated without apparent consequences. Governments become increasingly the embodiment of this collective will to self-absolutization, and in this connection the Antichrist would appear as the personification of this kind of government.

UNDERSTANDING THE GREAT BEAST

In the Bible, the figure of the Antichrist is expressed in words loaded with symbolism, principally that of the 'Beast' and the 'Dragon'. The Beast may be two entities or one duplicated in some way, and it is not easy to see whether this refers to a specific individual or a collective entity. There is first a beast with ten horns and seven heads, bearing a blasphemous name, which receives authority from the Dragon (an image of the devil):

> Men worshipped the dragon, for he had given his authority to the beast, and they worshipped the beast, saying 'Who is like the beast, and who can fight against it?'[4]

An orthodox explanation of this vision makes it a representation of Roman imperial power, in the form of seven Caesars, which is justified by the way in which time's cycles can make one period foreshadow and parallel another one in the distant future. However, it cannot be wholly equated with past events, because the events of the first century AD were not followed by Armageddon, the appearance of the New Jerusalem and the end of this world age. Thus the prophetic meaning must be allowed for, as in the first place there is so much in this text which has clearly not yet happened, and in the next place, the beast is said to blaspheme against God and to *make war on the saints* and to conquer them, as it achieves world power: 'And authority was given it over every tribe and people and tongue

---

4. Rev. 13:4 (Catholic R.S.V.).

and nation,'[5] and so it becomes almost universally an object of worship. However, there is said to be a second beast, which arose out of the earth as the first one arose out of the sea. This one ensures that the first one is worshipped, besides which,

> It works great signs, even making fire come down from heaven to earth in the sight of men . . . it deceives those who dwell on earth bidding them make an image for the beast which was wounded by the sword and lived . . . let him who has understanding reckon the number of the beast, for it is a human number, its number is six hundred and sixty-six.[6]

There are many things in need of explanation in these texts, but above all we need to understand the meaning of 'the Beast' (το θηριον, *to therion*). Two separate beings are so described, besides the being referred to as the Dragon, and this indicates that no one individual is referred to. Fortunately for the work of interpretation, the Great Beast does not appear only in the Bible, but can also be found in Plato's *Republic*, where an account of this being is given which leaves no doubt as to its essential nature:

> Each of these private teachers who work for pay, whom the politicians call Sophists and regard as their rivals, inculcates nothing else than these opinions of the multitude which they opine when they are assembled and calls this knowledge wisdom. It is as if a man were acquiring the knowledge of the humours and desires of a great strong beast which he had in his keeping, how it is to be approached and touched, and when and by what things it is made savage or gentle, yes, and the several sounds it is wont to utter on the occasion of each, and again what sounds uttered by another make it tame or fierce, and after mastering this knowledge by living with the creature and by lapse of time should call it wisdom, and should construct thereof a system and art and turn to the teaching of it, knowing nothing in reality about which of

5. Ibid., 13:7.
6. Ibid., 13:13–14 and 18. The wounded dragon, and the second Beast, who shares its power, are a demonic parody of the Father and Son in Trinity.

these opinions and desires is honourable or base, good or evil, just or unjust, but should apply all these terms to the judgements of the great beast, calling the things that pleased it good, and the things that vexed it bad, having no other account to render of them, but should call what is necessary just and honourable, never having observed how great is the real difference between the necessary and the good, and being incapable of explaining it to another. Do you not think, by heaven, that such a one would be a strange educator?[7]

Plato's point of view differs markedly from that of Saint John, but their differences do not necessarily concern the nature of the Beast in itself, but rather different views of its role in society and history. For Plato it is a great, formless, many-headed, sub-personal power which stifles all aspirations to the higher values, whereas for Saint John it is something bound for perdition which has the power to drag nearly everyone else with it in the latter days, whence the terror which it rouses. These positions are in any case compatible, and the essential reality involved is the unspiritual lower stratum of human collective consciousness, driven solely by the instinctive appetites and aversions of organic existence, and *per se* impervious to reason. While this most unredeemed element of mankind is present to some degree in the psycho-physical makeup of every social stratum, it is nevertheless the lower classes which, *qua* classes, come closest to being literally an embodiment of it, leaving aside the hidden potential of certain individuals. This view is also that of Cardinal Newman in an account of one of his letters (Autumn 1871) quoted by Joseph Pieper:

He [John Henry Newman] asked, who would be the Goths and Vandals destined to destroy modern civilization.... He gave himself the following answer: The lowest class, which is very great in numbers and unbelieving, will rise up out of the depths of modern cities and be the new scourge of God.[8]

7. Plato, *Republic* VI, 493 a–c, Paul Shorey, tr. See also Simone Weil, *Intimations of Christianity*, chap. 7.
8. Joseph Pieper, *The End of Time*. chap. 2 [5].

Religious belief and rational consciousness and judgement are inseparable because grace has intelligence just as much as love in its very essence. Although the converse, that intelligence should mean grace is not true when the intellective element is divorced from the rational, the cultivation of this faculty forms a vitally important basis for faith. Where minds are blocked against this development, they are not normally open to spiritual influences. The rise of social equality with its constant confusion between equal rights and equal possessions and attainments, means that society must accept anything that cannot be seen as a privilege, no matter how worthless it may be. This tendency becomes more pronounced with the passage of time, so that the Beast casts a lengthening shadow. The fact that this concerns a certain kind of collective entity pervading mankind does not nevertheless rule out the Antichrist as an individual, and one who would be the very incarnation and personification of this lower consciousness. At the same time, the Apocalypse indicates that there may well be more than one such individual, though in differing capacities.

Before considering the actions attributed to the Beast, the spiritual significance of the number 666 should be seen in the light of the system of meanings it is an instance of. This number can be derived by gematria in many ways, one of which shows it to be an expression of the name in question, that is, the Great Beast (το μεγα θηριον, *to mega therion*) since the Greek letters of this name add up to 666 when given their traditional numerical values.[9] If the letters for the Greek for 'cross', σταυρος (*stauros*), are given their numerical equivalents, their total with στ taken as six comes to 777. Finally, if the name of Jesus in Greek, Ιησους, is given its numerical equivalent in the same way, it comes to 888. (These three numbers are exactly divisible by the prime number 37, because 111 ÷ 37 = 3, whence 666, 777, and 888 give quotients of 18, 21, and 24 when divided by 37.) If the Cross, 777, is understood in its wider sense as the sacrifice or mortification of the lower possibilities of personhood, by way of

---

9. These are as follows:

α	β	γ	δ	ε	στ	ζ	η	θ	ι	κ	λ	μ	ν	ξ	ο	π	ρ	σ,ς	τ	υ	φ	χ	ψ	ω
1	2	3	4	5	6	7	8	9	10	20	30	40	50	60	70	80	100	200	300	400	500	600	700	800

which the grace of Jesus is shared in, all that is represented by 666 is that which is closed by nature against identification with any higher value, and which will be nothing but itself on a certain level.

THE INVERSION OF RELIGION

One of the most remarkable acts attributed to the Beast is that it wages war successfully against the saints. This is obviously not war in any literal sense, because holiness is not based on violence, and although it may mean persecution or martyrdoms, such things are in no way defeats from the spiritual point of view.[10] It could therefore more plausibly be a war of ideas and values, and the infiltration of false doctrine. Believers come to accept an increasing amount of teachings which are not those of the Holy Spirit, though they appear to be. Spiritual teachings are often foolishness from a natural point of view, while making sense on a higher, more essential level, but it is always possible for such teachings to be deformed into real foolishness without this being noticed by the majority who do not try to penetrate their beliefs intellectually.

The commonest example of this can be seen from the extent to which people fail to distinguish their faith from the socialist ideologies which were created to eliminate real Christianity by means of something which functions socially like it, while being voided of spiritual content. This shows how even orthodox religion can be made subservient to the unregenerate lower collective mind and will, of which the Beast is in effect the emblem and the incarnation. More generally, the New Dispensation, which was to apply only among Christians, is increasingly taken to be applicable without restriction to all conditions of mankind, and no less to those with no faith of any kind. Thus the New Dispensation is distorted into an *en bloc* validation of just about any human condition and disposition as though the truth required only that one should exist. Believers who take this for truth or a valid expansion of it are only right

10. This does not exclude actual violence from apocalyptic scenario, of course, as, for example, the name of the angel of the Bottomlesss Pit, *Apollyon*, means in the Latin Vulgate *Exterminans*, or in Greek 'destruction' or 'ruin' (Rev. 9:11).

inasmuch as it is certainly part of the Providential design for the world's time of ending. This is because it is only with such a universal pseudo-validation that the lowest possibilities of the world cycle can be realized without restriction, and thereby the end of the age. But this results from the impersonal aspect of God and the 'permissive' function of the divine Will, which has no direct connection with the spiritual good of mankind.

It appears that God's design and that of the devil come extremely close at a certain point, that is, where it is a question of enlightening and empowering the lowest class of mankind. This action can have two diametrically opposed consequences. It may lead to conversion and the assumption of a new and truly spiritual identity, or it may lead to the acceptance of every kind of advantage offered with no alteration to the original orientation and tendencies. In other words, the higher can meet the lower so that the lower can integrate with the higher, or so that the higher (what has been received from God) is reduced to a collaborator with the evil it sought to overcome. Numerically, the latter possibility is overwhelmingly the more prevalent, so that it forms the defining quality of the modern world. Such a union of power with an essential impotence is a formula for destruction.

Now that there is no longer any power on the social and political level able to balance that of the lower forces, the latter are able to take over the place which was traditionally held by legitimate power. Under these conditions leadership becomes more and more a misnomer in religion as much as in politics. At every least sign of resistance or displeasure from the Great Beast the institutional leaderships of religion, law, and politics hasten to appease it with the humility of paid servants, and ominously, no one even tries to entertain the idea that God might want anything it did not want. On the contrary, the teaching of the Beast is that service to God must be the same as service to it, and vice-versa; under this direction, the deviation that Pope Pius X once denounced as 'the substitution of man for God' becomes the whole programme of modernity. The lack of direct resistance to this hostile power from Christian sources is aggravated by an ingrained tendency to submit to worldly power and success, no matter how much one thinks one has renounced such things for oneself. This attitude was always justified by the belief that all power comes from God, so that submission to power must be indirectly submission to God. There is now no longer any relevance for this belief since the disappearance of nearly all traditional power structures. This means a time is beginning in which the price must be paid for an undemanding manner of being in the truth which prevailed in earlier ages when being subject to power could mean being subject to grace.

This price is ultimately a person, (or possibly a succession of persons), who becomes the head and mouthpiece of the collective animal, and it matters little whether he does this by formidable supernormal powers or whether he is merely the stooge of faceless controlling groups. In any case his terrifying power is really nothing apart from sin. What the Church has always taught about witches and sorcerers applies *a fortiori* to him, namely, that it is only because of the inveterate sinfulness in people that he has any power over them.

19

LIBERATION THROUGH KNOWLEDGE

SLAVES OF PLENITUDE

At this point it should not be hard to see that modernity as such is based ideologically on a denial of the traditional conception of time. This position is not maintained by public opinion so much as by the small minorities who control the political and educational systems of the world's wealthiest countries, though this is not to say that there is anything accidental about the situation. The resulting modern outlook brings with it a radical restriction of the social role of creativity inasmuch as all creative activities must now be pursued within a linear conception of time in which no part can repeat another.

Conversely, in ages when the repetitive element of cyclic time was accepted, and formed the background to all activities, the scope for creativity was at a maximum, as in Greco-Roman antiquity; there was no barrier to it other than the limits of the talents of those who engaged in it. The productions of such creativity were valued primarily in regard to the power and intelligence with which they were executed, while the originality of their content was a secondary issue. The exact inverse of this applies in cultures like that of the present time, where rectilinear time is a dogma. In this case, creativity can only mean *creativity in relation to history*, which confines it to things which have never been attempted before, and keeps it from the re-creation of things which were already part of a living tradition. Thus the novel content is everything, while the quality of execution is only subordinate. The field of creative endeavor is much reduced, therefore, since only a small minority has access to work which is sure of being historically original, while a correspondingly small proportion of the public can appreciate its significance. Thus far fewer people are able to participate in the creative functions of civilization, so that it could be said that the dogma of rectilinear time fosters the spread of barbarism and culture-substitutes which have a lowering effect on all values. This situation has been interpreted as a complete contrast to that of traditional man:

> Thus for traditional man, modern man affords the type neither of a free being nor a creator of history. On the contrary, the man of the archaic civilizations can be proud of his mode of existence, which allows him to be free and to create.... This *freedom in relation to his own history* [author's italics]—which for the modern is not only irreversible but constitutes human existence— cannot be claimed by the man who wills to be historical.[1]

The great irony here is that this immersion in history means that no one can even *make history* any longer, in a situation which I earlier called 'posthistorical'. The traditional civilizations referred to above have a greater quantity of cultural creation, while their ranges of themes will be relatively limited. In contrast to them, linear civilization displays a much greater variety in its productions, since experimentation and novelty are its lifeblood. At the same time, this creativity becomes increasingly confined to elites which the average man is neither able nor willing to associate with. This separation of the higher activities from increasing numbers of people is an inevitable feature of the age, since it serves to accelerate the downward trajectory of the final cycle.

An indifference to metaphysical knowledge and a scepticism as to its possibility is also a part of this kind of culture, and such scepticism inevitably embraces metaphysical theorems like the Principle of Plenitude. This is a perfect example of a mindset which affirms with all its might in practice what it denies in theory. The pursuit of historical originality at any price is metaphysically a programme for the realization of a maximum number of different possibilities,

---

1. Mircea Eliade, *The Myth of the Eternal Return*, chap. 4, p157.

simply because they are possibilities; a conviction that every known possibility must be realized as soon as it is known, regardless of its intrinsic value or lack of it. All this, of course, is neither more nor less than a collective human compliance with the way in which Plenitude operates in the universe as a whole. Christian morality is also significant in this context, with its emphasis on the sanctity of all human life, regardless of its social value. This can be seen as the operation of Plenitude in the propagation of all human possibilities for their own sake. Though this principle is based on love in the immediate context, its general outcome conforms precisely to Plenitude, so that these utterly different things combine inseparably.

However, modernity serves Plenitude, if not love, with all its energies, and with so much the more conviction because it has no notion of such a metaphysical principle being in control of it. Rather, the kind of awareness that metaphysics depends on is suppressed, and this is at least partly a result of modernity's unconscious conformity to Plenitude. Since the realization of novelty is the top priority, this will often be achieved at the price of intrinsic worth. As superior possibilities are so to speak 'used up', increasingly inferior ones will take over, and these will create an outlook of their own which will form a mental barrier against anything superior to them. This exhaustion of valuable possibilities appears in cultural, moral, and intellectual spheres at once, and in the extreme case it amounts to mere impoverishment, for all the novelty involved. There is no natural or physical necessity for this, since we are in principle free to realize whatever possibilities we choose. In practice, however, the control exerted by those with an ideological commitment to rectilinear historical time is enough to filter out all possibilities except those calculated to take some previous achievement a step further than it had been taken before, even though this development be trivial or pernicious.

Despite the negative effects of this ruling idea of historical time, there need be no doubt that it is part of the Providential plan for the world. No other conception of history could have the driving force to propel mankind all the way to the final bathos of the cycle. Without it, the free play of natural feeling would divert the course of history from developments which would be essentially anti-human, and the end-time would be delayed indefinitely. Only cultural control by the 'slaves of Plenitude' can ensure that the general happiness and welfare will always take second place to the historical process which holds the place of an idol. Poverty, for example, could have been overcome long ago if enormous resources had not been diverted into the development and production of more and more sophisticated and expensive replacements for technologies which were adequate enough. Such a world might have been adequately supplied, but would have been less technologically dynamic, and therefore not truly 'historical' as its masters understand the word. Related to this, there has been a huge expansion in the range of products which are not really necessary, even though this has to be at the expense of production of things which really are necessary. When one adds to these things the squandering of resources on war and preparation for war, that basic mechanism of history, the price paid for our dynamism should be clear enough.

Changes That Require Darkness

I have already remarked on the way in which slavish obedience to Plenitude results unintentionally from ignorance of and disbelief in such metaphysical principles. A parallel remark could be made in regard to the official disbelief in cyclic time. It is because this conception of time is rejected that the modern world is actually held in an iron grip by cyclic forces, and to a greater extent than ever before. Without moralizing about it, this is simply what is necessary to ensure that the end-time is approached. Thus, for example, a benighted or fog-bound traveler who is convinced that he is traveling in a straight line will not be alert to indications that he is really going round in circles. If he admitted that this could be happening, he could find how to get out of the situation, but not otherwise. So likewise with our conceptions of time. It cannot be over-emphasized that the cyclicity of time is not made known so that everyone can be more surely bound by it and locked into a system of pure repetition. Doctrinal misgivings over it are in this respect as wide of the mark as if it were thought that textbooks about diseases were written to teach people ways of making themselves ill.

By knowledge of the cyclic laws, life can be freed from their control in the ways that most matter. While a strong faith in God can do this even more directly, there is no inconsistency between the way of faith and that of knowledge, besides which, theoretical knowledge is under some conditions more easily imparted than faith. In regard to cyclic time, therefore, Christian thought after Saint Augustine could be reproached with the mistake of ignoring the superior possibilities of the cyclic idea. In other words, to escape the hostile effect of cyclic change, that is, its formal opposition to salvation, one need only realize that the mere fact that we know the cyclic laws means that our minds comprehend and transcend them, just as our rational being transcends the subtle influences of astral configurations. This is preferable by far to pretending that such laws are really not there.

When this pretence is made on behalf of society as a whole, the stage is set for the cyclic laws to take it over completely, even though some individual destinies may escape it by a strong religious faith. It is notorious that the only thing we learn from history is that society as a whole never learns from history, and this is to a large extent owing to precisely this lack of openness to the larger laws by which human life is contained. Ignorance and denial of cyclic laws is in effect the darkness in which, and in which alone, these laws can allow the working out of the worst possibilities. Their complete working out therefore requires that they be denied, in majority human thought, at least. There are in fact two opposite ways of reacting to the cyclic idea, one in the form of fatalism, and the other as a means of overcoming fate.

There is more than a passing connection between the attitude of religion to cyclic time and to astrology, although the two are by no means identical. Where astrology is concerned, there is no longer any need to deny that it is based on real knowledge, especially as it depends on phenomena which are increasingly substantiated by scientific discoveries made in the last few decades. Such denials by religious authorities were in any case really a matter of expediency, because the action of cosmic influences is always liable to appeal to our desire to avoid moral responsibility, and to act from interest rather than principle. So also in a parallel way with cyclic time. Responsible attitudes to one's own condition and that of the society to which one belongs are for some people weakened by the emotional effect of the idea of other worlds, among which this world is far from unique. Cosmic pluralism is usually morally relaxing, if only because it presents vistas of cosmic being for which human responsibility is necessarily impossible. That is felt to carry the meaning that responsibility is only a relative thing, or even an anomaly, and so of much less importance than if 'the world' was synonymous with our world. The best answer to this is that no truly sincere person would think of making his or her acceptance of moral responsibility wait upon a theory about the measurements of the universe.[2] However, these ideas lead us on to the next subject, the impact of cyclic change on moral absolutes.

MORAL RIGHT AND WRONG — ADJUSTABLE QUANTITIES?

Universal changes which affect moral standards prompt the question whether the amount of moral guilt in mankind is liable to vary according to the same laws. However, I have said little about this because morality is one of the least satisfactory parts of this subject, inasmuch as opposite moral conclusions can follow equally easily from the same data in this field. On the one hand, the cosmic process can seem to reduce moral responsibility; on the other hand, the descending process could mean a literal deepening of guilt. Taking the first of these alternatives, it can be seen that, although more and greater crimes will be committed toward the end of a world-cycle, they will inevitably form part of worsening conditions which will put more persons under pressure to act without principle. The increase in offences in turn brings a further worsening of conditions of life, and therewith a further increase in pressure to offend. Individuals involved in this process are usually confused as to whether they are agents or patients, that is, whether they are authors of their actions or whether they are merely instruments of outside forces.

2. Christian thought has never been unanimously either for or against cycles and astral influences. This disunity results from the two opposite ways of understanding cyclic laws just referred to. This is treated at greater length by Mircea Eliade in *The Myth of the Eternal Return*, chap. 4, 'The Terror of History'.

At the same time, the rise of physical and metaphysical entropy points to an increasing weakness and a lowering of the intelligence among the majority of those who live at such times. All this would by normal standards reduce moral responsibility. That the present-day human race is on average weaker in most ways than ever before is a conclusion which is also closely linked to the huge increase in world population which has taken place over the past two centuries. The connection between the rising numbers of a given species and the weakness of its individual members is explained by Dom Anscar Vonier as follows:

> Saint Thomas [Aquinas] remarks wisely that with material things, man not excluded, number supplements the weakness of the species; a species is saved from death, from disappearance, through its numbers, and the weaker the species, the greater its numbers.[3]

The elephant, for example, seldom needs its strength supported by numbers, whereas insect species are strong solely by virtue of their numbers. Such facts are coherent with a universal intuition that quantity and quality are linked in a way that makes either of them almost mathematically the inverse of the other. What these things mean in terms of increasing weakness and decrepitude can thus be quantified from the way in which world population has risen. It took the whole of recorded history to reach one thousand million by 1850, after which it reached two thousand million by 1930. By 1960 it was three thousand million, four thousand million in 1975, five thousand million in the 1980s, and is by now six thousand million. Total population has thus been multiplied by three in the seventy years from 1930. Mankind's descent into quantity could not be more dramatic. There is thus no doubt that the descending cosmic order militates against the qualitative aspect of personality, and therefore against moral responsibility, subject to any common sense view of human nature, at least. On this basis, one could even argue that the Antichrist and his associates would not be any more guilty than any other persons who have held equivalent positions in earlier times.

3. Dom Anscar Vonier, *The Angels*, chap. 4.

But such reasoning ignores the distinction between conscious guilt and objective guilt. It is possible to be objectively guilty by reason of the situation one unthinkingly forms part of, so that one's actions are so many prolongations of it. In this case, it would be possible for general guilt to increase to a maximum at certain times, though it may not be clear how this could be free from injustice to those involved. The former perspective of reduced responsibility can be shown to be tied to a view of personal identity for which everyone is born as a kind of blank tablet waiting to be inscribed by the forces of environment and upbringing. The idea of the soul implicit in this is only a very vague one, and it allows no meaning to the idea of a climactic collective guilt. However, this optimistic view conflicts with much that is known about heredity, since there are many indications that the beginning of life comprises much more than bare potentiality. In this case the time of conception would be one at which the whole state of being of which the parents formed part, besides their own heredity, would determine the kind of soul which was thereby drawn into incarnate life under the working of the Law of Cosmic Sympathy.[4] (One must suppose innumerable souls capable of this, each having its own spiritual potential for good or ill.) The idea of identity before birth is relevant whether one believes that each one is specially created at conception, or that souls pre-exist their embodied lives. Given this idea of the soul, every soul becomes incarnate only under the conditions which permit and facilitate the expression of its inherent possibilities. As those whose innate qualities imply a greater capacity for good would be born to those who live at times that allow the greatest scope for it, the equivalent must apply to capacity for evil. There would thus be no injustice in the idea of inherited guilt on this basis; every life would be in a real sense chosen.

Such is the second of the two possible moral deductions from the cyclic law, and it should suffice to show that the truth of the first of these two cannot simply be taken for granted.

4. A Plotinian and Stoic conception according to which the cosmic situations of all beings make manifest their inner tendencies.

DESTRUCTION AND TRANSFORMATION

What is bound to happen in the last times is, on a certain level, so destructive by nature that it can only appear to be a punishment to those who are directly subject to it, and this would be consistent with the idea of a special degree of guilt attaching to those concerned. But for all that, the destructive events on the material level in no way affect the Forms or essential causes of what is destroyed. Visible destruction is only the most negative aspect of a withdrawal of manifest realities into their unmanifest causes in a way which is both necessary and benign. This is what Joseph Pieper is referring to where he says:

> The end of time, inwardly as well as outwardly, will be utterly catastrophic in character, and history will debouch into its end as into a deliverance coming from outside (it does not come 'from outside', however, but from creation's innermost ground of being, which, of course, absolutely transcends creation).[5]

In other words, the physical destruction of a world is confined solely to the outward forms of reality, and not to their essential causes, besides which even the greatest destructive forces have access to no more than the final place-time coordinates of the things destroyed. Their being through all previous times cannot be affected by any evils which concern only their last extremities. What has been achieved in the past is therefore always secure in its own part of time, while its ultimate purposes are in any case not dependent on the phenomenal world. Pieper explains that, from his point of view, there is no reason for spiritual pessimism in an unspiritual world, on the grounds that the hope which results from belief in the final reintegration of things with their eternal causes makes all activities more meaningful in the here and now; the realization of the universal purpose covers that of all subordinate purposes.

The catastrophic denouement of history could never mean a failure in the purpose of creation to realize the ends it was intended for. This is because the final realization of this purpose is by definition impossible in time, that is, as long as this purpose is still confined

5. Joseph Pieper, *The End of Time*, chap. 2, [4].

within the temporal order where every supposed finality soon has to give way to something else. It is very hard to dissociate oneself from the dominant form of the world which results from a sense-orientated consciousness, even when one is largely free from its causes within oneself. It was in this connection, I believe, that Guénon maintained that the end of this world 'can never be anything but the end of an illusion.'[6] When the illusion is understood as falsified perception arising from the excess of the temporal condition, the implication is clear enough.

The only positive aspect of this kind of illusion is that it is fated to unmask itself by way of its own self-extension, because everything of this kind depends for its being on what it formally negates. The collapse of the illusion in this world will however not automatically mean any personal release from it for those who live at that time. For that to be the case, one must first have become dissociated from the cause of the evil in one's own lifetime. Failing this, one can only remain bound by the same illusion in the hereafter. Nevertheless, the self-neutralizing property of illusion shows how the perennial cosmology is beyond the usual alternatives of optimism and pessimism. To make this better understood, I have always emphasized the distinction between physical and archetypal realities, so that the pessimistic implications of universal history can be seen to be relevant only to physical or instantial reality. Corruption and decline in this unstable realm are only known to us because rational consciousness is founded upon the absolute realities of which the material ones are but the images. This axiological property of consciousness gives rise to one of the few counterbalancing forces to the decline of traditional religion in the Western world. Many persons now seek for themselves the inner wisdom traditions of the world's religions, whether they are members of them or not. This tendency is nurtured by the way in which everyone can now find all the greatest works of antiquity translated into their own language. Translation has removed what were once insuperable barriers in the path of authentic knowledge for the great majority, and this change has a Providential quality.

6. *The Reign of Quantity*, chap. 40, end of the final chapter.

At the same time, traditional religious exclusivism appears to have served its purpose, and where it is defended with open intolerance it is liable to do more harm than good. In such cases, an acceptance of external authority is not matched by an attempt to make one's own the truth which that authority stands for. Though the numbers of those who are prepared to take such spiritual responsibility for themselves are too small to reverse the overall situation, they do save it from being one of unmitigated degeneration. They are fore-runners of those who receive the final revelation of this world-age, prophesied by Joel:

> And it shall come to pass afterward, that I will pour out my spirit on all flesh; and your sons and daughters shall prophesy, your old men shall dream dreams and your young men shall see visions.[7]

Whatever happens, the luminous core of reality is always present and waiting for events to recall it to life. There is therefore nothing final in even the most catastrophic historical changes, because all temporal realities are manifestations of eternal originals which never cease to be re-manifested at times allowed by the cyclic order. Although destructive change is evil in itself, its evil is thus limited by the fact that it has no power to destroy the irreplaceable. This point is made by Frithjof Schuon where he quotes from the Sufis:

> The nature of evil, and not its inevitability, constitutes its condemnation ... one must not accept error, but one must be resigned to its existence. But beyond earthly destructions there is the Indestructible: 'Every form you see,' says Rumi, 'has its archetype in the divine world, beyond space; if the form perishes what matter, since its heavenly model is indestructible? Every beautiful form you have seen, every meaningful word you have heard—be not sorrowful because all this must be lost; such is not really the case. The divine Source is immortal and its outflowing gives water without cease; since neither the one nor the other can be stopped, whereof do you lament?... From the first moment

7. Joel 2:28, and see also Jer. 31:31–34.

when you entered this world of existence, a ladder has been set up before you.'[8]

For spiritual wisdom, therefore, the power of evil is much less than it is for the senses and for the imagination which is bound to the senses. When spiritual and natural evils go to extremes, they can even become useful, since they make it impossible to believe that this world is the world for which mankind was created. Extreme negation forces the mind to focus on what is being negated as long as it is not corrupted in the process. 'The age of the realization of the impossible,' as one traditionalist has called modernist culture, is in any case only a momentary sport of nature in comparison with the ages during which man was conscious of his true vocation and found the meaning of life in his attempts to realize it. The possibility of such a fulfilment is no less real on account of the influences which apparently belie it, and closer understanding of the short-lived substitutes for it is a sure means of making oneself inwardly free from their worst effects.

8. Frithjof Schuon, *Light on the Ancient Worlds*, chap. 4, pp 85–86.

INDEX

266 ✠ *Index*

Printed in the United States
2885